VERSES *by* VIRTUE

A Reference of Organized Bible Verses

VERSES *by* VIRTUE

A Reference of Organized Bible Verses

Jeffrey C. Dunn

ETERNAL LIGHT
PUBLISHING

Shining Forth the Light of Christ

Verses by Virtue: A Reference of Organized Bible Verses by Jeffrey C. Dunn

Post Office Box 4378
Davenport, IA 52808, U.S.A.
www.EternalLightPublishing.com

Copyright © 2008 by Jeffrey C. Dunn.
ISBN Hardcover edition: 978-0-9816718-0-2
ISBN Softcover edition: 978-0-9816718-1-9
Printed in the United States of America.

Table of Contents

Acknowledgments

Foremost, I offer my most sincere thanks to my parents who raised me in the path of righteousness. Superior thanks to my brother Michael and Father Daniel Wilder for having faith in me from the beginning. Many thanks to my family, Ramona Eidenmiller, Jim Jaeger, Jefree Schulte, Michael Bishop, Joan and Ton Anderson, Coleen and Tom Yucus, Gayle Thomas, Duane Loynes, Sr., Carole Vaughn, Betty Mehn, Paul Edleman, Chick West, the Wilkinson family, Daniel D'Aniello and David Wilder. Special thanks to Sharon Pfister and the St. Therese Foundation, Roger Colmark and Pat Hunt. I thank all these fine people for their support and selfless contributions.

I thank all of you who are fighting the good fight of faith. It always encourages me to see my brothers and sisters walking in Truth. With God on our side, we are destroying the forces of evil and spreading the Gospel of Peace throughout the lands. Let us all continue to fulfill the Great Commission Jesus gave us.

I give all the glory, praise, and honor that *Verses by Virtue* receives back to God. He, and He alone, is worthy to be praised. No author or musician or athlete or movie star took away the sins of the world. Jesus Christ, the Son of God, died for us so that we could live for Him. Thank You, Jesus.

How to Use This Book

Verses by Virtue can be read chapter by chapter as a normal book, but its power lies in its reference abilities. Use *Verses by Virtue* to find a Bible verse for special occasions such as weddings, graduations, birthday and anniversary cards, family gatherings, church events, Bible studies, prayer groups, and any other occasion that would benefit by including a passage from God's Word. Use the *Table of Contents* and *Index* to find verses easier and faster.

Verses by Virtue is a source of inspiration at your fingertips, providing you with courage when you feel afraid, hope when you feel in doubt, and confidence that Jesus is always with you no matter who you are, where you are, or what you are facing today.

Use *Verses by Virtue* as a Bible Study tool, or supplement an existing program with it. Prayer groups will be able to derive great discussions when including *Verses by Virtue* in the study. Use *Verses by Virtue* as an evangelistic tool to spread the Gospel of Christ to every creature in every place.

Of course, *Verses by Virtue* would not be complete without a Bible. This book captures a mere glimpse of the glory God has written in His book. Keep God's Word close to your heart throughout your life. Saturate your heart, mind, and tongue with Scripture, and God will saturate your life with His blessings.

Your word is a lamp to my feet
And a light to my path.

– Psalm 119:105 NASB

Chapter Contents

1 – VIRTUES OF VICTORY

2 - CALLS TO ACTION

3 - OVERCOMING PROBLEMS

4 - VICES TO AVOID

5 - CONCEPTS OF THE FAITH

Note to the Reader – NAB Psalms

Verse citations from the book of Psalms in the New American Bible (NAB) follow the Hebrew numbering of the verses which is often one verse more than other English translations. Most English translations do not include the superscriptions (e.g. "For the leader; with stringed instruments. A psalm of David.") in the first verse, whereas the NAB includes them as either part of or the entire first verse.

Introduction

As a believer and follower of Christ, I thoroughly enjoy every wonderful word in the Bible. It is essential to read and absorb God's Word to develop and strengthen your relationship with Christ our Savior. Before I wrote this book, when I was in need of God's Word, often I couldn't recall a particular verse that had supported me during difficult times in the past. Now, whenever a situation arises that calls for God's attention, I can turn to *Verses by Virtue* and keep the Bible first place in my life. It has served me well, and I want to share it with those whom it may help as well.

Verses by Virtue is organized into five chapters, each covering a different theme. Chapter 1, *Virtues of Victory*, highlights the essential virtues to live by that are found throughout the Bible. Chapter 2 pumps it up with *Calls to Action* that a Christian can perform in order to live as Christ did. Turn to Chapter 3 for help in *Overcoming Problems* that may occur in life. Remember, even Jesus faced hard times and tribulations, and He overcame them all by praying and trusting in the almighty power of God, and so can you! Chapter 4 introduces *Vices to Avoid*. Lastly, Chapter 5 covers other important areas of Christianity in *Concepts of the Faith*.

Thank you for turning to God and His Word to fulfill all your needs. God Bless you!

"Man shall not live by bread alone, but by every word that proceeds from the mouth of God."
– Matthew 4:4 NKJV

Virtues of Victory

1

Compassion

Your attitude should be the same as that of Christ Jesus.
>   - Philippians 2:5 NIV

All of you, be like-minded, be sympathetic, love one another, be compassionate and humble. Do not repay evil with evil or insult with insult. On the contrary, repay evil with blessing, because to this you were called so that you may inherit a blessing.
>   - 1 Peter 3:8-9 TNIV

He who has compassion on the poor
>   lends to the LORD,
>   and he will repay him for his good
>   deed.
>   - Proverbs 19:17 NAB

"And the King will answer and say to them, 'Assuredly, I say to you, inasmuch as you did it to one of the least of these My brethren, you did it to Me.' "
>   - Matthew 25:40 NKJV

"This is what the LORD Almighty said: 'Administer true justice; show mercy and compassion to one another.' "
>   - Zechariah 7:9 TNIV

The LORD's lovingkindnesses indeed
>   never cease,
> For His compassions never fail.
> They are new every morning;
> Great is Your faithfulness.
>   - Lamentations 3:22-23 NASB

"Love your enemies, bless those who curse you, do good to those who hate you, and pray for those who spitefully use you and persecute you."
- Matthew 5:44 NKJV

Yet the LORD longs to be gracious to you;
    he rises to show you compassion.
For the LORD is a God of justice.
    Blessed are all who wait for him!
- Isaiah 30:18 NIV

"For the LORD your God is gracious and compassionate, and will not turn His face away from you if you return to Him."
- 2 Chronicles 30:9 NASB

Be kind to one another, compassionate, forgiving one another as God has forgiven you.
- Ephesians 4:32 NAB

The LORD is gracious and compassionate,
    slow to anger and rich in love.
The LORD is good to all;
    he has compassion on all he has made.
- Psalm 145:8-9 NIV

See also **Generosity, Kindness, Love, Works**

Confidence

I can do all things through Christ who strengthens me.
>   - Philippians 4:13 NKJV

Let us be confident, then, in approaching the throne of grace, that we shall have mercy from him and find grace when we are in need of help.
>   - Hebrews 4:16 JB

If God is for us, who can be against us?
>   - Romans 8:31 NIV

I know that you can do all things,
   and that no purpose of yours can
       be hindered.
>   - Job 42:2 NAB

We have become partners of Christ, if only we hold our first confidence firm to the end.
>   - Hebrews 3:14 NRSV

Of this gospel I was appointed a herald and an apostle and a teacher. That is why I am suffering as I am. Yet I am not ashamed, because I know whom I have believed, and am convinced that he is able to guard what I have entrusted to him for that day.
>   - 2 Timothy 1:11-12 NIV

We are confident, I say, and willing rather to be absent from the body, and to be present with the Lord.
                              - 2 Corinthians 5:8 KJV

This is the confidence that we have in Him, that if we ask anything according to His will, He hears us. And if we know that He hears us, whatever we ask, we know that we have the petitions that we have asked of Him.
                              - 1 John 5:14-15 NKJV

I rejoice that in everything I have confidence in you.
                              - 2 Corinthians 7:16 NASB

We know that when He appears, we will be like Him, because we will see Him just as He is.
                              - 1 John 3:2 NASB

Because of Christ and our faith in him, we can now come boldly and confidently into God's presence.
                              - Ephesians 3:12 NLT

We have confidence in God and receive from him whatever we ask, because we keep his command-ments and do what pleases him.
                              - 1 John 3:21-22 NAB

I am sure of this, that He who started a good work in you will carry it on to completion until the day of Christ Jesus.
                              - Philippians 1:6 HCSB

Therefore, do not throw away your confidence, which has a great reward.
>
> - Hebrews 10:35 NASB

This is the confidence we have in approaching God: that if we ask anything according to his will, he hears us. And if we know that he hears us – whatever we ask – we know that we have what we asked of him.
>
> - 1 John 5:14-15 TNIV

In the fear of the LORD one has strong
> confidence,
>   and one's children will have a refuge.
>
> - Proverbs 14:26 NRSV

"For I know that my Redeemer lives,
>   and that at the last he will stand upon
>   the earth."
>
> - Job 19:25 NRSV

"Because of his grace he declared us righteous and gave us confidence that we will inherit eternal life."
>
> - Titus 3:7 NLT

We know that we have passed from death unto life, because we love the brethren.
>
> - 1 John 3:14 KJV

Pray also for me, that whenever I speak, words may be given me so that I will fearlessly make known the mystery of the gospel.
>
> - Ephesians 6:19 TNIV

"Blessed is the man who trusts in
        the LORD,
    whose confidence is in him.
He will be like a tree planted by the water
    that sends out its roots by the stream.
It does not fear when heat comes;
    its leaves are always green.
It has no worries in a year of drought
    and never fails to bear fruit."
                            - Jeremiah 17:7-8 NIV

The Lord shall be your confidence, firm and strong,
and shall keep your foot from being caught.
                            - Proverbs 3:26 AMP

See also **Courage, Peace of Mind, Perseverance**

Courage

"This is what the LORD says to you: 'Do not be afraid
or discouraged because of this vast army. For the battle is not yours, but God's.'"
                            - 2 Chronicles 20:15 NIV

"Behold, I give you the authority to trample on serpents and scorpions, and over all the power of the
enemy, and nothing shall by any means hurt you."
                            - Luke 10:19 NKJV

Keep alert, stand firm in your faith, be courageous, be strong.

- 1 Corinthians 16:13 NRSV

The LORD is my light and my salvation;
Whom shall I fear?
The LORD is the defense of my life;
Whom shall I dread?

- Psalm 27:1 NASB

My strength and my courage is the LORD,
    and he has been my savior.

- Exodus 15:2 NAB

"Be strong and of good courage; do not be afraid, nor be dismayed, for the LORD your God is with you wherever you go."

- Joshua 1:9 NKJV

I felt encouraged because the gracious hand of the LORD my God was on me.

- Ezra 7:28 NLT

Christ gives me the strength to face anything.

- Philippians 4:13 CEV

The wicked flee when no one is
        pursuing them,
but the righteous are as bold as a lion.

- Proverbs 28:1 HCSB

The Lord God is my Strength, my personal bravery, and my invincible army.

- Habakkuk 3:19 AMP

If God is for us, who can be against us?
- Romans 8:31 NAB

Wait on the LORD;
Be of good courage,
And He shall strengthen your heart;
Wait, I say, on the LORD!

- Psalm 27:14 NKJV

See also **Confidence, Soldier of God, Strength**

Discipline

"Blessed is the man whom God
        corrects;
    so do not despise the discipline of
        the Almighty.
For he wounds, but he also binds up;
    he injures, but his hands also heal."

- Job 5:17-18 NIV

A fool despises his father's
        instruction,
But he who receives correction
        is prudent.

- Proverbs 15:5 NKJV

Those who spare the rod of discipline
    hate their children.
  Those who love their children care
    enough to discipline them.
                 - Proverbs 13:24 NLT

"As many as I love, I rebuke and discipline."
                 - Revelation 3:19 HCSB

All discipline for the moment seems not to be joyful, but sorrowful; yet to those who have been trained by it, afterwards it yields the peaceful fruit of righteousness.
                 - Hebrews 12:11 NASB

Discipline yourselves, keep alert. Like a roaring lion your adversary the devil prowls around, looking for someone to devour. Resist him, steadfast in your faith, for you know that your brothers and sisters in all the world are undergoing the same kinds of suffering.
                 - 1 Peter 5:8-9 NRSV

My son, do not despise the chastening
    of the LORD,
Nor detest His correction;
For whom the LORD loves He corrects,
Just as a father the son in whom
    he delights.
                 - Proverbs 3:11-12 NKJV

As iron sharpens iron,
  so one man sharpens another.
                 - Proverbs 27:17 NIV

Examine yourselves as to whether you are in the faith. Test yourselves. Do you not know yourselves, that Jesus Christ is in you? – unless indeed you are disqualified. But I trust that you will know that we are not disqualified.

- 2 Corinthians 13:5-6 NKJV

But test and prove all things [until you can recognize] what is good; [to that] hold fast.

- 1 Thessalonians 5:21 AMP

Know then in your heart that as a man disciplines his son, so the LORD your God disciplines you.

- Deuteronomy 8:5 NIV

Listen to advice, accept correction,
    to be the wiser in the time to come.

- Proverbs 19:20 JB

Endure trials for the sake of discipline. God is treating you as children; for what child is there whom a parent does not discipline?

- Hebrews 12:7 NRSV

Correct me, O LORD, but with justice;
Not with Your anger, or You will bring me to
    nothing.

- Jeremiah 10:24 NASB

Search me, O God, and know my
        heart;
    test me and know my anxious
        thoughts.
See if there is any offensive way in me,
    and lead me in the way everlasting.
                            - Psalm 139:23-24 NIV

See also **Obedience, Perseverance**

Faith

"I have been crucified with Christ; it is no longer I who
live, but Christ lives in me; and the life which I now
live in the flesh I live by faith in the Son of God, who
loved me and gave Himself for me."
                            - Galatians 2:20 NKJV

For as the body without the spirit is dead, so faith
without works is dead also.
                            - James 2:26 KJV

"If you had faith like a mustard seed, you would say to
this mulberry tree, 'Be uprooted and be planted in the
sea'; and it would obey you."
                            - Luke 17:6 NASB

We walk by faith, not by sight.
                            - 2 Corinthians 5:7 NAB

Before faith came, we were kept in custody under the law, being shut up to the faith which was later to be revealed. Therefore the Law has become our tutor to lead us to Christ, so that we may be justified by faith. But now that faith has come, we are no longer under a tutor.

- Galatians 3:23-25 NASB

Though the fig tree may not
         blossom,
Nor fruit be on the vines;
Though the labor of the olive may
         fail,
And the fields yield no food;
Though the flock may be cut off
         from the fold,
And there be no herd in the stalls –
Yet I will rejoice in the LORD,
I will joy in the God of my salvation.

- Habakkuk 3:17-18 NKJV

'Everything is possible for anyone who has faith.'

- Mark 9:23 JB

"By faith in the name of Jesus, this man whom you see and know was made strong. It is Jesus' name and the faith that comes through him that has given this complete healing to him, as you can all see."

- Acts 3:16 NIV

You are all sons of God through faith in Christ Jesus.

- Galatians 3:26 HCSB

I pray that out of his glorious riches he may strengthen you with power through his Spirit in your inner being, so that Christ may dwell in your hearts through faith.

                            - Ephesians 3:16-17 TNIV

"I have prayed for you, that your faith may not fail."

                            - Luke 22:32 NASB

"A person is not justified by observing the law, but by faith in Jesus Christ. So we, too, have put our faith in Christ Jesus that we may be justified by faith in Christ and not by observing the law, because by observing the law no one will be justified."

                            - Galatians 2:16 TNIV

Your faith should not be in the wisdom of men but in the power of God.

                            - 1 Corinthians 2:5 NKJV

Because of Christ and our faith in him, we can now come boldly and confidently into God's presence.

                            - Ephesians 3:12 NLT

You were once alienated and hostile in mind because of your evil actions. But now He has reconciled you by His physical body through His death, to present you holy, faultless, and blameless before Him – if indeed you remain grounded and steadfast in the faith, and are not shifted away from the hope of the gospel that you heard.

                            - Colossians 1:21-23 HCSB

"The righteous will live by his faith."
> \- Habakkuk 2:4 NASB

I pray that you may be active in sharing your faith, so that you will have a full understanding of every good thing we have in Christ.
> \- Philemon 6 NIV

Blessed are they that have not seen, and yet have believed.
> \- John 20:29 KJV

Since we have been justified through faith, we have peace with God through our Lord Jesus Christ, through whom we have gained access by faith into this grace in which we now stand. And we rejoice in the hope of the glory of God.
> \- Romans 5:1-2 NIV

Fight the good fight of the faith. Take hold of the eternal life to which you were called when you made your good confession in the presence of many witnesses.
> \- 1 Timothy 6:12 TNIV

From childhood you have known the Holy Scriptures, which are able to make you wise for salvation through faith which is in Christ Jesus.
> \- 2 Timothy 3:15 NKJV

"O woman, great is your faith! Let it be done for you as you wish."
> \- Matthew 15:28 NAB

By faith Moses, when he had grown up, refused to be called the son of Pharaoh's daughter, choosing rather to endure ill-treatment with the people of God than to enjoy the passing pleasures of sin.
                                    - Hebrews 11:24-25 NASB

Take the shield of faith, with which you will be able to quench all the flaming arrows of the evil one.
                                    - Ephesians 6:16 NRSV

Build yourselves up on your most holy faith.
                                    - Jude 20 NRSV

Put on the breastplate of faith and love, and as a helmet, the hope of salvation.
                                    - 1 Thessalonians 5:8 NASB

Pursue righteousness, faith, love and peace, with those who call on the Lord from a pure heart.
                                    - 2 Timothy 2:22 NASB

Let us draw near to God with a sincere heart in full assurance of faith, having our hearts sprinkled to cleanse us from a guilty conscience and having our bodies washed with pure water.
                                    - Hebrews 10:22 TNIV

I pray that Christ will live in your hearts by faith.
                                    - Ephesians 3:17 NCV

By grace you have been saved through faith, and this is not your own doing; it is the gift of God.
                                    - Ephesians 2:8 NRSV

For his sake I have suffered the loss of all things, and I regard them as rubbish, in order that I may gain Christ and be found in him, not having a righteousness of my own that comes from the law, but one that comes through faith in Christ, the righteousness from God based on faith.

> - Philippians 3:8-9 NRSV

You see that his faith and his actions were working together, and his faith was made complete by what he did.

> - James 2:22 TNIV

Set an example for those who believe, in speech, conduct, love, faith, and purity.

> - 1 Timothy 4:12 NAB

Now faith is the substance of things hoped for, the evidence of things not seen.

> - Hebrews 11:1 NKJV

I can do all things through Christ who strengthens me.

> - Philippians 4:13 NKJV

'If you have faith, everything you ask for in prayer you will receive.'

> - Matthew 21:22 JB

Without faith it is impossible to please God, for whoever would approach him must believe that he exists and that he rewards those who seek him.

> - Hebrews 11:6 NRSV

These trials will show that your faith is genuine. It is being tested as fire tests and purifies gold – though your faith is far more precious than mere gold. So when your faith remains strong through many trials, it will bring you much praise and glory and honor on the day when Jesus Christ is revealed to the whole world.

- 1 Peter 1:7 NLT

"Stand up and go; your faith has made you well."
- Luke 17:19 NASB

Be on your guard, stand firm in the faith, be courageous, be strong.
- 1 Corinthians 16:13 NAB

Faith comes from what is heard, and what is heard comes through the word of Christ.
- Romans 10:17 NAB

Did you receive the Spirit by the works of the law or by hearing with faith? So then, does God supply you with the Spirit and work miracles among you by the works of the law or by hearing with faith?
- Galatians 3:2,5 HCSB

But let him ask in faith, with no doubting, for he who doubts is like a wave of the sea driven and tossed by the wind.
- James 1:6 NKJV

Let us run with endurance the race that is set before us, looking unto Jesus, the author and finisher of our faith.
- Hebrews 12:1-2 NKJV

Whatever has been born of God conquers the world. This is the victory that has conquered the world: our faith.

> - 1 John 5:4 HCSB

For in the gospel a righteousness from God is revealed, a righteousness that is by faith from first to last, just as it is written: "The righteous will live by faith."

> - Romans 1:17 NIV

By faith we understand that the worlds were prepared by the word of God, so that what is seen was made from things that are not visible.

> - Hebrews 11:3 NRSV

"Have faith in God. For assuredly, I say to you, whoever says to this mountain, 'Be removed and be cast into the sea,' and does not doubt in his heart, but believes that those things he says will be done, he will have whatever he says."

> - Mark 11:22-23 NKJV

See also **All Things Are Possible, Believing, Hope, Works**

Fear of the Lord

"The fear of the LORD is the beginning
        of wisdom,
And the knowledge of the Holy One is
        understanding."
                                    - Proverbs 9:10 NKJV

For as high as the heavens are above the earth,
        so great is his love for those who fear him.
                                    - Psalm 103:11 TNIV

Happy are those who fear the LORD,
who greatly delight in his commandments.
                                    - Psalm 112:1 NRSV

"The LORD your God you shall fear; and He will deliver
you from the hand of all your enemies."
                                    - 2 Kings 17:39 NASB

The angel of the LORD encamps
        around those who fear Him,
And rescues them.
                                    - Psalm 34:7 NASB

Since we are receiving a kingdom which cannot be
shaken, let us have grace, by which we may serve God
acceptably with reverence and godly fear. For our God
is a consuming fire.
                                    - Hebrews 12:28-29 NKJV

The fear of the LORD is a fountain of life,
turning people from the snares of death.
                    - Proverbs 14:27 HCSB

"Fear God and give him glory, for his time has come to
sit in judgment. Worship him who made heaven and
earth and sea and springs of water."
                    - Revelation 14:7 NAB

"Do not fear those who kill the body but are unable to
kill the soul; but rather fear Him who is able to destroy both soul and body in hell."
                    - Matthew 10:28 NASB

"But to you who fear My name
The Sun of Righteousness shall
        arise
With healing in His wings."
                    - Malachi 4:2 NKJV

In the fear of the LORD one has strong
        confidence,
    and one's children will have a refuge.
                    - Proverbs 14:26 NRSV

"You must always act in the fear of the LORD, with
faithfulness and an undivided heart."
                    - 2 Chronicles 19:9 NLT

God is greatly to be feared in the
        assembly of the saints,
And to be held in reverence by all
        those around Him.
                    - Psalm 89:7 NKJV

The reward of humility and fear of the LORD
   is riches, honor and life.
                     - Proverbs 22:4 NAB

Be not wise in thine own eyes: fear the LORD, and depart from evil.
                     - Proverbs 3:7 KJV

"You shall walk after the LORD your God and fear Him,
and keep His commandments and obey His voice; you
shall serve Him and hold fast to Him."
                     - Deuteronomy 13:4 NKJV

The earth has yielded its produce;
God, our God, blesses us.
God blesses us,
That all the ends of the earth may fear Him.
                     - Psalm 67:6-7 NASB

Fear the LORD, you his saints,
   for those who fear him lack nothing.
                     - Psalm 34:9 NIV

The Lord takes pleasure in those who reverently and
worshipfully fear Him, in those who hope in His mercy
and loving-kindness.
                     - Psalm 147:11 AMP

Since we have these promises, dear friends, let us purify ourselves from everything that contaminates body
and spirit, perfecting holiness out of reverence for
God.
                     - 2 Corinthians 7:1 TNIV

The eyes of the LORD are on those
     who fear him,
  on those whose hope is in his unfailing love,
to deliver them from death
    and keep them alive in famine.
                        - Psalm 33:18-19 NIV

Surely his salvation is at hand for those
     who fear him,
  that his glory may dwell in our land.
                        - Psalm 85:9 NRSV

Charm is deceitful and beauty is
     passing,
But a woman who fears the LORD,
     she shall be praised.
                        - Proverbs 31:30 NKJV

The secret of the LORD is with those
     who fear Him,
And He will show them His covenant.
                        - Psalm 25:14 NKJV

Indeed I know that it shall be well with those who fear
God, for their reverence toward him.
                        - Ecclesiastes 8:12 NAB

Let all the earth fear the LORD;
Let all the inhabitants of the world
     stand in awe of Him.
                        - Psalm 33:8 NASB

He will bless those who fear the LORD,
  both small and great.
                        - Psalm 115:13 NRSV

Fear God and keep his commandments,
>for this is the whole duty of man.
>>- Ecclesiastes 12:13 NIV

The fear of the LORD prolongs days,
But the years of the wicked will be
>shortened.
>>- Proverbs 10:27 NKJV

He fulfills the desires of those who fear him;
>he hears their cry and saves them.
>>- Psalm 145:19 TNIV

Blessed are all who fear the LORD,
>who walk in his ways.
>>- Psalm 128:1 NIV

The fear of the LORD leads to life,
And he who has it will abide in
>satisfaction;
He will not be visited with evil.
>>- Proverbs 19:23 NKJV

In every nation he who venerates and has a reverential fear for God, treating Him with worshipful obedience and living uprightly, is acceptable to Him and sure of being received and welcomed [by Him].
>- Acts 10:35 AMP

See also **Obedience, Respect**

Forgiveness

As God's chosen people, holy and dearly loved, clothe yourselves with compassion, kindness, humility, gentleness and patience. Bear with each other and forgive one another if any of you has a grievance against someone. Forgive as the Lord forgave you.
                                    - Colossians 3:12-13 TNIV

"If you forgive others their trespasses, your heavenly Father will also forgive you."
                                    - Matthew 6:14 NRSV

If we walk in the light as He is in the light, we have fellowship with one another, and the blood of Jesus Christ His Son cleanses us from all sin.
                                    - 1 John 1:7 NKJV

"All the prophets testify about Him that through His name everyone who believes in Him will receive forgiveness of sins."
                                    - Acts 10:43 HCSB

Praise the LORD, my soul,
    and forget not all his benefits –
who forgives all your sins
    and heals all your diseases,
who redeems your life from the pit
    and crowns you with love and compassion,
who satisfies your desires with good things
    so that your youth is renewed like the eagle's.
                                    - Psalm 103:2-5 TNIV

"You have cast all my sins behind
    Your back."
           - Isaiah 38:17 NKJV

"It is I who sweep away your transgressions
for My own sake
and remember your sins no more."
           - Isaiah 43:25 HCSB

Get rid of all bitterness, rage and anger, brawling and slander, along with every form of malice. Be kind and compassionate to one another, forgiving each other, just as in Christ God forgave you.
           - Ephesians 4:31-32 NIV

Create in me a clean heart, O God,
And renew a steadfast spirit within
        me.
           - Psalm 51:10 NKJV

In him we have redemption through his blood, the forgiveness of sins, in accordance with the riches of God's grace.
           - Ephesians 1:7 NIV

"Repent and be baptized, every one of you, in the name of Jesus Christ for the forgiveness of your sins. And you will receive the gift of the Holy Spirit."
           - Acts 2:38 TNIV

If we confess our sins, He is faithful and just to forgive us our sins and to cleanse us from all unrighteousness.
           - 1 John 1:9 NKJV

"But You are a God of forgiveness,
Gracious and compassionate,
Slow to anger and abounding in
        lovingkindness;
And You did not forsake them."
                    - Nehemiah 9:17 NASB

Let the wicked forsake their way,
    and the unrighteous their thoughts;
let them return to the LORD, that he
        may have mercy on them,
    and to our God, for he will abundantly
        pardon.
                        - Isaiah 55:7 NRSV

For Your name's sake, O Lord, pardon my iniquity and
my guilt, for [they are] great.
                        - Psalm 25:11 AMP

Wash me thoroughly from my
        iniquity,
    and cleanse me from my sin.
                    - Psalm 51:2 NRSV

"And forgive us our sins,
    as we have forgiven those who sin
        against us."
                        - Matthew 6:12 NLT

Purge me with hyssop, and I shall be clean: wash me,
and I shall be whiter than snow.
                        - Psalm 51:7 KJV

As far as the east is from the west,
so far has He removed
our transgressions from us.
                    - Psalm 103:12 HCSB

For You, Lord, are good, and ready
            to forgive,
And abundant in mercy to all those
        who call upon You.
                    - Psalm 86:5 NKJV

"If your brother sins against you, rebuke him; and if
he repents, forgive him. And if he sins against you
seven times in a day, and seven times in a day returns
to you, saying, 'I repent,' you shall forgive him."
                    - Luke 17:3-4 NKJV

Blessed is he whose transgression is forgiven, whose
sin is covered.
                    - Psalm 32:1 KJV

Let us draw near to God with a sincere heart in full
assurance of faith, having our hearts sprinkled to
cleanse us from a guilty conscience and having our
bodies washed with pure water.
                    - Hebrews 10:22 TNIV

He will again have compassion on us;
He will vanquish our iniquities.
You will cast all our sins
into the depths of the sea.
                    - Micah 7:19 HCSB

"Come now, and let us reason
        together,"
Says the LORD,
"Though your sins are as scarlet,
They will be as white as snow;
Though they are red like crimson,
They will be like wool."
                    - Isaiah 1:18 NASB

See also **Letting Go of the Past, Mercy, Repentance,
    Reconciliation**

Generosity

"Bring all the tithes into the
        storehouse,
That there may be food in My house,
And try Me now in this,"
Says the LORD of hosts,
"If I will not open for you the windows
        of heaven
And pour out for you such blessing
That there will not be room enough
        to receive it."
                    - Malachi 3:10 NKJV

Those who are kind to the poor lend to
        the LORD,
    and he will reward them for what they
        have done.
                    - Proverbs 19:17 TNIV

"From everyone to whom much has been given, much will be required; and from the one to whom much has been entrusted, even more will be demanded."
                                        - Luke 12:48 NRSV

You will be enriched in every way for your great generosity, which will produce thanksgiving to God through us.
                                        - 2 Corinthians 9:11 NRSV

He has given freely to the poor,
His righteousness endures forever;
His horn will be exalted in honor.
                                        - Psalm 112:9 NASB

One person gives freely,
yet gains more;
another withholds what is right,
only to become poor.
                                        - Proverbs 11:24 HCSB

"Then the King will say to those on his right, 'Come, you who are blessed by my Father; take your inheritance, the kingdom prepared for you since the creation of the world. For I was hungry and you gave me something to eat, I was thirsty and you gave me something to drink, I was a stranger and you invited me in, I needed clothes and you clothed me, I was sick and you looked after me, I was in prison and you came to visit me.' "
                                        - Matthew 25:34-36 NIV

The wicked borrow, and do not pay back,
but the righteous are generous and keep giving.
- Psalm 37:21 NRSV

Command them to do good, to be rich in good deeds,
and to be generous and willing to share. In this way
they will lay up treasure for themselves as a firm
foundation for the coming age, so that they may take
hold of the life that is truly life.
- 1 Timothy 6:18-19 TNIV

A generous person will be blessed,
for he shares his food with the poor.
- Proverbs 22:9 HCSB

"If you extend your soul to the
hungry
And satisfy the afflicted soul,
Then your light shall dawn in the
darkness,
And your darkness shall be as the
noonday."
- Isaiah 58:10 NKJV

Give generously...and do so without a grudging heart;
then because of this the LORD your God will bless you
in all your work and in everything you put your hand
to.
- Deuteronomy 15:10 NIV

Each man should give what he has decided in his
heart to give, not reluctantly or under compulsion, for
God loves a cheerful giver.
- 2 Corinthians 9:7 NIV

A generous person will be enriched,
and one who gives water will get water.
- Proverbs 11:25 NRSV

See also **Compassion, Giving, Kindness, Works**

Grace

By the grace of God I am what I am, and His grace toward me was not in vain; but I labored more abundantly than they all, yet not I, but the grace of God which was with me.
- 1 Corinthians 15:10 NKJV

For by grace you are saved through faith, and this is not from yourselves; it is God's gift.
- Ephesians 2:8 HCSB

He said to me, "My grace is sufficient for you, for My strength is made perfect in weakness."
- 2 Corinthians 12:9 NKJV

The grace of our Lord overflowed for me with the faith and love that are in Christ Jesus.
- 1 Timothy 1:14 NRSV

I do not set aside the grace of God; for if righteousness comes through the law, then Christ died for nothing.
- Galatians 2:21 HCSB

In Him we have redemption through His blood, the forgiveness of our trespasses, according to the riches of His grace.
                    - Ephesians 1:7 NASB

He saved us through the washing of rebirth and renewal by the Holy Spirit, whom he poured out on us generously through Jesus Christ our Savior, so that, having been justified by his grace, we might become heirs having the hope of eternal life.
                    - Titus 3:5-7 TNIV

He mocks those who mock,
but gives grace to the humble.
                    - Proverbs 3:34 HCSB

Since we have been justified through faith, we have peace with God through our Lord Jesus Christ, through whom we have gained access by faith into this grace in which we now stand.
                    - Romans 5:1-2 TNIV

Be strong in the grace that is in Christ Jesus.
                    - 2 Timothy 2:1 NAB

Let us therefore approach the throne of grace with boldness, so that we may receive mercy and find grace to help in time of need.
                    - Hebrews 4:16 NRSV

God saved us and called us to live a holy life. He did this, not because we deserved it, but because that was his plan from before the beginning of time – to show us his grace through Christ Jesus.

- 2 Timothy 1:9 NLT

We have different gifts, according to the grace given to each of us.

- Romans 12:6 TNIV

You know the grace of our Lord Jesus Christ, that though he was rich, yet for your sakes he became poor, so that you through his poverty might become rich.

- 2 Corinthians 8:9 NIV

Let your conversation be always full of grace, seasoned with salt, so that you may know how to answer everyone.

- Colossians 4:6 TNIV

Since we are receiving a kingdom which cannot be shaken, let us have grace, by which we may serve God acceptably with reverence and godly fear. For our God is a consuming fire.

- Hebrews 12:28-29 NKJV

We have conducted ourselves in the world...with integrity and godly sincerity. We have done so, relying not on worldly wisdom but on God's grace.

- 2 Corinthians 1:12 TNIV

Grow in the grace and knowledge of our Lord and Savior Jesus Christ.
> \- 2 Peter 3:18 NASB

Sin will not rule over you, because you are not under law but under grace.
> \- Romans 6:14 HCSB

See also **Receiving, Reconciliation, Salvation**

Happiness

This is the day the LORD has made;
  let us rejoice and be glad in it.
> \- Psalm 118:24 NIV

I have learned how to be content with whatever I have.
> \- Philippians 4:11 NLT

Be glad and rejoice with all your
      heart,
The LORD has taken away your
      judgments,
He has cast out your enemy.
The King of Israel, the LORD, is in
      your midst;
You shall see disaster no more.
> \- Zephaniah 3:14-15 NKJV

Happy are the people whose God is the LORD.
                    - Psalm 144:15 NCV

I know that there is nothing better for people than to be happy and to do good while they live.
                    - Ecclesiastes 3:12 TNIV

You have put gladness in my heart.
                    - Psalm 4:7 NRSV

If they obey and serve Him, they shall spend their days in prosperity and their years in pleasantness and joy.
                    - Job 36:11 AMP

Happy are those who fear the LORD,
     who greatly delight in God's commands.
                    - Psalm 112:1 NAB

Serve the LORD with gladness;
Come before His presence with singing.
                    - Psalm 100:2 NKJV

Godliness with contentment is great gain.
                    - 1 Timothy 6:6 KJV

The LORD has done great things for us,
     and we are filled with joy.
                    - Psalm 126:3 NIV

The fear of the LORD leads to life,
And he who has it will abide in
     satisfaction.
           - Proverbs 19:23 NKJV

Happy are those who consider the
     poor;
  the LORD delivers them in the day
    of trouble.
           - Psalm 41:1 NRSV

"You will go out in joy
  and be led forth in peace;
the mountains and hills
  will burst into song before you,
and all the trees of the field
  will clap their hands."
           - Isaiah 55:12 NIV

A cheerful heart is good medicine,
  but a broken spirit saps a person's
    strength.
           - Proverbs 17:22 NLT

I rejoiced with those who said to me,
  "Let us go to the house of the LORD."
           - Psalm 122:1 TNIV

See also **Joy, Rejoice**

Holiness

Since we have these promises, dear friends, let us purify ourselves from everything that contaminates body and spirit, perfecting holiness out of reverence for God.

- 2 Corinthians 7:1 NIV

Put off, concerning your former conduct, the old man which grows corrupt according to the deceitful lusts, and be renewed in the spirit of your mind, and that you put on the new man which was created according to God, in true righteousness and holiness.

- Ephesians 4:22-24 NKJV

Like the Holy One who called you, be holy yourselves also in all your behavior; because it is written, "You shall be holy, for I am holy."

- 1 Peter 1:15-16 NASB

God saved us and called us to live a holy life.

- 2 Timothy 1:9 NLT

Pursue peace with all people, and holiness, without which no one will see the Lord.

- Hebrews 12:14 NKJV

Now that you have been set free from sin and have become slaves to God, the benefit you reap leads to holiness, and the result is eternal life.

- Romans 6:22 NIV

God did not call us to live in immorality, but in holiness.

                    - 1 Thessalonians 4:7 GNT

Take no part in and have no fellowship with the fruitless deeds and enterprises of darkness, but instead [let your lives be so in contrast as to] expose and reprove and convict them.

                    - Ephesians 5:11 AMP

In speech, conduct, love, faith and purity, show yourself an example of those who believe.

                    - 1 Timothy 4:12 NASB

Do you not know that you are the temple of God and that the Spirit of God dwells in you? For the temple of God is holy, which temple you are.

                    - 1 Corinthians 3:16-17 NKJV

"Wash yourselves, make yourselves clean;
Remove the evil of your deeds from My sight.
Cease to do evil."

                    - Isaiah 1:16 NASB

His divine power has given us everything required for life and godliness, through the knowledge of Him who called us by His own glory and goodness.

                    - 2 Peter 1:3 HCSB

Train yourself in godliness, for, while physical training is of some value, godliness is valuable in every way, holding promise for both the present life and the life to come.

                    - 1 Timothy 4:7-8 NRSV

"Come out from among them
And be separate, says the Lord.
Do not touch what is unclean,
And I will receive you."
                    - 2 Corinthians 6:17 NKJV

God's solid foundation stands firm, sealed with this
inscription: "The Lord knows those who are his," and,
"Everyone who confesses the name of the Lord must
turn away from wickedness."
                    - 2 Timothy 2:19 TNIV

Do not be deceived: "Evil company corrupts good habits."
                    - 1 Corinthians 15:33 NKJV

Do not be yoked together with unbelievers. For what
do righteousness and wickedness have in common?
Or what fellowship can light have with darkness?
                    - 2 Corinthians 6:14 NIV

See also **Righteousness, Pureness of Heart**

Honesty

A false balance is an abomination
    to the LORD,
But a just weight is His delight.
                                    - Proverbs 11:1 NASB

Each of you must put off falsehood and speak truthfully to his neighbor, for we are all members of one
body.
                                    - Ephesians 4:25 NIV

"Do not cheat anyone by using false measures of
length, weight, or quantity. Use honest scales, honest
weights, and honest measures."
                                    - Leviticus 19:35-36 GNT

If anyone competes in athletics, he is not crowned unless he competes according to the rules.
                                    - 2 Timothy 2:5 NKJV

Lying lips are an abomination to the
        LORD,
    but those who are truthful are
        his delight.
                                    - Proverbs 12:22 NAB

We intend to do what is right not only in the Lord's
sight but also in the sight of others.
                                    - 2 Corinthians 8:21 NRSV

"Speak the truth to each other, and render true and sound judgment in your courts."
                              - Zechariah 8:16 TNIV

Masters, give your bondservants what is just and fair, knowing that you also have a Master in heaven.
                              - Colossians 4:1 NKJV

See also **Honor, Integrity, Truth**

Honor

Pray for us. We are sure that we have a clear conscience and desire to live honorably in every way.
                              - Hebrews 13:18 NIV

A man's pride will bring him low,
But the humble in spirit will retain honor.
                              - Proverbs 29:23 NKJV

"If anyone serves Me, he must follow Me; and where I am, there My servant will be also; if anyone serves Me, the Father will honor him."
                              - John 12:26 NASB

It is honorable for a man to stop
        striving,
Since any fool can start a quarrel.
                              - Proverbs 20:3 NKJV

They have distributed freely, they have
        given to the poor;
    their righteousness endures forever;
    their horn is exalted in honor.
                            - Psalm 112:9 NRSV

"Riches and honor come from You, and You rule over
all."
                            - 1 Chronicles 29:12 NASB

"Worthy are you, Lord our God,
    to receive glory and honor and power,
for you created all things;
    because of your will they came to
        be and were created."
                            - Revelation 4:11 NAB

The one who oppresses the poor insults
        their Maker,
but one who is kind to the needy honors Him.
                            - Proverbs 14:31 HCSB

The name of our Lord Jesus will be honored because
of the way you live, and you will be honored along
with him.
                            - 2 Thessalonians 1:12 NLT

" 'Those who honor Me I will honor.' "
                            - 1 Samuel 2:30 NASB

The wise inherit honor,
    but fools get only shame.
                            - Proverbs 3:35 TNIV

"I do not receive honor from men."
                                    - John 5:41 NKJV

Beloved, I urge you...to abstain from the desires of the flesh that wage war against the soul. Conduct your-selves honorably among the Gentiles, so that, though they malign you as evildoers, they may see your ho-norable deeds and glorify God when he comes to judge.
                                    - 1 Peter 2:11-12 NRSV

Honor God by accepting each other, as Christ has ac-cepted you.
                                    - Romans 15:7 CEV

See also **Honesty, Integrity**

Hope

Now hope does not disappoint, because the love of God has been poured out in our hearts by the Holy Spirit who was given to us.
                                    - Romans 5:5 NKJV

May the God of hope fill you with all joy and peace as you trust in him, so that you may overflow with hope by the power of the Holy Spirit.
                                    - Romans 15:13 NIV

We know that when He appears, we will be like Him, because we will see Him just as He is. And everyone who has this hope fixed on Him purifies himself, just as He is pure.

> - 1 John 3:2-3 NASB

"I know the plans I have for you," declares the LORD, "plans to prosper you and not to harm you, plans to give you hope and a future."

> - Jeremiah 29:11 TNIV

The eyes of the LORD are on those
    who fear him,
  on those whose hope is in his unfailing love,
to deliver them from death
    and keep them alive in famine.

> - Psalm 33:18-19 NIV

Having such a hope, we use great boldness in our speech.

> - 2 Corinthians 3:12 NASB

Everything that was written in the past was written to teach us, so that through the endurance taught in the Scriptures and the encouragement they provide we might have hope.

> - Romans 15:4 TNIV

You faithfully answer our prayers with
    awesome deeds,
  O God our savior.
You are the hope of everyone on earth,
    even those who sail on distant seas.

> - Psalm 65:5 NLT

May integrity and uprightness protect
    me,
  because my hope, LORD, is in you.
- Psalm 25:21 TNIV

We rejoice in the hope of the glory of God.
- Romans 5:2 HCSB

The Lord takes pleasure in those who reverently and worshipfully fear Him, in those who hope in His mercy and loving-kindness.
- Psalm 147:11 AMP

Let us put on faith and love for a breastplate, and the hope of salvation for a helmet.
- 1 Thessalonians 5:8 JB

He saved us through the washing of rebirth and renewal by the Holy Spirit, whom he poured out on us generously through Jesus Christ our Savior, so that, having been justified by his grace, we might become heirs having the hope of eternal life.
- Titus 3:5-7 TNIV

I do not mean that I am already as God wants me to be. I have not yet reached that goal, but I continue trying to reach it and to make it mine. Christ wants me to do that, which is the reason he made me his.
- Philippians 3:12 NCV

Do not be a terror to me;
You are my hope in the day of doom.
- Jeremiah 17:17 NKJV

It is good to hope in silence
　　for the saving help of the LORD.
　　　　　　　　- Lamentations 3:26 NAB

Now in this hope we were saved, yet hope that is seen
is not hope, because who hopes for what he sees? But
if we hope for what we do not see, we eagerly wait for
it with patience.
　　　　　　　　- Romans 8:24-25 HCSB

"Then you will know that I am the LORD;
　　those who hope in me will not be disappointed."
　　　　　　　　- Isaiah 49:23 TNIV

Be of good courage,
And He shall strengthen your heart,
All you who hope in the LORD.
　　　　　　　　- Psalm 31:24 NKJV

See also **All Things Are Possible, Believing, Faith,
　　Perseverance**

Humility

"For everyone who exalts himself will be humbled, and he who humbles himself will be exalted."
- Luke 14:11 NASB

Whoever will humble himself therefore and become like this little child [trusting, lowly, loving, forgiving] is greatest in the kingdom of heaven.
- Matthew 18:4 AMP

The humble He guides in justice,
And the humble He teaches His way.
- Psalm 25:9 NKJV

"God opposes the proud
but favors the humble."
- James 4:6 NLT

Though I am free and belong to no one, I have made myself a slave to everyone, to win as many as possible.
- 1 Corinthians 9:19 TNIV

For the LORD takes pleasure in His
people;
He will beautify the humble with
salvation.
- Psalm 149:4 NKJV

With humility comes wisdom.
- Proverbs 11:2 HCSB

If anyone among you considers himself wise in this age, let him become a fool so as to become wise.

- 1 Corinthians 3:18 NAB

For I am the least of the apostles, who am not worthy to be called an apostle.... But by the grace of God I am what I am, and His grace toward me was not in vain.

- 1 Corinthians 15:9-10 NKJV

"The LORD gave, and the LORD has taken away; blessed be the name of the LORD."

- Job 1:21 NRSV

The humble will be filled with fresh joy
        from the LORD.
    The poor will rejoice in the Holy One
        of Israel.

- Isaiah 29:19 NLT

All of you, be of one mind, sympathetic, loving toward one another, compassionate, humble.

- 1 Peter 3:8 NAB

Man's pride causes his humiliation,
    but he who is humble of spirit obtains honor.

- Proverbs 29:23 NAB

Do what the elders tell you, and all wrap yourselves in humility to be servants of each other.

- 1 Peter 5:5 JB

A servant of the Lord must not quarrel but be gentle to all, able to teach, patient, in humility correcting those who are in opposition, if God perhaps will grant them repentance, so that they may know the truth.
- 2 Timothy 2:24-25 NKJV

The LORD has told you what is good,
and this is what he requires of you:
to do what is right, to love mercy,
and to walk humbly with your God.
- Micah 6:8 NLT

Remind the people to be subject to rulers and authorities, to be obedient, to be ready to do whatever is good, to slander no one, to be peaceable and considerate, and to show true humility toward all men.
- Titus 3:1-2 NIV

In humility regard others as better than yourselves.
- Philippians 2:3 NRSV

Humble yourselves [feeling very insignificant] in the presence of the Lord, and He will exalt you [He will lift you up and make your lives significant].
- James 4:10 AMP

Humble yourselves under the mighty hand of God, that He may exalt you at the proper time, casting all your anxiety on Him, because He cares for you.
- 1 Peter 5:6-7 NASB

"We have no power against this great multitude that is coming against us; nor do we know what to do, but our eyes are upon You."
                    - 2 Chronicles 20:12 NKJV

You rescue the humble,
    but you humiliate the proud.
                        - Psalm 18:27 NLT

"Blessed are the poor in spirit,
    for theirs is the kingdom of heaven."
                    - Matthew 5:3 NAB

Better is one day in your courts
    than a thousand elsewhere;
I would rather be a doorkeeper in the
        house of my God
    than dwell in the tents of the wicked.
                        - Psalm 84:10 NIV

The LORD sustains the humble
    but casts the wicked to the ground.
                    - Psalm 147:6 TNIV

By humility and the fear of the LORD
Are riches and honor and life.
                    - Proverbs 22:4 NKJV

See also **Thanksgiving**

Integrity

Better is the poor who walks in his
      integrity
Than one perverse in his ways,
      though he be rich.
- Proverbs 28:6 NKJV

May integrity and uprightness protect
      me,
      because my hope is in you.
- Psalm 25:21 NIV

We have conducted ourselves in the world...with integrity and godly sincerity. We have done so, relying not on worldly wisdom but on God's grace.
- 2 Corinthians 1:12 TNIV

Vindicate me, O LORD, for I have
      walked in my integrity,
And I have trusted in the LORD without
      wavering.
- Psalm 26:1 NASB

The integrity of the upright guides them,
      but the unfaithful are destroyed by their duplicity.
- Proverbs 11:3 TNIV

The just man walketh in his integrity: his children are blessed after him.
- Proverbs 20:7 KJV

But as for me, I will walk in my integrity; redeem me
and be merciful and gracious to me.

- Psalm 26:11 AMP

See also **Honesty, Honor, Truth**

Joy

"You now have sorrow; but I will see you again and
your heart will rejoice, and your joy no one will take
from you."

- John 16:22 NKJV

You have turned my mourning into dancing;
    you have taken off my sackcloth
    and clothed me with joy.

- Psalm 30:11 NRSV

The humble will be filled with fresh joy
        from the LORD.
    The poor will rejoice in the Holy One
        of Israel.

- Isaiah 29:19 NLT

"I have said these things to you so that my joy may be
in you, and that your joy may be complete."

- John 15:11 NRSV

The LORD has done great things for us,
    and we are filled with joy.
                        - Psalm 126:3 TNIV

Shout for joy, O heavens! And rejoice,
        O earth!
Break forth into joyful shouting, O
        mountains!
For the LORD has comforted His people
And will have compassion on His afflicted.
                        - Isaiah 49:13 NASB

Restore to me the joy of Your salvation
And sustain me with a willing spirit.
                        - Psalm 51:12 NASB

It gave me great joy to have some brothers come and
tell about your faithfulness to the truth and how you
continue to walk in the truth. I have no greater joy
than to hear that my children are walking in the truth.
                        - 3 John 3-4 NIV

My soul shall be joyful in the LORD: it shall rejoice in
his salvation.
                        - Psalm 35:9 KJV

May the God of hope fill you with all joy and peace as
you trust in him, so that you may overflow with hope
by the power of the Holy Spirit.
                        - Romans 15:13 TNIV

"Don't be dejected and sad, for the joy of the LORD is
your strength!"
                        - Nehemiah 8:10 NLT

Make a joyful shout to God, all the
          earth!
Sing out the honor of His name;
Make His praise glorious.
                              - Psalm 66:1-2 NKJV

"You will go out in joy
    and be led forth in peace;
the mountains and hills
    will burst into song before you,
and all the trees of the field
    will clap their hands."
                              - Isaiah 55:12 NIV

If they obey and serve Him, they shall spend their
days in prosperity and their years in pleasantness and
joy.
                              - Job 36:11 AMP

"Ask and you will receive, so that your joy may be
complete."
                              - John 16:24 NAB

Delight yourself in the LORD;
And He will give you the desires of
          your heart.
                              - Psalm 37:4 NASB

"There will be more joy in heaven over one sinner who
repents than over ninety-nine righteous persons who
need no repentance."
                              - Luke 15:7 NRSV

See also **Happiness, Praise, Rejoice**

Justice

Don't be deceived: God is not mocked. For whatever a man sows he will also reap, because the one who sows to his flesh will reap corruption from the flesh, but the one who sows to the Spirit will reap eternal life from the Spirit.
- Galatians 6:7-8 HCSB

Learn to do right! Seek justice, relieve the oppressed, and correct the oppressor. Defend the fatherless, plead for the widow.
- Isaiah 1:17 AMP

He who sows sparingly will also reap sparingly, and he who sows bountifully will also reap bountifully.
- 2 Corinthians 9:6 NASB

"Judge not, that you be not judged. For with what judgment you judge, you will be judged; and with the measure you use, it will be measured back to you."
- Matthew 7:1-2 NKJV

"He is the Rock, His work is perfect;
For all His ways are justice,
A God of truth and without injustice;
Righteous and upright is He."
- Deuteronomy 32:4 NKJV

"This is what the LORD Almighty says: 'Administer true justice; show mercy and compassion to one another.'"
- Zechariah 7:9 NIV

He leads the humble in justice,
And He teaches the humble His way.
                                    - Psalm 25:9 NASB

The evil do not understand justice,
    but those who seek the LORD understand it
        completely.
                                    - Proverbs 28:5 NRSV

Every morning He brings His
        justice to light;
He never fails.
                                    - Zephaniah 3:5 NKJV

Hate evil and love what is good;
    turn your courts into true halls of justice.
                                    - Amos 5:15 NLT

Whatever you do, work at it with all your heart, as
working for the Lord, not for men, since you know that
you will receive an inheritance from the Lord as a reward. It is the Lord Christ you are serving. Anyone
who does wrong will be repaid for his wrong, and there
is no favoritism.
                                    - Colossians 3:23-25 NIV

"Speak the truth to each other, and render true and
sound judgment in your courts."
                                    - Zechariah 8:16 TNIV

The Lord will reward each one of you for whatever
good you do, whether you are slave or free.
                                    - Ephesians 6:8 TNIV

Masters, give your bondservants what is just and fair, knowing that you also have a Master in heaven.
                                    - Colossians 4:1 NKJV

For I, the LORD, love justice.
                                    - Isaiah 61:8 NASB

"Maintain justice
    and do what is right,
for my salvation is close at hand
    and my righteousness will soon be revealed."
                                    - Isaiah 56:1 NIV

Let justice run down like waters and righteousness as a mighty and ever-flowing stream.
                                    - Amos 5:24 AMP

Near is the day of the LORD
    for all the nations!
As you have done, so shall it be done
        to you,
    your deed shall come back upon
        your own head.
                                    - Obadiah 15 NAB

"I, the LORD, search the heart,
I test the mind,
Even to give every man according to
        his ways,
According to the fruit of his doings."
                                    - Jeremiah 17:10 NKJV

Yet the LORD longs to be gracious to you;
   he rises to show you compassion.
For the LORD is a God of justice.
   Blessed are all who wait for him!
- Isaiah 30:18 NIV

See also **Judgment**

Kindness

Accept each other just as Christ has accepted you so that God will be given glory.
- Romans 15:7 NLT

Let us not become weary in doing good, for at the proper time we will reap a harvest if we do not give up. Therefore, as we have opportunity, let us do good to all people.
- Galatians 6:9-10 TNIV

Be kind to one another, tenderhearted, forgiving one another, even as God in Christ forgave you.
- Ephesians 4:32 NKJV

Bear one another's burdens, and in this way you will fulfill the law of Christ.
- Galatians 6:2 NRSV

He who oppresses the poor blasphemes
> his Maker,
> but he who is kind to the needy glorifies
> > him.
>> - Proverbs 14:31 NAB

As for you, brothers, never tire of doing what is right.
> - 2 Thessalonians 3:13 NIV

"And the King will answer and say to them, 'Assuredly, I say to you, inasmuch as you did it to one of the least of these My brethren, you did it to Me.' "
> - Matthew 25:40 NKJV

Let your gentleness be evident to all.
> - Philippians 4:5 TNIV

A man who has friends must himself
> be friendly,
But there is a friend who sticks
> closer than a brother.
>> - Proverbs 18:24 NKJV

Those who are kind to the poor lend to
> the LORD,
> and he will reward them for what they
> > have done.
>> - Proverbs 19:17 TNIV

"Treat people the same way you want them to treat you."
> - Matthew 7:12 NASB

Encourage one another and build up each other, as indeed you are doing.
> \- 1 Thessalonians 5:11 NRSV

We are God's masterpiece. He has created us anew in Christ Jesus, so we can do the good things he planned for us long ago.
> \- Ephesians 2:10 NLT

See also **Compassion, Generosity, Love, Works**

Knowledge

For it is the God who commanded light to shine out of darkness, who has shone in our hearts to give the light of the knowledge of the glory of God in the face of Jesus Christ.
> \- 2 Corinthians 4:6 NKJV

Yes, everything else is worthless when compared with the infinite value of knowing Christ Jesus my Lord.
> \- Philippians 3:8 NLT

For the LORD gives wisdom,
   from his mouth come knowledge and
      understanding.
> \- Proverbs 2:6 NAB

The fear of the LORD is the beginning
     of wisdom,
and the knowledge of the Holy One
     is understanding.
          - Proverbs 9:10 HCSB

The mind of the intelligent seeks knowledge,
But the mouth of fools feeds on folly.
          - Proverbs 15:14 NASB

Grow in the grace and knowledge of our Lord and Savior Jesus Christ.
          - 2 Peter 3:18 NASB

Let us pursue the knowledge of the LORD.
          - Hosea 6:3 NKJV

His divine power has given us everything required for life and godliness, through the knowledge of Him who called us by His own glory and goodness.
          - 2 Peter 1:3 HCSB

A wise man is more powerful than
     a strong man,
and a man of knowledge than a
     man of might.
          - Proverbs 24:5 NAB

In Him all the treasures of wisdom and knowledge are hidden.
          - Colossians 2:3 HCSB

Make every effort to support your faith with goodness, and goodness with knowledge, and knowledge with self-control, and self-control with endurance, and endurance with godliness, and godliness with mutual affection, and mutual affection with love. For if these things are yours and are increasing among you, they keep you from being ineffective and unfruitful in the knowledge of our Lord Jesus Christ.

- 2 Peter 1:5-8 NRSV

See also **Understanding, Wisdom**

Life

"I have come that they may have life, and that they may have it more abundantly."

- John 10:10 NKJV

To be controlled by human nature results in death; to be controlled by the Spirit results in life and peace.

- Romans 8:6 GNT

This is how God showed his love among us: He sent his one and only Son into the world that we might live through him.

- 1 John 4:9 NIV

If the Spirit of Him who raised Jesus from the dead dwells in you, He who raised Christ Jesus from the dead will also give life to your mortal bodies through His Spirit who dwells in you.

- Romans 8:11 NASB

For the law of the spirit of life in Christ Jesus has freed you from the law of sin and death.
- Romans 8:2 NAB

Live a life of love, just as Christ loved us and gave himself up for us as a fragrant offering and sacrifice to God.
- Ephesians 5:2 NIV

"I am the resurrection and the life. He who believes in Me, though he may die, he shall live. And whoever lives and believes in Me shall never die."
- John 11:25-26 NKJV

We know that we have passed from death unto life, because we love the brethren.
- 1 John 3:14 KJV

If a law had been given which was able to impart life, then righteousness would indeed have been based on law.
- Galatians 3:21 NASB

Understanding is a wellspring of life to those who have it.
- Proverbs 16:22 AMP

Because of his great love for us, God, who is rich in mercy, made us alive with Christ even when we were dead in transgressions.
- Ephesians 2:4-5 NIV

"The Spirit of God has made me;
    the breath of the Almighty gives me life."
- Job 33:4 TNIV

Whoever finds me [Wisdom] finds life and draws forth
and obtains favor from the Lord.
                              - Proverbs 8:35 AMP

This is the testimony: God gave us eternal life, and
this life is in his Son. Whoever has the Son has life;
whoever does not have the Son of God does not have
life.
                              - 1 John 5:11-12 NRSV

The fear of the LORD is a fountain of life,
turning people from the snares of death.
                              - Proverbs 14:27 HCSB

"I am the Light of the world; he who follows Me will not
walk in the darkness, but will have the Light of life."
                              - John 8:12 NASB

Blessed are those who persevere under trial, because
when they have stood the test, they will receive the
crown of life that God has promised to those who love
him.
                              - James 1:12 TNIV

You endowed me with life,
     watched each breath of mine with tender care.
                              - Job 10:12 JB

You have a full and true life in Christ, who is ruler
over all rulers and powers.
                              - Colossians 2:10 NCV

The fear of the LORD leads to life,
And he who has it will abide in
      satisfaction;
He will not be visited with evil.
                 - Proverbs 19:23 NKJV

Our Savior Jesus Christ...has abolished death and brought life and immortality to light through the gospel.
                 - 2 Timothy 1:10 NKJV

I am Alpha and Omega, the beginning and the end. I will freely give water from the life-giving fountain to everyone who is thirsty.
                 - Revelation 21:6 CEV

And you [He made alive], when you were dead (slain) by [your] trespasses and sins.
                 - Ephesians 2:1 AMP

I will never forget your precepts;
    through them you give me life.
                 - Psalm 119:93 NAB

"I call heaven and earth as witnesses today against you, that I have set before you life and death, blessing and cursing; therefore choose life, that both you and your descendants may live; that you may love the LORD your God, that you may obey His voice, and that you may cling to Him, for He is your life and the length of your days."
                 - Deuteronomy 30:19-20 NKJV

"I am the way and the truth and the life. No one comes to the Father except through me."
>   - John 14:6 NIV

I shall not die, but live, and declare the works of the LORD.
>   - Psalm 118:17 KJV

For with You is the fountain of life;
In Your light we see light.
>   - Psalm 36:9 NASB

"He is not God of the dead but of the living, because all are living to Him."
>   - Luke 20:38 HCSB

His divine power has granted to us everything pertaining to life and godliness, through the true knowledge of Him who called us by His own glory and excellence.
>   - 2 Peter 1:3 NASB

"I am the bread of life. He who comes to Me shall never hunger, and he who believes in Me shall never thirst."
>   - John 6:35 NKJV

"Enter through the narrow gate. For wide is the gate and broad is the road that leads to destruction, and many enter through it. But small is the gate and narrow the road that leads to life, and only a few find it."
>   - Matthew 7:13-14 TNIV

See also **Eternal Life, Live in Christ**

Longsuffering

Therefore I take pleasure in infirmities, in reproaches, in needs, in persecutions, in distresses, for Christ's sake. For when I am weak, then I am strong.

- 2 Corinthians 12:10 NKJV

It is better, if it is God's will, to suffer for doing good than for doing evil.

- 1 Peter 3:17 NIV

"Blessed are you when people insult you and persecute you, and falsely say all kinds of evil against you because of Me. Rejoice and be glad, for your reward in heaven is great; for in the same way they persecuted the prophets who were before you."

- Matthew 5:11-12 NASB

Take as an example of hardship and patience, brothers, the prophets who spoke in the name of the Lord.

- James 5:10 NAB

"If the world hates you, you know that it has hated Me before it hated you."

- John 15:18 NASB

When we are cursed, we bless; when we are persecuted, we endure it; when we are slandered, we answer kindly.

- 1 Corinthians 4:12-13 NIV

"Whoever does not bear his cross and come after Me cannot be My disciple."

- Luke 14:27 NKJV

Of this gospel I was appointed a herald and an apostle and a teacher. That is why I am suffering as I am. Yet I am not ashamed, because I know whom I have believed, and am convinced that he is able to guard what I have entrusted to him for that day.

- 2 Timothy 1:11-12 NIV

Therefore we do not lose heart. Even though our outward man is perishing, yet the inward man is being renewed day by day.

- 2 Corinthians 4:16 NKJV

How is it to your credit if you receive a beating for doing wrong and endure it? But if you suffer for doing good and you endure it, this is commendable before God. To this you were called, because Christ suffered for you, leaving you an example, that you should follow in his steps.

- 1 Peter 2:20-21 TNIV

For to this end we both labor and suffer reproach, because we trust in the living God, who is the Savior of all men, especially of those who believe.

- 1 Timothy 4:10 NKJV

Yet if any of you suffers as a Christian, do not consider it a disgrace, but glorify God because you bear this name.

- 1 Peter 4:16 NRSV

Though I am free and belong to no one, I have made myself a slave to everyone, to win as many as possible.
- 1 Corinthians 9:19 TNIV

We went through fire and through water,
Yet You brought us out into a place of abundance.
- Psalm 66:12 NASB

By faith Moses, when he became of age, refused to be called the son of Pharaoh's daughter, choosing rather to suffer affliction with the people of God than to enjoy the passing pleasures of sin.
- Hebrews 11:24-25 NKJV

It has been granted to you on behalf of Christ not only to believe on him, but also to suffer for him.
- Philippians 1:29 NIV

Even if you should suffer for what is right, you are blessed. "Do not fear their threats; do not be frightened."
- 1 Peter 3:14 TNIV

"Blessed are those who have been persecuted for the sake of righteousness, for theirs is the kingdom of heaven."
- Matthew 5:10 NASB

Keep a clear head about everything, endure hardship, do the work of an evangelist, fulfill your ministry.
- 2 Timothy 4:5 HCSB

Since Christ suffered for us in the flesh, arm yourselves also with the same mind, for he who has suffered in the flesh has ceased from sin, that he no
longer should live the rest of his time in the flesh for
the lusts of men, but for the will of God.

- 1 Peter 4:1-2 NKJV

The Spirit himself testifies with our spirit that we are
God's children. Now if we are children, then we are
heirs – heirs of God and co-heirs with Christ, if indeed
we share in his sufferings in order that we may also
share in his glory.

- Romans 8:16-17 TNIV

If you are reproached for the name of Christ, blessed
are you, for the Spirit of glory and of God rests upon
you. On their part He is blasphemed, but on your part
He is glorified.

- 1 Peter 4:14 NKJV

For this reason I obtained mercy, that in me first
Jesus Christ might show all longsuffering, as a pattern to those who are going to believe on Him for everlasting life.

- 1 Timothy 1:16 NKJV

After you have suffered for a little while, the God of all
grace, who called you to His eternal glory in Christ,
will Himself perfect, confirm, strengthen and establish
you.

- 1 Peter 5:10 NASB

We also rejoice in our sufferings, because we know
that suffering produces perseverance; perseverance,
character; and character, hope.

- Romans 5:3-4 NIV

For his sake I have suffered the loss of all things, and I regard them as rubbish, in order that I may gain Christ and be found in him, not having a righteousness of my own that comes from the law, but one that comes through faith in Christ, the righteousness from God based on faith.
                              - Philippians 3:8-9 NRSV

"Love your enemies, bless those who curse you, do good to those who hate you, and pray for those who spitefully use you and persecute you."
                              - Matthew 5:44 NKJV

"The LORD gave, and the LORD has taken away; blessed be the name of the LORD."
                              - Job 1:21 NRSV

Though the fig tree does not bud
    and there are no grapes on the vines,
though the olive crop fails
    and the fields produce no food,
though there are no sheep in the pen
    and no cattle in the stalls,
yet I will rejoice in the LORD,
    I will be joyful in God my Savior.
                              - Habakkuk 3:17-18 NIV

Beloved, do not think it strange concerning the fiery trial which is to try you, as though some strange thing happened to you; but rejoice to the extent that you partake of Christ's sufferings, that when His glory is revealed, you may also be glad with exceeding joy.
                              - 1 Peter 4:12-13 NKJV

See also **Persecution, Perseverance**

Love

"You have heard that it was said, 'You shall love your neighbor and hate your enemy.' But I say to you, love your enemies, bless those who curse you, do good to those who hate you, and pray for those who spitefully use you and persecute you."
- Matthew 5:43-44 NKJV

Love never fails. But where there are prophecies, they will cease; where there are tongues, they will be stilled; where there is knowledge, it will pass away.
- 1 Corinthians 13:8 NIV

My lips will glorify You
because Your faithful love is better than life.
- Psalm 63:3 HCSB

For God so loved the world that he gave his only Son, so that everyone who believes in him might not perish but might have eternal life.
- John 3:16 NAB

God's love was revealed among us in this way: God sent his only Son into the world so that we might live through him. In this is love, not that we loved God but that he loved us and sent his Son to be the atoning sacrifice for our sins.
- 1 John 4:9-10 NRSV

Your unfailing love, O LORD, is as vast as the heavens; your faithfulness reaches beyond the clouds.
- Psalm 36:5 NLT

The entire law is fulfilled in keeping this one command: "Love your neighbor as yourself."
- Galatians 5:14 TNIV

Love covers all offenses.
- Proverbs 10:12 NAB

I pray that you and all God's holy people will have the power to understand the greatness of Christ's love – how wide and how long and how high and how deep that love is. Christ's love is greater than anyone can ever know, but I pray that you will be able to know that love. Then you can be filled with the fullness of God.
- Ephesians 3:18-19 NCV

The LORD is with me to the end.
    LORD, your love endures forever.
- Psalm 138:8 NAB

See how great a love the Father has bestowed on us, that we would be called children of God; and such we are.
- 1 John 3:1 NASB

"Sow for yourselves righteousness,
    reap the fruit of unfailing love."
- Hosea 10:12 TNIV

And now these three remain: faith, hope and love. But the greatest of these is love.
- 1 Corinthians 13:13 NIV

Do not owe anyone anything, except to love one another, for the one who loves another has fulfilled the law. Love does no wrong to a neighbor. Love, therefore, is the fulfillment of the law.
- Romans 13:8,10 HCSB

Although you have not seen him, you love him; and even though you do not see him now, you believe in him and rejoice with an indescribable and glorious joy, for you are receiving the outcome of your faith, the salvation of your souls.
- 1 Peter 1:8-9 NRSV

Because of his great love for us, God, who is rich in mercy, made us alive with Christ even when we were dead in transgressions.
- Ephesians 2:4-5 NIV

The LORD protects all those who love him.
- Psalm 145:20 NLT

As the elect of God, holy and beloved, put on tender mercies, kindness, humility, meekness, longsuffering; bearing with one another, and forgiving one another, if anyone has a complaint against another; even as Christ forgave you, so you also must do. But above all these things put on love, which is the bond of perfection.
- Colossians 3:12-14 NKJV

Whoever loves his brother lives in the light, and there is nothing in him to make him stumble.
- 1 John 2:10 NIV

Pray for the peace of Jerusalem! May they prosper who love you [the Holy City]!
                              - Psalm 122:6 AMP

"Though the mountains be shaken
    and the hills be removed,
yet my unfailing love for you will not be shaken
    nor my covenant of peace be removed,"
    says the LORD, who has compassion on you.
                              - Isaiah 54:10 TNIV

God's gift was not a spirit of timidity, but the Spirit of power, and love, and self-control.
                              - 2 Timothy 1:7 JB

The love of God has been poured out within our hearts through the Holy Spirit who was given to us.
                              - Romans 5:5 NASB

The LORD is gracious and compassionate,
    slow to anger and rich in love.
The LORD is good to all;
    he has compassion on all he has made.
                              - Psalm 145:8-9 TNIV

Keep yourselves in the love of God and wait for the mercy of our Lord Jesus Christ that leads to eternal life.
                              - Jude 21 NAB

"I give you a new commandment: love one another. Just as I have loved you, you must also love one another. By this all people will know that you are My disciples, if you have love for one another."
                              - John 13:34-35 HCSB

I will sing of the LORD's great love forever;
   with my mouth I will make your faithfulness
      known through all generations.
                              - Psalm 89:1 NIV

You were called for freedom, brothers. But do not use
this freedom as an opportunity for the flesh; rather,
serve one another through love.
                              - Galatians 5:13 NAB

The LORD's unfailing love
   surrounds those who trust in him.
                              - Psalm 32:10 TNIV

If I give all my possessions to feed the poor, and if I
surrender my body to be burned, but do not have love,
it profits me nothing.
                              - 1 Corinthians 13:3 NASB

Let no one despise or think less of you because of your
youth, but be an example (pattern) for the believers in
speech, in conduct, in love, in faith, and in purity.
                              - 1 Timothy 4:12 AMP

We love Him because He first loved us.
                              - 1 John 4:19 NKJV

This is how we know what love is: Jesus Christ laid
down his life for us. And we ought to lay down our
lives for our brothers.
                              - 1 John 3:16 NIV

"Greater love has no one than this, than to lay down one's life for his friends."
                                        - John 15:13 NKJV

God demonstrates His own love toward us, in that while we were yet sinners, Christ died for us.
                                        - Romans 5:8 NASB

Let us put on faith and love for a breastplate, and the hope of salvation for a helmet.
                                        - 1 Thessalonians 5:8 JB

This is the commandment we have from him: whoever loves God must also love his brother.
                                        - 1 John 4:21 NAB

"I will give you a new heart and put a new spirit within you; I will remove your heart of stone and give you a heart of flesh."
                                        - Ezekiel 36:26 HCSB

The faithful love of the LORD never ends!
    His mercies never cease.
                                        - Lamentations 3:22 NLT

This is love: that we walk in obedience to his commands. As you have heard from the beginning, his command is that you walk in love.
                                        - 2 John 6 TNIV

Pursue righteousness, faith, love and peace, with those who call on the Lord from a pure heart.
                                        - 2 Timothy 2:22 NASB

I am persuaded that neither death nor life, nor angels nor principalities nor powers, nor things present nor things to come, nor height nor depth, nor any other created thing, shall be able to separate us from the love of God which is in Christ Jesus our Lord.

- Romans 8:38-39 NKJV

Pursue love and strive for the spiritual gifts.

- 1 Corinthians 14:1 NRSV

I pray that Christ will live in your hearts by faith and that your life will be strong in love and be built on love.

- Ephesians 3:17 NCV

Whoever keeps His word, in him the love of God has truly been perfected.

- 1 John 2:5 NASB

For the love of Christ compels us.

- 2 Corinthians 5:14 NKJV

Now this is His command: that we believe in the name of His Son Jesus Christ, and love one another as He commanded us.

- 1 John 3:23 HCSB

Let all that you do be done in love.

- 1 Corinthians 16:14 NRSV

Be devoted to one another in brotherly love. Honor one another above yourselves. Never be lacking in zeal, but keep your spiritual fervor, serving the Lord.

- Romans 12:10-11 NIV

We know that we have passed from death to life because we love our brothers.
                              - 1 John 3:14 NAB

Live a life of love, just as Christ loved us and gave
himself up for us as a fragrant offering and sacrifice to
God.
                              - Ephesians 5:2 NIV

Let brotherly love continue.
                              - Hebrews 13:1 KJV

Now that you have purified your souls by your obedience to the truth so that you have genuine mutual
love, love one another deeply from the heart.
                              - 1 Peter 1:22 NRSV

This is the message which you have heard from the
beginning, that we should love one another.
                              - 1 John 3:11 NASB

"If you love Me, you will keep My commandments."
                              - John 14:15 NASB

Love must be sincere.
                              - Romans 12:9 NIV

Beloved, let us love one another, because love is from
God; everyone who loves is born of God and knows
God. Whoever does not love does not know God, for
God is love.
                              - 1 John 4:7-8 NRSV

Above all, maintain constant love for one another, for love covers a multitude of sins.

> \- 1 Peter 4:8 NRSV

We must not love in word or speech, but in deed and truth.

> \- 1 John 3:18 HCSB

" 'You shall love the LORD your God with all your heart, with all your soul, with all your strength, and with all your mind,' and 'your neighbor as yourself.' "

> \- Luke 10:27 NKJV

Let the morning bring me word of your
    unfailing love,
  for I have put my trust in you.
Show me the way I should go,
  for to you I lift up my soul.

> \- Psalm 143:8 NIV

Beloved, since God loved us so much, we also ought to love one another. ...If we love one another, God lives in us, and his love is perfected in us.

> \- 1 John 4:11-12 NRSV

If I speak in the tongues of men and of angels, but have not love, I am only a resounding gong or a clanging cymbal. If I have the gift of prophecy and can fathom all mysteries and all knowledge, and if I have a faith that can move mountains, but have not love, I am nothing.

> \- 1 Corinthians 13:1-2 NIV

For love is as strong as death.

> \- Song of Solomon 8:6 AMP

All of you, be of one mind, sympathetic, loving toward one another, compassionate, humble.
                    - 1 Peter 3:8 NAB

There is no fear in love, but perfect love casts out fear.
                    - 1 John 4:18 NRSV

A friend loves at all times.
                    - Proverbs 17:17 HCSB

By this we know that we love the children of God, when we love God and obey his commandments. For the love of God is this, that we obey his commandments.
                    - 1 John 5:2-3 NRSV

God is love. Whoever lives in love lives in God, and God in him.
                    - 1 John 4:16 NIV

Love is patient; love is kind; love is not envious or boastful or arrogant or rude. It does not insist on its own way; it is not irritable or resentful; it does not rejoice in wrongdoing, but rejoices in the truth. It bears all things, believes all things, hopes all things, endures all things.
                    - 1 Corinthians 13:4-7 NRSV

See also **Compassion, Forgiveness, Kindness, Mercy, Passion of Jesus**

Loyalty

"Do not fear any of those things which you are about to suffer. Indeed, the devil is about to throw some of you into prison, that you may be tested, and you will have tribulation ten days. Be faithful until death, and I will give you the crown of life."
                    - Revelation 2:10 NKJV

If we are faithless, He remains faithful, for He cannot deny Himself.
                    - 2 Timothy 2:13 NASB

"Don't ask me to leave you and turn back. Wherever you go, I will go; wherever you live, I will live. Your people will be my people, and your God will be my God. Wherever you die, I will die, and there I will be buried. May the LORD punish me severely if I allow anything but death to separate us!"
                    - Ruth 1:16-17 NLT

It gave me great joy to have some brothers come and tell about your faithfulness to the truth and how you continue to walk in the truth.
                    - 3 John 3 NIV

"Devote yourselves completely to the LORD our God, walking in his statutes and keeping his commandments."
                    - 1 Kings 8:61 NRSV

"Whoever is faithful in very little is also faithful in much, and whoever is unrighteous in very little is also unrighteous in much."
                                   - Luke 16:10 HCSB

A faithful man shall abound with blessings.
                                   - Proverbs 28:20 AMP

"For the eyes of the LORD run to and fro throughout the whole earth, to show Himself strong on behalf of those whose heart is loyal to Him."
                                   - 2 Chronicles 16:9 NKJV

I thank Christ Jesus our Lord, who has given me strength, and who judged me faithful enough to call me into his service.
                                   - 1 Timothy 1:12 JB

God is faithful and will not let you be tried beyond your strength; but with the trial he will also provide a way out, so that you may be able to bear it.
                                   - 1 Corinthians 10:13 NAB

Your testimonies are righteous forever.
                                   - Psalm 119:144 NASB

"There has not failed one word of all His good promise."
                                   - 1 Kings 8:56 NKJV

Never let loyalty and faithfulness leave you.
Tie them around your neck;
write them on the tablet of your heart.
Then you will find favor and high regard
in the sight of God and man.
- Proverbs 3:3-4 HCSB

"The LORD rewards every man for his righteousness
and faithfulness."
- 1 Samuel 26:23 TNIV

I will sing of the LORD's great love forever;
with my mouth I will make your faithfulness
known
through all generations.
- Psalm 89:1 TNIV

"You must always act in the fear of the LORD, with
faithfulness and an undivided heart."
- 2 Chronicles 19:9 NLT

Through the LORD's mercies we are
not consumed,
Because His compassions fail not.
They are new every morning;
Great is Your faithfulness.
- Lamentations 3:22-23 NKJV

O LORD, you are my God;
I will exalt you and praise your name,
for in perfect faithfulness
you have done marvelous things,
things planned long ago.
- Isaiah 25:1 NIV

Your unfailing love, O LORD, is as vast as the heavens;
    your faithfulness reaches beyond the clouds.
                                    - Psalm 36:5 NLT

The Lord is faithful; he will strengthen you and guard
you from the evil one.
                            - 2 Thessalonians 3:3 NAB

Let us hold fast the confession of our hope without
wavering, for He who promised is faithful.
                            - Hebrews 10:23 NASB

" 'Well done, good and faithful servant; you were faithful over a few things, I will make you ruler over many
things. Enter into the joy of your lord.' "
                            - Matthew 25:21 NKJV

See also **Faith, Obedience, Promise, Trust**

Mercy

For as the heavens are high above
        the earth,
So great is His mercy toward those
        who fear Him.
                            - Psalm 103:11 NKJV

Those who oppress the poor insult their
        Maker,
    but those who are kind to the needy honor him.
                            - Proverbs 14:31 NRSV

Let the wicked forsake his way,
And the unrighteous man his
          thoughts;
Let him return to the LORD,
And He will have mercy on him;
And to our God,
For He will abundantly pardon.
                    - Isaiah 55:7 NKJV

Let us therefore approach the throne of grace with
boldness, so that we may receive mercy and find grace
to help in time of need.
                    - Hebrews 4:16 NRSV

He saved us, not because of righteous things we had
done, but because of his mercy.
                    - Titus 3:5 TNIV

Judgment will be merciless to one who has shown no
mercy; mercy triumphs over judgment.
                    - James 2:13 NASB

The LORD has told you what is good,
    and this is what he requires of you:
to do what is right, to love mercy,
    and to walk humbly with your God.
                    - Micah 6:8 NLT

I will sing of Your power;
Yes, I will sing aloud of Your mercy
          in the morning;
                    - Psalm 59:16 NKJV

For thy mercy is great above the heavens: and thy
truth reacheth unto the clouds.
                          - Psalm 108:4 KJV

The favors of the LORD are not exhausted,
    his mercies are not spent;
They are renewed each morning,
    so great is his faithfulness.
                          - Lamentations 3:22-23 NAB

" 'Break away now from your sins by doing righteousness and from your iniquities by showing mercy to the
poor.' "
                          - Daniel 4:27 NASB

Oh, give thanks to the LORD, for He
        is good!
For His mercy endures forever.
                          - Psalm 106:1 NKJV

Do not, O LORD, withhold your mercy
        from me;
let your steadfast love and your faithfulness
        keep me safe forever.
                          - Psalm 40:11 NRSV

"This is what the LORD of Heaven's Armies says: Judge
fairly, and show mercy and kindness to one another."
                          - Zechariah 7:9 NLT

On those who waver, have mercy.
                          - Jude 22 NAB

For You, Lord, are good, and ready
          to forgive,
And abundant in mercy to all those
          who call upon You.
                    - Psalm 86:5 NKJV

Since it is by God's mercy that we are engaged in this
ministry, we do not lose heart.
                    - 2 Corinthians 4:1 NRSV

Let Your tender mercies come to me,
          that I may live;
For Your law is my delight.
                    - Psalm 119:77 NKJV

Blessed are the merciful: for they shall obtain mercy.
                    - Matthew 5:7 KJV

Because of his great love for us, God, who is rich in
mercy, made us alive with Christ even when we were
dead in transgressions.
                    - Ephesians 2:4-5 TNIV

The LORD is gracious and full of
          compassion,
Slow to anger and great in mercy.
The LORD is good to all,
And His tender mercies are over all
          His works.
                    - Psalm 145:8-9 NKJV

See also **Compassion, Generosity**

Obedience

If you fully obey the LORD your God and carefully follow all his commands I give you today, the LORD your God will set you high above all the nations on earth.
                                    - Deuteronomy 28:1 NIV

"Whoever practices and teaches these commands will be called great in the kingdom of heaven."
                                    - Matthew 5:19 NIV

Let every soul be subject to the governing authorities. For there is no authority except from God, and the authorities that exist are appointed by God. Therefore whoever resists the authority resists the ordinance of God, and those who resist will bring judgment on themselves.
                                    - Romans 13:1-2 NKJV

This is love: that we walk in obedience to his commands. As you have heard from the beginning, his command is that you walk in love.
                                    - 2 John 6 TNIV

We also have as our ambition, whether at home or absent, to be pleasing to Him.
                                    - 2 Corinthians 5:9 NASB

If they obey and serve Him, they shall spend their days in prosperity and their years in pleasantness and joy.
                                    - Job 36:11 AMP

Obey your earthly masters with respect and fear, and with sincerity of heart, just as you would obey Christ.

- Ephesians 6:5 TNIV

"Devote yourselves completely to the LORD our God, walking in his statutes and keeping his command-ments."

- 1 Kings 8:61 NRSV

Whoever keeps His word, in him the love of God has truly been perfected. By this we know that we are in Him: the one who says he abides in Him ought himself to walk in the same manner as He walked.

- 1 John 2:5-6 NASB

If you abide in My word [hold fast to My teachings and live in accordance with them], you are truly My dis-ciples.

- John 8:31 AMP

Do all things without complaining and disputing, that you may become blameless and harmless, children of God without fault in the midst of a crooked and per-verse generation, among whom you shine as lights in the world.

- Philippians 2:14-15 NKJV

Happy are those who fear the LORD,
    who greatly delight in God's commands.

- Psalm 112:1 NAB

Having been perfected, He became the author of eter-nal salvation to all who obey Him.

- Hebrews 5:9 NKJV

Remind the people to be subject to rulers and authorities, to be obedient, to be ready to do whatever is good, to slander no one, to be peaceable and considerate, and to show true humility toward all men.

- Titus 3:1-2 NIV

Whatever we ask we receive from Him, because we keep His commandments and do the things that are pleasing in His sight.

- 1 John 3:22 NASB

"Keep the mandate of the LORD, your God, following his ways and observing his statutes, commands, ordinances, and decrees..., that you may succeed in whatever you do, wherever you turn."

- 1 Kings 2:3 NAB

The world and its desire are passing away, but those who do the will of God live forever.

- 1 John 2:17 NRSV

"If anyone loves Me, he will keep My word. My Father will love him, and We will come to him and make Our home with him."

- John 14:23 HCSB

Blessed are all who fear the LORD,
    who walk in obedience to him.

- Psalm 128:1 TNIV

"Honor your father and your mother, that your days may be prolonged in the land which the LORD your God gives you."

- Exodus 20:12 NASB

Obey your leaders and submit to their authority. They keep watch over you as men who must give an account. Obey them so that their work will be a joy, not a burden, for that would be of no advantage to you.

- Hebrews 13:17 NIV

You were cleansed from your sins when you obeyed the truth.

- 1 Peter 1:22 NLT

Fear God and keep his commandments,
    for this is the whole duty of man.

- Ecclesiastes 12:13 NIV

"You shall walk after the LORD your God and fear Him, and keep His commandments and obey His voice; you shall serve Him and hold fast to Him."

- Deuteronomy 13:4 NKJV

This is how we are sure that we have come to know Him: by keeping His commands.

- 1 John 2:3 HCSB

"Keep this Book of the Law always on your lips; meditate on it day and night, so that you may be careful to do everything written in it. Then you will be prosperous and successful."

- Joshua 1:8 TNIV

Children, obey your parents in the Lord, for this is right. "Honor your father and mother" – this is the first commandment with a promise: "so that it may be well with you and you may live long on the earth."

- Ephesians 6:1-3 NRSV

"Has the LORD as much delight in burnt
    offerings and sacrifices
As in obeying the voice of the LORD?
Behold, to obey is better than sacrifice,
And to heed than the fat of rams."
                           - 1 Samuel 15:22 NASB

But Peter and the other apostles answered and said:
"We ought to obey God rather than men."
                           - Acts 5:29 NKJV

"Not everyone who says to Me, 'Lord, Lord,' will enter
the kingdom of heaven, but he who does the will of My
Father who is in heaven will enter."
                           - Matthew 7:21 NASB

"We are witnesses of these things, and so is the Holy
Spirit, whom God has given to those who obey him."
                           - Acts 5:32 TNIV

Everyone has heard about your obedience, so I rejoice
because of you; but I want you to be wise about what
is good, and innocent about what is evil.
                           - Romans 16:19 TNIV

"If you love Me, you will keep My commandments."
                           - John 14:15 NASB

I will climb up to my watchtower
    and stand at my guardpost.
There I will wait to see what the LORD says
    and how he will answer my complaint.
                           - Habakkuk 2:1 NLT

If you are willing and obedient, you shall eat the good of the land.
                                            - Isaiah 1:19 AMP

" 'Because you have kept My command to persevere, I also will keep you from the hour of trial which shall come upon the whole world.' "
                                            - Revelation 3:10 NKJV

By this we know that we love the children of God, when we love God and obey his commandments. For the love of God is this, that we obey his command-ments. And his commandments are not burdensome.
                                            - 1 John 5:2-3 NRSV

"I delight to do Your will, my God;
Your instruction resides within me."
                                            - Psalm 40:8 HCSB

Submit yourselves to every ordinance of man for the Lord's sake, whether to the king as supreme, or to governors, as to those who are sent by him for the punishment of evildoers and for the praise of those who do good. For this is the will of God, that by doing good you may put to silence the ignorance of foolish men.
                                            - 1 Peter 2:13-15 NKJV

See also **Loyalty**

Patience

But those who wait on the LORD
Shall renew their strength;
They shall mount up with wings like
    eagles,
They shall run and not be weary,
They shall walk and not faint.
                   - Isaiah 40:31 NKJV

We who live by the Spirit eagerly wait to receive by
faith the righteousness God has promised to us.
                   - Galatians 5:5 NLT

A servant of the Lord must not quarrel but be gentle to
all, able to teach, patient, in humility correcting those
who are in opposition, if God perhaps will grant them
repentance, so that they may know the truth.
                 - 2 Timothy 2:24-25 NKJV

On that day it will be said,
"Look, this is our God;
we have waited for Him, and He has saved us.
This is the LORD; we have waited for Him.
Let us rejoice and be glad in His salvation."
                   - Isaiah 25:9 HCSB

I waited patiently for the LORD;
And He inclined to me and heard my cry.
                   - Psalm 40:1 NASB

The patient in spirit is better than the proud in spirit.
                 - Ecclesiastes 7:8 KJV

Be patient, therefore, beloved, until the coming of the Lord. The farmer waits for the precious crop from the earth, being patient with it until it receives the early and the late rains. You also must be patient. Strengthen your hearts, for the coming of the Lord is near.

- James 5:7-8 NRSV

But if we hope for what we do not yet have, we wait for it patiently.

- Romans 8:25 NIV

Don't say, "I'll pay you back for the wrong
      you did."
   Wait for the LORD, and he will make
         things right.

- Proverbs 20:22 NCV

But as for me, I will look to the LORD,
   I will wait for the God of my salvation;
   my God will hear me.

- Micah 7:7 NRSV

Be patient with all.

- 1 Thessalonians 5:14 NAB

The LORD is good to those who wait
      for Him,
To the soul who seeks Him.
It is good that one should hope and
      wait quietly
For the salvation of the LORD.

- Lamentations 3:25-26 NKJV

I will climb up to my watchtower
   and stand at my guardpost.
There I will wait to see what the LORD says
   and how he will answer my complaint.
                        - Habakkuk 2:1 NLT

Having patiently waited, he obtained the promise.
                        - Hebrews 6:15 NASB

"Then you will know that I am the LORD;
   those who wait for me shall not be put to shame."
                        - Isaiah 49:23 NRSV

Preach the Word; be prepared in season and out of season; correct, rebuke and encourage – with great patience and careful instruction.
                        - 2 Timothy 4:2 NIV

Wait on the LORD;
Be of good courage,
And He shall strengthen your heart;
Wait, I say, on the LORD!
                        - Psalm 27:14 NKJV

My brethren, count it all joy when you fall into various trials, knowing that the testing of your faith produces patience. But let patience have its perfect work, that you may be perfect and complete, lacking nothing.
                        - James 1:2-4 NKJV

Be still and rest in the Lord; wait for Him and patiently lean yourself upon Him.
                        - Psalm 37:7 AMP

Therefore the LORD waits to be gracious
  to you;
 therefore he will rise up to show
  mercy to you.
For the LORD is a God of justice;
 blessed are all those who wait for him.
      - Isaiah 30:18 NRSV

Brothers and sisters, as an example of patience in the face of suffering, take the prophets who spoke in the name of the Lord.
      - James 5:10 TNIV

"For the vision is yet for the appointed time;
It hastens toward the goal and it will not fail.
Though it tarries, wait for it;
For it will certainly come, it will not delay."
      - Habakkuk 2:3 NASB

See also **Peace, Perseverance**

Peace

Since we have been justified through faith, we have peace with God through our Lord Jesus Christ.
      - Romans 5:1 TNIV

Blessed are the peacemakers: for they shall be called the children of God.
      - Matthew 5:9 KJV

"Peace be with you! As the Father has sent me, I am sending you."
                              - John 20:21 NIV

"Repent, then, and turn to God, so that your sins may be wiped out, that times of refreshing may come from the Lord."
                              - Acts 3:19 NIV

God is not the author of confusion, but of peace.
                    - 1 Corinthians 14:33 KJV

By waiting and by calm you
        shall be saved,
    in quiet and in trust your
        strength lies.
                    - Isaiah 30:15 NAB

How wonderful it is, how pleasant,
    for God's people to live together in harmony!
                    - Psalm 133:1 GNT

"These things I have spoken to you, so that in Me you may have peace. In the world you have tribulation, but take courage; I have overcome the world."
                    - John 16:33 NASB

"Now acquaint yourself with Him,
        and be at peace;
    Thereby good will come to you."
                    - Job 22:21 NKJV

"You will go out in joy
   and be led forth in peace;
the mountains and hills
   will burst into song before you,
and all the trees of the field
   will clap their hands."
                          - Isaiah 55:12 TNIV

Pray for the peace of Jerusalem: they shall prosper
that love thee.
                          - Psalm 122:6 KJV

"We sought the LORD our God, and he has given us
peace on every side."
                          - 2 Chronicles 14:7 NLT

The mind controlled by the sinful nature is death, but
the mind controlled by the Spirit is life and peace.
                          - Romans 8:6 TNIV

For He Himself is our peace.
                          - Ephesians 2:14 NASB

"You will keep him in perfect
            peace,
Whose mind is stayed on You,
Because he trusts in You."
                          - Isaiah 26:3 NKJV

Rejoice, be made complete, be comforted, be like-
minded, live in peace; and the God of love and peace
will be with you.
                          - 2 Corinthians 13:11 NASB

" ' "The LORD bless you
    and keep you;
the LORD make his face shine upon you
    and be gracious to you;
the LORD turn his face toward you
    and give you peace." ' "
                        - Numbers 6:24-26 NIV

He made peace with everything in heaven
        and on earth
    by means of Christ's blood on the cross.
                        - Colossians 1:20 NLT

A heart at peace gives life to the body.
                        - Proverbs 14:30 TNIV

The peace of God, which surpasses all understanding,
will guard your hearts and minds through Christ Jesus.
                        - Philippians 4:7 NKJV

Pursue righteousness, faith, love, and peace, along
with those who call on the Lord with purity of heart.
                        - 2 Timothy 2:22 NAB

Let the peace of Christ rule in your hearts, since as
members of one body you were called to peace.
                        - Colossians 3:15 NIV

Live in harmony with one another.
                        - Romans 12:16 TNIV

Now may the Lord of peace Himself grant you His peace (the peace of His kingdom) at all times and in all ways [under all circumstances and conditions, whatever comes].

- 2 Thessalonians 3:16 AMP

May the God of hope fill you with all joy and peace as you trust in him, so that you may overflow with hope by the power of the Holy Spirit.

- Romans 15:13 NIV

"Let them turn away from evil and do
        good;
    let them seek peace and pursue it."

- 1 Peter 3:11 NRSV

This is what the LORD says:
"Stand at the crossroads and look;
    ask for the ancient paths,
ask where the good way is, and walk in it,
    and you will find rest for your souls."

- Jeremiah 6:16 NIV

He lets me lie down in green pastures;
He leads me beside quiet waters.

- Psalm 23:2 HCSB

Great peace have those who
        love Your law,
And nothing causes them to
        stumble.

- Psalm 119:165 NKJV

Those who are peacemakers will plant seeds of peace and reap a harvest of righteousness.
                                        - James 3:18 NLT

"Though the mountains be shaken
    and the hills be removed,
yet my unfailing love for you will not be shaken
    nor my covenant of peace be removed,"
    says the LORD, who has compassion on you.
                                        - Isaiah 54:10 TNIV

Pursue peace with all people, and holiness, without which no one will see the Lord.
                                        - Hebrews 12:14 NKJV

When a man's ways are pleasing to
        the LORD,
    he makes even his enemies live
        at peace with him.
                                        - Proverbs 16:7 NIV

If it is possible, as far as it depends on you, live at peace with everyone.
                                        - Romans 12:18 TNIV

"Peace I leave with you, My peace I give to you; not as the world gives do I give to you. Let not your heart be troubled, neither let it be afraid."
                                        - John 14:27 NKJV

See also **Patience, Peace of Mind**

Peace of Mind

Yea, though I walk through the
     valley of the shadow of death,
I will fear no evil;
For You are with me;
Your rod and Your staff, they comfort
     me.
                    - Psalm 23:4 NKJV

"I am with you always, even to the end of the age."
                    - Matthew 28:20 NASB

"Therefore do not worry about tomorrow, for tomorrow will worry about its own things. Sufficient for the day is its own trouble."
                    - Matthew 6:34 NKJV

We know that if the earthly tent we live in is destroyed, we have a building from God, an eternal house in heaven, not built by human hands.
                    - 2 Corinthians 5:1 NIV

My God will fully satisfy every need of yours according to his riches in glory in Christ Jesus.
                    - Philippians 4:19 NRSV

When you lie down, you need not
     be afraid,
   when you rest, your sleep
     will be sweet.
                    - Proverbs 3:24 NAB

"I have given you authority to trample on snakes and scorpions and to overcome all the power of the enemy; nothing will harm you."
- Luke 10:19 TNIV

The God of peace will crush Satan under your feet shortly.
- Romans 16:20 NKJV

"Do not be afraid or discouraged, for the LORD your God is with you wherever you go."
- Joshua 1:9 HCSB

He Himself has said, "I will never leave you nor forsake you." So we may boldly say:
"The LORD is my helper;
I will not fear.
What can man do to me?"
- Hebrews 13:5-6 NKJV

The Lord will perfect that which concerns me;
Your mercy and loving-kindness, O Lord, endure forever.
- Psalm 138:8 AMP

"Let not your heart be troubled; you believe in God, believe also in Me. In My Father's house are many mansions; if it were not so, I would have told you. I go to prepare a place for you. And if I go and prepare a place for you, I will come again and receive you to Myself; that where I am, there you may be also. And where I go you know, and the way you know."
- John 14:1-4 NKJV

God has not given us a spirit of fear, but of power and
of love and of a sound mind.
> - 2 Timothy 1:7 NKJV

"Come to me, all you who are weary and burdened,
and I will give you rest. Take my yoke upon you and
learn from me, for I am gentle and humble in heart,
and you will find rest for your souls. For my yoke is
easy and my burden is light."
> - Matthew 11:28-30 TNIV

If God is for us, who can be against us?
> - Romans 8:31 NIV

See also **Confidence, Peace, Promise, Worry**

Perseverance

We also glory in our sufferings, because we know that
suffering produces perseverance; perseverance, character; and character, hope.
> - Romans 5:3-4 TNIV

"And you will be hated by all for My name's sake. But
he who endures to the end shall be saved."
> - Mark 13:13 NKJV

If you faint in the day of adversity, your strength is
small.
> - Proverbs 24:10 AMP

How is it to your credit if you receive a beating for doing wrong and endure it? But if you suffer for doing good and you endure it, this is commendable before God. To this you were called, because Christ suffered for you, leaving you an example, that you should follow in his steps.

- 1 Peter 2:20-21 TNIV

Do you not know that those who run in a race all run, but only one receives the prize? Run in such a way that you may win.

- 1 Corinthians 9:24 NASB

I can do all things through Christ who strengthens me.

- Philippians 4:13 NKJV

Restore to me the joy of Your salvation
And sustain me with a willing spirit.

- Psalm 51:12 NASB

Stand firm and hold fast to the traditions that you were taught by us, either by word of mouth or by our letter.

- 2 Thessalonians 2:15 NRSV

Indeed we count them blessed who endure. You have heard of the perseverance of Job and seen the end intended by the Lord – that the Lord is very compassionate and merciful.

- James 5:11 NKJV

Therefore, my beloved, be steadfast, immovable, always excelling in the work of the Lord, because you know that in the Lord your labor is not in vain.
                              - 1 Corinthians 15:58 NRSV

The one who looks intently into the perfect law of freedom and perseveres in it, and is not a forgetful hearer but a doer who acts – this person will be blessed in what he does.
                              - James 1:25 HCSB

We went through fire and through water,
Yet You brought us out into a place of abundance.
                              - Psalm 66:12 NASB

" 'Because you have kept My command to persevere, I also will keep you from the hour of trial which shall come upon the whole world.' "
                              - Revelation 3:10 NKJV

Keep a clear head about everything, endure hardship, do the work of an evangelist, fulfill your ministry.
                              - 2 Timothy 4:5 HCSB

Encourage one another day after day, as long as it is still called "Today," so that none of you will be hardened by the deceitfulness of sin.
                              - Hebrews 3:13 NASB

For Christ's love compels us.
                              - 2 Corinthians 5:14 NIV

Since it is by God's mercy that we are engaged in this ministry, we do not lose heart.
                              - 2 Corinthians 4:1 NRSV

Stand fast therefore in the liberty by which Christ has made us free, and do not be entangled again with a yoke of bondage.
                              - Galatians 5:1 NKJV

Let us hold fast the confession of our hope without wavering, for He who promised is faithful.
                              - Hebrews 10:23 NASB

You were once alienated and hostile in mind because of your evil actions. But now He has reconciled you by His physical body through His death, to present you holy, faultless, and blameless before Him – if indeed you remain grounded and steadfast in the faith, and are not shifted away from the hope of the gospel that you heard.
                              - Colossians 1:21-23 HCSB

If we have died with Him, we shall also live with Him. If we endure, we shall also reign with Him.
                              - 2 Timothy 2:11-12 AMP

Pray without ceasing.
                              - 1 Thessalonians 5:17 NRSV

Be sober, be vigilant; because your adversary the devil walks about like a roaring lion, seeking whom he may devour. Resist him, steadfast in the faith, knowing that the same sufferings are experienced by your brotherhood in the world.
                              - 1 Peter 5:8-9 NKJV

We do not give up; even though our outer person is being destroyed, our inner person is being renewed day by day.

- 2 Corinthians 4:16 HCSB

Let us not grow weary while doing good, for in due season we shall reap if we do not lose heart.

- Galatians 6:9 NKJV

Though he stumble, he will not fall,
   for the LORD upholds him with his hand.

- Psalm 37:24 NIV

Create in me a clean heart, O God,
And renew a steadfast spirit within
      me.

- Psalm 51:10 NASB

For we have become partakers of Christ if we hold the beginning of our confidence steadfast to the end.

- Hebrews 3:14 NKJV

God blesses those who patiently endure testing and temptation. Afterward they will receive the crown of life that God has promised to those who love him.

- James 1:12 NLT

And as for you, brethren, do not become weary or lose heart in doing right [but continue in well-doing without weakening].

- 2 Thessalonians 3:13 AMP

When ridiculed, we bless; when persecuted, we endure; when slandered, we respond gently.
- 1 Corinthians 4:12-13 NAB

Brethren, I do not count myself to have apprehended; but one thing I do, forgetting those things which are behind and reaching forward to those things which are ahead, I press toward the goal for the prize of the upward call of God in Christ Jesus.
- Philippians 3:13-14 NKJV

I am willing to endure anything if it will bring salvation and eternal glory in Christ Jesus to those God has chosen.
- 2 Timothy 2:10 NLT

Whatever was written previously was written for our instruction, that by endurance and by the encouragement of the scriptures we might have hope.
- Romans 15:4 NAB

Now it is God who makes both us and you stand firm in Christ. He anointed us, set his seal of ownership on us, and put his Spirit in our hearts.
- 2 Corinthians 1:21 NIV

Keep alert, stand firm in your faith, be courageous, be strong.
- 1 Corinthians 16:13 NRSV

Do not rejoice over me, O my enemy;
    when I fall, I shall rise;
when I sit in darkness,
    the LORD will be a light to me.
- Micah 7:8 NRSV

O LORD, by Your favor You have made
   my mountain to stand strong.
               - Psalm 30:7 NASB

For now we live, if you stand firm in the Lord.
          - 1 Thessalonians 3:8 HCSB

We are hard-pressed on every side, yet not crushed;
we are perplexed, but not in despair; persecuted, but
not forsaken; struck down, but not destroyed – always
carrying about in the body the dying of the Lord Jesus, that the life of Jesus also may be manifested in
our body.
          - 2 Corinthians 4:8-10 NKJV

For you have need of endurance, so that when you
have done the will of God, you may receive what was
promised.
          - Hebrews 10:36 NASB

I don't mean to say that I have already achieved these
things or that I have already reached perfection. But I
press on to possess that perfection for which Christ
Jesus first possessed me.
          - Philippians 3:12 NLT

I would have lost heart, unless I
     had believed
That I would see the goodness of
     the LORD
In the land of the living.
          - Psalm 27:13 NKJV

Since we are surrounded by so great a cloud of witnesses, let us lay aside every weight, and the sin which so easily ensnares us, and let us run with endurance the race that is set before us, looking unto Jesus, the author and finisher of our faith, who for the joy that was set before Him endured the cross, despising the shame, and has sat down at the right hand of the throne of God.

- Hebrews 12:1-2 NKJV

See also **Longsuffering, Patience**

Pureness of Heart

Whatever is true, whatever is noble, whatever is right, whatever is pure, whatever is lovely, whatever is admirable – if anything is excellent or praiseworthy – think about such things.

- Philippians 4:8 TNIV

Blessed are the pure in heart: for they shall see God.

- Matthew 5:8 KJV

"The LORD does not see as man sees; for man looks at the outward appearance, but the LORD looks at the heart."

- 1 Samuel 16:7 NKJV

As the water reflects the face,
so the heart reflects the person.

- Proverbs 27:19 HCSB

"I strive always to keep my conscience clear before
God and man."
- Acts 24:16 NIV

Who may ascend into the hill of the LORD?
And who may stand in His holy place?
He who has clean hands and a pure heart,
Who has not lifted up his soul to falsehood
And has not sworn deceitfully.
- Psalm 24:3-4 NASB

Those who live according to the sinful nature have
their minds set on what that nature desires; but those
who live in accordance with the Spirit have their
minds set on what the Spirit desires.
- Romans 8:5 TNIV

Create in me a pure heart, O God,
    and renew a steadfast spirit within me.
- Psalm 51:10 TNIV

Do not let your adornment be merely outward –
arranging the hair, wearing gold, or putting on fine
apparel – rather let it be the hidden person of the
heart, with the incorruptible beauty of a gentle and
quiet spirit, which is very precious in the sight of God.
- 1 Peter 3:3-4 NKJV

He who loves a pure heart and whose
        speech is gracious
    will have the king for his friend.
- Proverbs 22:11 NIV

Pray for us, for we are confident that we have a clear conscience, wishing to act rightly in every respect.
                              - Hebrews 13:18 NAB

May the words of my mouth and the
          meditation of my heart
     be pleasing in your sight,
     O LORD, my Rock and my Redeemer.
                              - Psalm 19:14 NIV

Now flee from youthful lusts and pursue righteousness, faith, love and peace, with those who call on the Lord from a pure heart.
                              - 2 Timothy 2:22 NASB

See also **Holiness, Righteousness**

Respect

Do not rebuke an older man harshly, but exhort him as if he were your father. Treat younger men as brothers, older women as mothers, and younger women as sisters, with absolute purity.
                              - 1 Timothy 5:1-2 NIV

Be devoted to one another in brotherly love. Honor one another above yourselves.
                              - Romans 12:10 NIV

"Honor your father and your mother as the LORD your God has commanded you."
                                    - Deuteronomy 5:16 NCV

Pay your obligations to everyone: taxes to those you owe taxes, tolls to those you owe tolls, respect to those you owe respect, and honor to those you owe honor.
                                    - Romans 13:7 HCSB

" 'You shall rise up before the grayheaded and honor the aged, and you shall revere your God.' "
                                    - Leviticus 19:32 NASB

Then shall I not be ashamed, when I have respect unto all thy commandments.
                                    - Psalm 119:6 KJV

Likewise you younger people, submit yourselves to your elders. Yes, all of you be submissive to one another, and be clothed with humility.
                                    - 1 Peter 5:5 NKJV

See also **Fear of the Lord, Humility, Obedience**

Righteousness

For his sake I have suffered the loss of all things, and I regard them as rubbish, in order that I may gain Christ and be found in him, not having a righteousness of my own that comes from the law, but one that comes through faith in Christ, the righteousness from God based on faith.

- Philippians 3:8-9 NRSV

Do not be unequally yoked together with unbelievers. For what fellowship has righteousness with lawlessness? And what communion has light with darkness?

- 2 Corinthians 6:14 NKJV

The prayer of a righteous person is powerful and effective.

- James 5:16 TNIV

Awake to righteousness, and do not sin; for some do not have the knowledge of God.

- 1 Corinthians 15:34 NKJV

The righteous man will flourish like the
    palm tree,
He will grow like a cedar in Lebanon.

- Psalm 92:12 NASB

Who can find a virtuous wife?
For her worth is far above rubies.

- Proverbs 31:10 NKJV

It is not the hearers of the law who are righteous in God's sight, but the doers of the law who will be justified.
                              - Romans 2:13 NRSV

For the LORD is righteous, He loves
        righteousness;
The upright will behold His face.
                              - Psalm 11:7 NASB

"For the eyes of the Lord are on the
        righteous
    and his ears are attentive to their
        prayer."
                              - 1 Peter 3:12 NIV

He Himself bore our sins in His body on the cross, so that we might die to sin and live to righteousness; for by His wounds you were healed.
                              - 1 Peter 2:24 NASB

"Blessed are those who hunger and thirst for
        righteousness,
    for they will be filled."
                              - Matthew 5:6 NIV

I will greatly rejoice in the LORD,
    my whole being shall exult in my God;
for he has clothed me with the garments of salvation,
    he has covered me with the robe of righteousness.
                              - Isaiah 61:10 NRSV

Those who are peacemakers will plant seeds of peace and reap a harvest of righteousness.
                              - James 3:18 NLT

When the whirlwind passes, the wicked
    is no more,
But the righteous has an everlasting
    foundation.
            - Proverbs 10:25 NASB

The wicked borrow, and do not pay back,
    but the righteous are generous and keep giving.
            - Psalm 37:21 NRSV

For physical training is of some value, but godliness
has value for all things, holding promise for both the
present life and the life to come.
            - 1 Timothy 4:8 NIV

The righteous is delivered from trouble,
And it comes to the wicked instead.
            - Proverbs 11:8 NKJV

According to his promise we await new heavens and a
new earth in which righteousness dwells.
            - 2 Peter 3:13 NAB

For You, O LORD, will bless the righteous;
With favor You will surround him as with
    a shield.
            - Psalm 5:12 NKJV

Cast your burden upon the LORD and
    He will sustain you;
He will never allow the righteous to
    be shaken.
            - Psalm 55:22 NASB

Say to the righteous that it shall be well with them, for they shall eat the fruit of their deeds.
- Isaiah 3:10 AMP

We who live by the Spirit eagerly wait to receive by faith the righteousness God has promised to us.
- Galatians 5:5 NLT

Pursue righteousness, faith, love, and peace, along with those who call on the Lord with purity of heart.
- 2 Timothy 2:22 NAB

A little that a righteous man has
Is better than the riches of many wicked.
- Psalm 37:16 NKJV

Put away the old self of your former way of life, corrupted through deceitful desires, and be renewed in the spirit of your minds, and put on the new self, created in God's way in righteousness and holiness of truth.
- Ephesians 4:22-24 NAB

If a law had been given that was able to give life, then righteousness would certainly be by the law.
- Galatians 3:21 HCSB

But you, O man of God, ...pursue righteousness, godliness, faith, love, patience, gentleness.
- 1 Timothy 6:11 NKJV

The salvation of the righteous comes
    from the LORD;
  he is their stronghold in time of
    trouble.
                 - Psalm 37:39 TNIV

They have distributed freely, they have
    given to the poor;
  their righteousness endures forever;
  their horn is exalted in honor.
                 - Psalm 112:9 NRSV

"Break off your sins by being righteous, and your iniquities by showing mercy to the poor."
                 - Daniel 4:27 NKJV

"The LORD rewards every man for his righteousness and faithfulness."
                 - 1 Samuel 26:23 NIV

He restores my soul;
He guides me in the paths of righteousness
For His name's sake.
                 - Psalm 23:3 NASB

You have been set free from sin and have become slaves to righteousness.
                 - Romans 6:18 TNIV

In every nation he who venerates and has a reverential fear for God, treating Him with worshipful obedience and living uprightly, is acceptable to Him and sure of being received and welcomed [by Him].
                 - Acts 10:35 AMP

"The righteous will live by his faith."
                    - Habakkuk 2:4 NASB

"Sow for yourselves righteousness,
    reap the fruit of unfailing love,
and break up your unplowed ground;
    for it is time to seek the LORD,
until he comes
    and showers righteousness on you."
                    - Hosea 10:12 NIV

The righteous cry out, and the LORD hears them;
    he delivers them from all their troubles.
                    - Psalm 34:17 TNIV

"Come out from among unbelievers,
    and separate yourselves from them,
        says the LORD.
Don't touch their filthy things,
    and I will welcome you."
                    - 2 Corinthians 6:17 NLT

Fasten the belt of truth around your waist, and put on
the breastplate of righteousness.
                    - Ephesians 6:14 NRSV

Godliness with contentment is great gain.
                    - 1 Timothy 6:6 KJV

For in the gospel a righteousness from God is revealed, a righteousness that is by faith from first to
last, just as it is written: "The righteous will live by
faith."
                    - Romans 1:17 NIV

For the LORD God is a sun and shield;
The LORD gives grace and glory;
No good thing does He withhold from those who
     walk uprightly.
                   - Psalm 84:11 NASB

We are concerned for what is honorable not only in the sight of the Lord but also in the sight of others.
                   - 2 Corinthians 8:21 NAB

He believed in the LORD, and He accounted it to him for righteousness.
                   - Genesis 15:6 NKJV

"The righteous will shine like the sun in the kingdom of their Father."
                   - Matthew 13:43 NIV

The path of the just is like the
     shining sun,
That shines ever brighter unto the
     perfect day.
                   - Proverbs 4:18 NKJV

For we are to God the fragrance of Christ among those who are being saved and among those who are perishing.
                   - 2 Corinthians 2:15 NKJV

Let justice run down like waters and righteousness as a mighty and ever-flowing stream.
                   - Amos 5:24 AMP

See also **Holiness, Pureness of Heart**

Self-Control

He who is slow to anger is better
　　than the mighty,
And he who rules his spirit, than he
　　who captures a city.
　　　　　　　　- Proverbs 16:32 NASB

Make your own attitude that of Christ Jesus.
　　　　　　　　- Philippians 2:5 HCSB

Be clear minded and self-controlled so that you can
pray.
　　　　　　　　- 1 Peter 4:7 NIV

If your enemy is hungry, give him food to eat;
　　if he is thirsty, give him water to drink.
In doing this, you will heap burning coals
　　　　on his head,
　　and the LORD will reward you.
　　　　　　　　- Proverbs 25:21-22 TNIV

Set an example for those who believe, in speech, conduct, love, faith, and purity.
　　　　　　　　- 1 Timothy 4:12 NAB

Beloved, do not avenge yourselves, but rather give
place to wrath; for it is written, "Vengeance is Mine, I
will repay," says the Lord.
　　　　　　　　- Romans 12:19 NKJV

Like the Holy One who called you, be holy yourselves
also in all your behavior.
                    - 1 Peter 1:15 NASB

A soft answer turns away wrath,
but a harsh word stirs up anger.
                    - Proverbs 15:1 NRSV

"Be angry, and do not sin": do not let the sun go down
on your wrath, nor give place to the devil.
                    - Ephesians 4:26-27 NKJV

A fool gives full vent to his anger,
   but a wise man keeps himself under control.
                    - Proverbs 29:11 NIV

Whatever happens, conduct yourselves in a manner
worthy of the gospel of Christ.
                    - Philippians 1:27 NIV

He who is slow to wrath has great
         understanding,
But he who is impulsive exalts folly.
                    - Proverbs 14:29 NKJV

See also **Anger, Forgiveness, Patience, Revenge**

Selflessness

Let no one seek his own good, but that of his neighbor.

- 1 Corinthians 10:24 NASB

The person who sows sparingly will also reap sparingly, and the person who sows generously will also reap generously. Each person should do as he has decided in his heart – not out of regret or out of necessity, for God loves a cheerful giver.

- 2 Corinthians 9:6-7 HCSB

Each of you should look not only to your own interests, but also to the interests of others.

- Philippians 2:4 NIV

Happy are those who consider the
        poor;
    the Lord delivers them in the day
        of trouble.

- Psalm 41:1 NRSV

Warn those who are unruly, comfort the fainthearted, uphold the weak, be patient with all. See that no one renders evil for evil to anyone, but always pursue what is good both for yourselves and for all.

- 1 Thessalonians 5:14-15 NKJV

One person gives freely,
yet gains more;
another withholds what is right,
only to become poor.

- Proverbs 11:24 HCSB

Carry each other's burdens, and in this way you will fulfill the law of Christ.

- Galatians 6:2 NIV

See also **Generosity, Giving, Helping Others**

Strength

And He said to me, "My grace is sufficient for you, for My strength is made perfect in weakness." Therefore most gladly I will rather boast in my infirmities, that the power of Christ may rest upon me.

- 2 Corinthians 12:9 NKJV

I can do all things through Him who strengthens me.

- Philippians 4:13 NASB

But those who hope in the LORD
     will renew their strength.
They will soar on wings like eagles;
     they will run and not grow weary,
     they will walk and not be faint.

- Isaiah 40:31 TNIV

'You will receive power when the Holy Spirit comes on you.'

- Acts 1:8 JB

I pray that out of his glorious riches he may strengthen you with power through his Spirit in your inner being, so that Christ may dwell in your hearts through faith.

- Ephesians 3:16-17 NIV

I am grateful to Christ Jesus our Lord, who has strengthened me, because he judged me faithful and appointed me to his service.

- 1 Timothy 1:12 NRSV

Wait on the LORD;
Be of good courage,
And He shall strengthen your heart;
Wait, I say, on the LORD!

- Psalm 27:14 NKJV

"In Your hand are power and might, and it is in Your hand to make great and to give strength to all."

- 1 Chronicles 29:12 HCSB

My strength and my courage is the LORD,
   and he has been my savior.

- Exodus 15:2 NAB

In the day when I cried out, You
      answered me,
And made me bold with strength in
      my soul.

- Psalm 138:3 NKJV

Therefore I take pleasure in infirmities, in reproaches, in necessities, in persecutions, in distresses for Christ's sake: for when I am weak, then am I strong.
                                                    - 2 Corinthians 12:10 KJV

A wise man has great power,
    and a man of knowledge increases
        strength.
                                                    - Proverbs 24:5 NIV

After you have suffered for a little while, the God of all grace, who called you to His eternal glory in Christ, will Himself perfect, confirm, strengthen and establish you.
                                                    - 1 Peter 5:10 NASB

God is my strength and power: and he maketh my way perfect.
                                                    - 2 Samuel 22:33 KJV

"By faith in the name of Jesus, this man whom you see and know was made strong."
                                                    - Acts 3:16 NIV

Be strong in the Lord and in the strength of His might. Put on the full armor of God, so that you will be able to stand firm against the schemes of the devil.
                                                    - Ephesians 6:10-11 NASB

You have been a strength to the poor,
A strength to the needy in his distress,
A refuge from the storm,
A shade from the heat.
                                                    - Isaiah 25:4 NKJV

The Lord stood by me and strengthened me, so that through me the [Gospel] message might be fully proclaimed.

- 2 Timothy 4:17 AMP

The Lord God is my Strength, my personal bravery, and my invincible army.

- Habakkuk 3:19 AMP

Truly I am full of power by the spirit of the LORD.

- Micah 3:8 KJV

" 'Fear not, for I am with you;
Be not dismayed, for I am your God.
I will strengthen you,
Yes, I will help you,
I will uphold you with My righteous
    right hand.' "

- Isaiah 41:10 NKJV

"Be strong and courageous. Do not be afraid; do not be discouraged, for the LORD your God will be with you wherever you go."

- Joshua 1:9 TNIV

Be on your guard, stand firm in the faith, be courageous, be strong.

- 1 Corinthians 16:13 NAB

"Do not grieve, because your strength comes from rejoicing in the LORD."

- Nehemiah 8:10 HCSB

O LORD, by Your favor You have made
    my mountain to stand strong.
                    - Psalm 30:7 NASB

Be strong in the grace that is in Christ Jesus.
                    - 2 Timothy 2:1 NAB

He gives power to the weak,
And to those who have no might He
    increases strength.
                    - Isaiah 40:29 NKJV

You are complete in Him, who is the head of all principality and power.
                    - Colossians 2:10 NKJV

In returning and rest you shall be
    saved;
  in quietness and in trust shall
    be your strength.
                    - Isaiah 30:15 NRSV

The LORD is the strength of my life; of whom shall I be
afraid?
                    - Psalm 27:1 KJV

The salvation of the righteous comes
    from the LORD;
  he is their stronghold in time of
    trouble.
                    - Psalm 37:39 TNIV

See also **Courage, Soldier of God**

Understanding

I pray that you and all God's holy people will have the power to understand the greatness of Christ's love – how wide and how long and how high and how deep that love is. Christ's love is greater than anyone can ever know, but I pray that you will be able to know that love. Then you can be filled with the fullness of God.

- Ephesians 3:18-19 NCV

Brothers and sisters, do not be children in your thinking; rather, be infants in evil, but in thinking be adults.

- 1 Corinthians 14:20 NRSV

He who is slow to anger has great
    understanding,
But he who is quick-tempered exalts folly.

- Proverbs 14:29 NASB

I pray that you may be active in sharing your faith, so that you will have a full understanding of every good thing we have in Christ.

- Philemon 6 NIV

For the LORD gives wisdom,
    from his mouth come knowledge and
      understanding.

- Proverbs 2:6 NAB

Evil men do not understand justice,
But those who seek the LORD understand
    all things.
                      - Proverbs 28:5 NASB

The righteousness of Your
    testimonies is everlasting;
Give me understanding, and I shall live.
                      - Psalm 119:144 NKJV

Understanding is a wellspring of life to those who have
it.
                      - Proverbs 16:22 AMP

"There is a spirit in man,
And the breath of the Almighty gives him
    understanding."
                      - Job 32:8 NKJV

The fear of the LORD is the beginning
    of wisdom,
And the knowledge of the Holy One is
    understanding.
                      - Proverbs 9:10 NASB

So then do not be foolish, but understand what the
will of the Lord is.
                      - Ephesians 5:17 NASB

We know that the Son of God has come and has given
us understanding so that we may know the true One.
We are in the true One – that is, in His Son Jesus
Christ. He is the true God and eternal life.
                      - 1 John 5:20 HCSB

Blessed is the man who finds
     wisdom,
  the man who gains understanding.
                              - Proverbs 3:13 NIV

Then he opened their minds so they could understand
the Scriptures.
                              - Luke 24:45 TNIV

See also **Knowledge, Wisdom**

Wisdom

"The fear of the LORD is the beginning
     of wisdom,
  and knowledge of the Holy One is
     understanding."
                              - Proverbs 9:10 NIV

If any of you is lacking in wisdom, ask God, who gives
to all generously and ungrudgingly, and it will be giv-
en you.
                              - James 1:5 NRSV

Wisdom is better than weapons of war.
                              - Ecclesiastes 9:18 HCSB

Whoever finds me [Wisdom] finds life and draws forth
and obtains favor from the Lord.
                              - Proverbs 8:35 AMP

Walk with wise men and you will become wise.
                    - Proverbs 13:20 NAB

In Him all the treasures of wisdom and knowledge are hidden.
                    - Colossians 2:3 HCSB

Be wise in the way you act toward outsiders; make the most of every opportunity. Let your conversation be always full of grace, seasoned with salt, so that you may know how to answer everyone.
                    - Colossians 4:5-6 TNIV

A fool gives full vent to his anger,
    but a wise man keeps himself under control.
                    - Proverbs 29:11 NIV

When pride comes, disgrace comes;
    but with the humble is wisdom.
                    - Proverbs 11:2 NAB

The wisdom from above is first pure, then peaceable, gentle, willing to yield, full of mercy and good fruits, without a trace of partiality or hypocrisy.
                    - James 3:17 NRSV

Wisdom excels folly as light excels darkness.
                    - Ecclesiastes 2:13 NASB

From childhood you have known the Holy Scriptures, which are able to make you wise for salvation through faith which is in Christ Jesus.
                    - 2 Timothy 3:15 NKJV

Teach us to number our days,
    that we may gain a heart of wisdom.
                        - Psalm 90:12 TNIV

The wise inherit honor,
    but fools get only shame.
                        - Proverbs 3:35 TNIV

For the LORD gives wisdom,
    from his mouth come knowledge and
        understanding.
                        - Proverbs 2:6 NAB

"Those who are wise will shine like the brightness of
the heavens, and those who lead many to righteousness, like the stars for ever and ever."
                        - Daniel 12:3 NIV

A wise man is more powerful than
    a strong man,
  and a man of knowledge than a
    man of might.
                        - Proverbs 24:5 NAB

"For I will give you words and wisdom that none of
your adversaries will be able to resist or contradict."
                        - Luke 21:15 NIV

The reward given by wisdom is success.
                        - Ecclesiastes 10:10 JB

How blessed is the man who finds wisdom
And the man who gains understanding.
                                    - Proverbs 3:13 NASB

"Behold, I send you out as sheep in the midst of
wolves. Therefore be wise as serpents and harmless as
doves."
                                    - Matthew 10:16 NKJV

Wisdom is the principal thing;
Therefore get wisdom.
And in all your getting, get
        understanding.
                                    - Proverbs 4:7 NKJV

The quiet words of the wise are more
        to be heeded
    than the shouts of a ruler of fools.
                                    - Ecclesiastes 9:17 NIV

See also **Knowledge, Understanding**

Calls to Action

2

Believing

"He who believes in Me, as the Scripture has said, out of his heart will flow rivers of living water."
                                    - John 7:38 NKJV

Jesus said to the centurion, "Go; it shall be done for you as you have believed." And the servant was healed that very moment.
                                    - Matthew 8:13 NASB

"All that you ask for in prayer, believe that you will receive it and it shall be yours."
                                    - Mark 11:24 NAB

"I assure you: The one who believes in Me will also do the works that I do. And he will do even greater works than these, because I am going to the Father."
                                    - John 14:12 HCSB

"I am the resurrection and the life; he who believes in Me will live even if he dies, and everyone who lives and believes in Me will never die."
                                    - John 11:25-26 NASB

Without faith it is impossible to please God, for whoever would approach him must believe that he exists and that he rewards those who seek him.
                                    - Hebrews 11:6 NRSV

Since we believe that Jesus died and was raised to life again, we also believe that when Jesus returns, God will bring back with him the believers who have died.
- 1 Thessalonians 4:14 NLT

"Blessed are those who have not seen and yet have believed."
- John 20:29 TNIV

For God so loved the world, that he gave his only begotten Son, that whosoever believeth in him should not perish, but have everlasting life.
- John 3:16 KJV

"If you can believe, all things are possible to him who believes."
- Mark 9:23 NKJV

"Believe in the LORD your God, and you will be established; believe in His prophets, and you will succeed."
- 2 Chronicles 20:20 HCSB

"I am the bread of life. He who comes to Me shall never hunger, and he who believes in Me shall never thirst."
- John 6:35 NKJV

"He who hears My word and believes in Him who sent Me has everlasting life, and shall not come into judgment, but has passed from death into life."
- John 5:24 NKJV

Although you have not seen him, you love him; and even though you do not see him now, you believe in him and rejoice with an indescribable and glorious joy, for you are receiving the outcome of your faith, the salvation of your souls.

- 1 Peter 1:8-9 NRSV

"All the prophets testify about Him that through His name everyone who believes in Him will receive forgiveness of sins."

- Acts 10:43 HCSB

"Don't be afraid; just believe."

- Mark 5:36 TNIV

For I am not ashamed of the gospel of Christ, for it is the power of God to salvation for everyone who believes.

- Romans 1:16 NKJV

"Did I not say to you that if you believe, you will see the glory of God?"

- John 11:40 NASB

Happy are the people whose God is the LORD.

- Psalm 144:15 NCV

Yet to all who received him, to those who believed in his name, he gave the right to become children of God.

- John 1:12 NIV

If you confess with your mouth that Jesus is Lord and believe in your heart that God raised him from the dead, you will be saved. For one believes with the heart and so is justified, and one confesses with the mouth and so is saved.

- Romans 10:9-10 NAB

He believed in the LORD, and He accounted it to him for righteousness.

- Genesis 15:6 NKJV

Christ has already accomplished the purpose for which the law was given. As a result, all who believe in him are made right with God.

- Romans 10:4 NLT

"Believe in the Lord Jesus, and you will be saved – you and your household."

- Acts 16:31 TNIV

"I have come as Light into the world, so that everyone who believes in Me will not remain in darkness."

- John 12:46 NASB

"Whoever says to this mountain, 'Be lifted up and thrown into the sea,' and does not doubt in his heart but believes that what he says will happen, it shall be done for him."

- Mark 11:23 NAB

"If you believe, you will receive whatever you ask for in prayer."

- Matthew 21:22 NIV

He who believes in Me [who adheres to, trusts in, relies on, and has faith in Me] has (now possesses) eternal life.

- John 6:47 AMP

Now this is His command: that we believe in the name
of His Son Jesus Christ, and love one another as He
commanded us.

- 1 John 3:23 HCSB

See also **All Things Are Possible, Faith, Hope**

Blessing

Blessed be the God and Father of our Lord Jesus
Christ, who has blessed us with every spiritual blessing in the heavenly places in Christ.

- Ephesians 1:3 NKJV

Blessed is he whose transgression is forgiven, whose
sin is covered.

- Psalm 32:1 KJV

" ' "The LORD bless you
      and keep you;
the LORD make his face shine upon you
      and be gracious to you;
the LORD turn his face toward you
      and give you peace." ' "

- Numbers 6:24-26 NIV

The Lord your God has blessed you in all the work of your hand.
>   - Deuteronomy 2:7 AMP

Blessed are all who fear the LORD,
    who walk in obedience to him.
>   - Psalm 128:1 TNIV

Enter into His gates with thanksgiving,
And into His courts with praise.
Be thankful to Him, and bless His name.
>   - Psalm 100:4 NKJV

Oh, taste and see that the LORD is
        good;
Blessed is the man who trusts in
        Him!
>   - Psalm 34:8 NKJV

Bless those who persecute you: never curse them, bless them.
>   - Romans 12:14 JB

God is able to provide you with every blessing in abundance, so that by always having enough of everything, you may share abundantly in every good work.
>   - 2 Corinthians 9:8 NRSV

" 'I will send down showers in season; there will be showers of blessing.' "
>   - Ezekiel 34:26 TNIV

A faithful man shall abound with blessings.
>   - Proverbs 28:20 AMP

You prepare a table before me
in the presence of my enemies;
you anoint my head with oil;
my cup overflows.
- Psalm 23:5 NRSV

I will bless the LORD at all times: his praise shall continually be in my mouth.
- Psalm 34:1 KJV

"Blessed is he who is not offended because of Me."
- Matthew 11:6 NKJV

My mouth will speak your praises,
LORD;
all flesh will bless your holy name
forever.
- Psalm 145:21 NAB

The earth has yielded its produce;
God, our God, blesses us.
God blesses us,
That all the ends of the earth may fear Him.
- Psalm 67:6-7 NASB

"Stand up and bless the LORD
your God
Forever and ever!
Blessed be Your glorious name,
Which is exalted above all blessing
and praise!"
- Nehemiah 9:5 NKJV

"Blessed are you when people insult you and persecute you, and falsely say all kinds of evil against you
because of Me. Rejoice and be glad, for your reward in
heaven is great."

> \- Matthew 5:11-12 NASB

A generous person will be blessed,
for he shares his food with the poor.

> \- Proverbs 22:9 HCSB

He will bless those who fear the LORD,
   both small and great.

> \- Psalm 115:13 NRSV

All of you, be like-minded, be sympathetic, love one
another, be compassionate and humble. Do not repay
evil with evil or insult with insult. On the contrary,
repay evil with blessing, because to this you were
called so that you may inherit a blessing.

> \- 1 Peter 3:8-9 TNIV

You crown the year with Your goodness,
And Your paths drip with abundance.

> \- Psalm 65:11 NKJV

Blessed is the man who finds
      wisdom,
   the man who gains understanding.

> \- Proverbs 3:13 NIV

For You, O LORD, will bless the righteous;
With favor You will surround him as with
      a shield.

> \- Psalm 5:12 NKJV

Give generously...and do so without a grudging heart; then because of this the LORD your God will bless you in all your work and in everything you put your hand to.

- Deuteronomy 15:10 NIV

Even if you should suffer for what is right, you are blessed. "Do not fear their threats; do not be frightened."

- 1 Peter 3:14 TNIV

"Love your enemies, bless those who curse you, do good to those who hate you, and pray for those who spitefully use you and persecute you."

- Matthew 5:44 NKJV

May God be gracious to us and bless us
    and make his face shine upon us.

- Psalm 67:1 NIV

"Bring the whole tithe into the storehouse, that there may be food in my house. Test me in this," says the LORD Almighty, "and see if I will not throw open the floodgates of heaven and pour out so much blessing that you will not have room enough for it."

- Malachi 3:10 NIV

See also **Favor of God, Prosper, Victory**

Confessing Christ

If you confess with your mouth, "Jesus is Lord," and believe in your heart that God raised Him from the dead, you will be saved. With the heart one believes, resulting in righteousness, and with the mouth one confesses, resulting in salvation.
                    - Romans 10:9-10 HCSB

"Whoever confesses Me before men, him I will also confess before My Father who is in heaven."
                    - Matthew 10:32 NKJV

Fight the good fight of the faith. Take hold of the eternal life to which you were called when you made your good confession in the presence of many witnesses.
                    - 1 Timothy 6:12 TNIV

This is how you can recognize the Spirit of God: Every spirit that acknowledges that Jesus Christ has come in the flesh is from God.
                    - 1 John 4:2 TNIV

Let us continually offer up to God a sacrifice of praise, that is, the fruit of our lips that confess His name.
                    - Hebrews 13:15 HCSB

Whoever confesses the Son has the Father as well.
                    - 1 John 2:23 NAB

I am not ashamed of the gospel, because it is the power of God that brings salvation to everyone who believes.

- Romans 1:16 TNIV

Pray on my behalf, that utterance may be given to me in the opening of my mouth, to make known with boldness the mystery of the gospel, for which I am an ambassador in chains; that in proclaiming it I may speak boldly, as I ought to speak.

- Ephesians 6:19-20 NASB

"As I live, says the LORD,
Every knee shall bow to Me,
And every tongue shall confess to God."

- Romans 14:11 NKJV

Whenever you eat this bread and drink this cup, you proclaim the Lord's death until he comes.

- 1 Corinthians 11:26 NIV

God's solid foundation stands firm, sealed with this inscription: "The Lord knows those who are his," and, "Everyone who confesses the name of the Lord must turn away from wickedness."

- 2 Timothy 2:19 TNIV

God also has highly exalted Him and given Him the name which is above every name, that at the name of Jesus every knee should bow, of those in heaven, and of those on earth, and of those under the earth, and that every tongue should confess that Jesus Christ is Lord, to the glory of God the Father.

- Philippians 2:9-11 NKJV

Whoever confesses that Jesus is the Son of God, God abides in him, and he in God.
                    - 1 John 4:15 NASB

"Blessed is he who is not offended because of Me."
                    - Luke 7:23 NKJV

See also **Ministry, Speaking Boldly, Works**

Exemplify

Let no one despise or think less of you because of your youth, but be an example (pattern) for the believers in speech, in conduct, in love, in faith, and in purity.
                    - 1 Timothy 4:12 AMP

Be shepherds of God's flock that is under your care, watching over them – not because you must, but because you are willing, as God wants you to be; not pursuing dishonest gain, but eager to serve; not lording it over those entrusted to you, but being examples to the flock. And when the Chief Shepherd appears, you will receive the crown of glory that will never fade away.
                    - 1 Peter 5:2-4 TNIV

Follow my example, as I follow the example of Christ.
                    - 1 Corinthians 11:1 NCV

"So if I, your Lord and Teacher, have washed your feet, you also ought to wash one another's feet. For I have set you an example, that you also should do as I have done to you."

- John 13:14-15 NRSV

Beloved, do not imitate what is evil, but what is good. He who does good is of God, but he who does evil has not seen God.

- 3 John 11 NKJV

Brothers and sisters, as an example of patience in the face of suffering, take the prophets who spoke in the name of the Lord.

- James 5:10 TNIV

For this reason I obtained mercy, that in me first Jesus Christ might show all longsuffering, as a pattern to those who are going to believe on Him for everlasting life.

- 1 Timothy 1:16 NKJV

Beloved, I urge you...to abstain from the desires of the flesh that wage war against the soul. Conduct yourselves honorably among the Gentiles, so that, though they malign you as evildoers, they may see your honorable deeds and glorify God when he comes to judge.

- 1 Peter 2:11-12 NRSV

Therefore be imitators of God [copy Him and follow His example], as well-beloved children [imitate their father].

- Ephesians 5:1 AMP

If you endure suffering even when you have done right, God will bless you for it. It was to this that God called you, for Christ himself suffered for you and left you an example, so that you would follow in his steps.
- 1 Peter 2:20-21 GNT

See also **Ministry, Works**

Giving

"Remember the words of the Lord Jesus, that He said, 'It is more blessed to give than to receive.'"
- Acts 20:35 NKJV

Each of you should give what you have decided in your heart to give, not reluctantly or under compulsion, for God loves a cheerful giver.
- 2 Corinthians 9:7 TNIV

Honor the LORD with your wealth,
    with first fruits of all your produce.
- Proverbs 3:9 NAB

Do not forget to do good and to share, for with such sacrifices God is well pleased.
- Hebrews 13:16 NKJV

He has given freely to the poor,
His righteousness endures forever;
His horn will be exalted in honor.
- Psalm 112:9 NASB

Every man shall give as he is able, according to the blessing of the Lord your God which He has given you.

- Deuteronomy 16:17 AMP

One person gives freely,
yet gains more;
another withholds what is right,
only to become poor.

- Proverbs 11:24 HCSB

God is able to provide you with every blessing in abundance, so that by always having enough of everything, you may share abundantly in every good work.

- 2 Corinthians 9:8 NRSV

Then Jesus, looking at him, loved him, and said to him, "One thing you lack: Go your way, sell whatever you have and give to the poor, and you will have treasure in heaven; and come, take up the cross, and follow Me."

- Mark 10:21 NKJV

"Silver and gold I do not have, but what I do have I give you: In the name of Jesus Christ of Nazareth, rise up and walk."

- Acts 3:6 NKJV

Give generously...and do so without a grudging heart; then because of this the LORD your God will bless you in all your work and in everything you put your hand to.

- Deuteronomy 15:10 NIV

"And as you go, preach, saying, 'The kingdom of heaven is at hand.' Heal the sick, raise the dead, cleanse the lepers, cast out demons. Freely you received, freely give."

- Matthew 10:7-8 NASB

The wicked man borrows without meaning to repay,
but a virtuous man is generous and open-handed.

- Psalm 37:21 JB

Those who are taught the word must share in all good things with their teacher.

- Galatians 6:6 NRSV

Command those who are rich in this present world not to be arrogant nor to put their hope in wealth, which is so uncertain, but to put their hope in God, who richly provides us with everything for our enjoyment. Command them to do good, to be rich in good deeds, and to be generous and willing to share. In this way they will lay up treasure for themselves as a firm foundation for the coming age, so that they may take hold of the life that is truly life.

- 1 Timothy 6:17-19 NIV

See also **Generosity, Helping Others, Receiving, Selflessness, Works**

Glory

For you were bought at a price; therefore glorify God in your body and in your spirit, which are God's.
- 1 Corinthians 6:20 NKJV

May the God who gives endurance and encouragement give you a spirit of unity among yourselves as you follow Christ Jesus, so that with one heart and mouth you may glorify the God and Father of our Lord Jesus Christ.
- Romans 15:5-6 NIV

The heavens declare the glory of God;
    the skies proclaim the work of his
        hands.
- Psalm 19:1 NIV

"This sickness is not to end in death, but for the glory of God, so that the Son of God may be glorified by it."
- John 11:4 NASB

"Yours, O LORD, are the greatness, the power, the glory, the victory, and the majesty; for all that is in the heavens and on the earth is yours; yours is the kingdom, O LORD, and you are exalted as head above all."
- 1 Chronicles 29:11 NRSV

My lips will glorify You
because Your faithful love is better than life.
- Psalm 63:3 HCSB

"Fear God, and give Him glory, because the hour of
His judgment has come; worship Him who made the
heaven and the earth and sea and springs of waters."
                              - Revelation 14:7 NASB

Rise up in splendor! Your light has
        come,
    the glory of the Lord shines upon
        you.
                              - Isaiah 60:1 NAB

"He who glories, let him glory in the LORD."
                              - 2 Corinthians 10:17 NKJV

In Christ Jesus, then, I have legitimate reason to glory
(exult) in my work for God [in what through Christ
Jesus I have accomplished concerning the things of
God].
                              - Romans 15:17 AMP

"Worthy are you, Lord our God,
    to receive glory and honor and power,
for you created all things;
    because of your will they came to
        be and were created."
                              - Revelation 4:11 NAB

So, whether you eat or drink, or whatever you do, do
everything for the glory of God.
                              - 1 Corinthians 10:31 NRSV

If you are reproached for the name of Christ, blessed are you, for the Spirit of glory and of God rests upon you. On their part He is blasphemed, but on your part He is glorified.

- 1 Peter 4:14 NKJV

Glorify the LORD with me;
    let us exalt his name together.

- Psalm 34:3 TNIV

Give to the LORD the glory due
        His name;
Bring an offering, and come
        before Him.
Oh, worship the LORD in the
        beauty of holiness!

- 1 Chronicles 16:29 NKJV

And they glorified God [as the Author and Source of what had taken place] in me.

- Galatians 1:24 AMP

Call on Me in the day of trouble; I will deliver you, and you shall honor and glorify Me.

- Psalm 50:15 AMP

We constantly pray for you, that our God may make you worthy of his calling, and that by his power he may bring to fruition your every desire for goodness and your every deed prompted by faith. We pray this so that the name of our Lord Jesus may be glorified in you, and you in him, according to the grace of our God and the Lord Jesus Christ.

- 2 Thessalonians 1:11-12 TNIV

Receive one another, just as Christ also received us, to the glory of God.

- Romans 15:7 NKJV

"Let not the wise man glory in
    his wisdom,
Let not the mighty man glory in
    his might,
Nor let the rich man glory in
    his riches;
But let him who glories glory in this,
That he understands and knows Me,
That I am the LORD, exercising
    lovingkindness, judgment, and
    righteousness in the earth.
For in these I delight," says the LORD.

- Jeremiah 9:23-24 NKJV

Who is the King of glory?
The LORD strong and mighty,
The LORD mighty in battle.

- Psalm 24:8 NASB

The Word became flesh and made his dwelling among us. We have seen his glory, the glory of the One and Only, who came from the Father, full of grace and truth.

- John 1:14 NIV

"By this is my Father glorified, that you bear much fruit and become my disciples."

- John 15:8 NAB

Declare His glory among the nations, His marvelous works among all peoples.

- 1 Chronicles 16:24 AMP

To him who is able to keep you from falling and to present you before his glorious presence without fault and with great joy – to the only God our Savior be glory, majesty, power and authority, through Jesus Christ our Lord, before all ages, now and forevermore!

- Jude 24-25 NIV

"Let your light shine before men in such a way that they may see your good works, and glorify your Father who is in heaven."

- Matthew 5:16 NASB

See also **Honor, Praise**

Helping Others

My brothers and sisters, if one of you should wander from the truth and someone should bring them back, remember this: Whoever turns a sinner from the way of error will save them from death and cover over a multitude of sins.

- James 5:19-20 TNIV

Bear one another's burdens, and so fulfill the law of Christ.

- Galatians 6:2 NKJV

"Even the Son of Man did not come to be served, but to serve."
                                      - Mark 10:45 NASB

Encourage one another day after day, as long as it is still called "Today," so that none of you will be hardened by the deceitfulness of sin.
                                      - Hebrews 3:13 NASB

Be hospitable to one another without complaining.
                                      - 1 Peter 4:9 HCSB

Let the word of Christ dwell in you richly, as in all wisdom you teach and admonish one another.
                                      - Colossians 3:16 NAB

Therefore, as we have opportunity, let us do good to all people, especially to those who belong to the family of believers.
                                      - Galatians 6:10 NIV

In a church meeting I would rather speak five understandable words to help others than ten thousand words in an unknown language.
                                      - 1 Corinthians 14:19 NLT

You were called for freedom, brothers. But do not use this freedom as an opportunity for the flesh; rather, serve one another through love.
                                      - Galatians 5:13 NAB

"Do to others whatever you would have them do to you. This is the law and the prophets."
- Matthew 7:12 NAB

Two people are better than one,
　　because they get more done by
　　　　working together.
If one falls down,
　　the other can help him up.
- Ecclesiastes 4:9-10 NCV

"So if I, your Lord and Teacher, have washed your feet, you also ought to wash one another's feet. For I have set you an example, that you also should do as I have done to you."
- John 13:14-15 NRSV

See also **Generosity, Giving, Selflessness, Works**

Live in Christ

If anyone is in Christ, he is a new creation; old things have passed away; behold, all things have become new.
- 2 Corinthians 5:17 NKJV

Count yourselves dead to sin but alive to God in Christ Jesus.
- Romans 6:11 NIV

"For in Him we live and move and exist."
                              - Acts 17:28 HCSB

We know that the Son of God has come and has given
us understanding so that we may know the true One.
We are in the true One – that is, in His Son Jesus
Christ. He is the true God and eternal life.
                              - 1 John 5:20 HCSB

God did not choose us to suffer his anger, but to possess salvation through our Lord Jesus Christ, who
died for us in order that we might live together with
him.
                              - 1 Thessalonians 5:9-10 GNT

Through the law I died to the law, that I might live for
God.
                              - Galatians 2:19 NAB

For we do not live to ourselves alone and we do not die
to ourselves alone. If we live, we live to the Lord; and if
we die, we die to the Lord. So, whether we live or die,
we belong to the Lord.
                              - Romans 14:7-8 TNIV

"If anyone loves Me, he will keep My word. My Father
will love him, and We will come to him and make Our
home with him."
                              - John 14:23 HCSB

God is love. Whoever lives in love lives in God, and
God in him.
                              - 1 John 4:16 NIV

"I have been crucified with Christ; it is no longer I who live, but Christ lives in me; and the life which I now live in the flesh I live by faith in the Son of God, who loved me and gave Himself for me."
                                      - Galatians 2:20 NKJV

For to me, to live is Christ and to die is gain.
                                      - Philippians 1:21 NIV

"Behold, I stand at the door and knock. If anyone hears My voice and opens the door, I will come in to him and dine with him, and he with Me."
                                      - Revelation 3:20 NKJV

Beloved, since God loved us so much, we also ought to love one another. ...If we love one another, God lives in us, and his love is perfected in us.
                                      - 1 John 4:11-12 NRSV

He died for all, so that they who live might no longer live for themselves, but for Him who died and rose again on their behalf.
                                      - 2 Corinthians 5:15 NASB

I pray that Christ will live in your hearts by faith and that your life will be strong in love and be built on love.
                                      - Ephesians 3:17 NCV

Now if we have died with Christ, we believe that we shall also live with Him, knowing that Christ, having been raised from the dead, is never to die again.
                                      - Romans 6:8-9 NASB

For his sake I have suffered the loss of all things, and
I regard them as rubbish, in order that I may gain
Christ and be found in him, not having a righteous-
ness of my own that comes from the law, but one that
comes through faith in Christ, the righteousness from
God based on faith.
                              - Philippians 3:8-9 NRSV

We who live by the Spirit eagerly wait to receive by
faith the righteousness God has promised to us.
                              - Galatians 5:5 NLT

Those who live according to the sinful nature have
their minds set on what that nature desires; but those
who live in accordance with the Spirit have their
minds set on what the Spirit desires.
                              - Romans 8:5 TNIV

See also **Eternal Life, Life, Seek God, Walk in Christ**

Ministry

"Go therefore and make disciples of all the nations, baptizing them in the name of the Father and of the Son and of the Holy Spirit, teaching them to observe all things that I have commanded you; and lo, I am with you always, even to the end of the age."
- Matthew 28:19-20 NKJV

I am grateful to Christ Jesus our Lord, who has strengthened me, because he judged me faithful and appointed me to his service.
- 1 Timothy 1:12 NRSV

"By this everyone will know that you are my disciples, if you love one another."
- John 13:35 TNIV

"You will receive power when the Holy Spirit has come upon you, and you will be My witnesses in Jerusalem, in all Judea and Samaria, and to the ends of the earth."
- Acts 1:8 HCSB

"Thus it is written, and thus it was necessary for the Christ to suffer and to rise from the dead the third day, and that repentance and remission of sins should be preached in His name to all nations, beginning at Jerusalem. And you are witnesses of these things."
- Luke 24:46-48 NKJV

I pray that you may be active in sharing your faith, so that you will have a full understanding of every good thing we have in Christ.

　　　　　　　　　- Philemon 6 NIV

Declare His glory among the nations, His marvelous works among all peoples.

　　　　　　　　　- 1 Chronicles 16:24 AMP

We are ambassadors for Christ, as though God were pleading through us: we implore you on Christ's behalf, be reconciled to God.

　　　　　　　　　- 2 Corinthians 5:20 NKJV

This Jesus God raised up, and of that all we [His disciples] are witnesses.

　　　　　　　　　- Acts 2:32 AMP

Of this gospel I was appointed a herald and an apostle and a teacher.

　　　　　　　　　- 2 Timothy 1:11 TNIV

As shoes for your feet put on whatever will make you ready to proclaim the gospel of peace.

　　　　　　　　　- Ephesians 6:15 NRSV

There are diversities of gifts, but the same Spirit. There are differences of ministries, but the same Lord. And there are diversities of activities, but it is the same God who works all in all.

　　　　　　　　　- 1 Corinthians 12:4-6 NKJV

Do not cast me away from Your presence
And do not take Your Holy Spirit from me.
Restore to me the joy of Your salvation
And sustain me with a willing spirit.
Then I will teach transgressors Your ways,
And sinners will be converted to You.
- Psalm 51:11-13 NASB

I am willing to endure anything if it will bring salvation and eternal glory in Christ Jesus to those God has chosen.
- 2 Timothy 2:10 NLT

Pray also for me, that whenever I open my mouth, words may be given me so that I will fearlessly make known the mystery of the gospel, for which I am an ambassador in chains. Pray that I may declare it fearlessly, as I should.
- Ephesians 6:19-20 NIV

"Peace be with you. As the Father has sent me, so I send you."
- John 20:21 NAB

How beautiful on the mountains
    are the feet of those who bring good news,
who proclaim peace,
    who bring good tidings,
    who proclaim salvation.
- Isaiah 52:7 TNIV

In a church meeting I would rather speak five understandable words to help others than ten thousand words in an unknown language.
- 1 Corinthians 14:19 NLT

"Those who are wise will shine like the brightness of the heavens, and those who lead many to righteousness, like the stars for ever and ever."
                                                    - Daniel 12:3 TNIV

You yourselves are our letter, written on our hearts, known and read by everybody. You show that you are a letter from Christ, the result of our ministry, written not with ink but with the Spirit of the living God, not on tablets of stone but on tablets of human hearts.
                                          - 2 Corinthians 3:2-3 NIV

I shall not die, but live, and declare the works of the LORD.
                                                    - Psalm 118:17 KJV

Do not be ashamed of the testimony of our Lord, nor of me His prisoner, but share with me in the sufferings for the gospel according to the power of God, who has saved us and called us with a holy calling, not according to our works, but according to His own purpose and grace which was given to us in Christ Jesus before time began.
                                                - 2 Timothy 1:8-9 NKJV

You shall speak My words to them whether they will hear or refuse to hear.
                                                    - Ezekiel 2:7 AMP

Since it is by God's mercy that we are engaged in this ministry, we do not lose heart.
                                          - 2 Corinthians 4:1 NRSV

"The Spirit of the Lord GOD is upon Me,
Because the LORD has anointed Me
To preach good tidings to the poor;
He has sent Me to heal the brokenhearted,
To proclaim liberty to the captives,
And the opening of the prison to those who are
      bound;
To proclaim the acceptable year of the LORD,
And the day of vengeance of our God;
To comfort all who mourn."
                      - Isaiah 61:1-2 NKJV

Preach the Word; be prepared in season and out of season; correct, rebuke and encourage – with great patience and careful instruction.
                      - 2 Timothy 4:2 NIV

The gifts he gave were that some would be apostles, some prophets, some evangelists, some pastors and teachers, to equip the saints for the work of ministry, for building up the body of Christ, until all of us come to the unity of the faith and of the knowledge of the Son of God, to maturity, to the measure of the full stature of Christ.
                      - Ephesians 4:11-13 NRSV

Sing to the LORD, all the earth.
Proclaim His salvation from day to day.
Declare His glory among the nations,
His wonderful works among all peoples.
                      - 1 Chronicles 16:23-24 HCSB

Keep a clear head about everything, endure hardship, do the work of an evangelist, fulfill your ministry.
                      - 2 Timothy 4:5 HCSB

"And now, Lord, look at their threats, and grant to your servants to speak your word with all boldness, while you stretch out your hand to heal, and signs and wonders are performed through the name of your holy servant Jesus."
                              - Acts 4:29-30 NRSV

"And as you go, preach, saying, 'The kingdom of heaven is at hand.' Heal the sick, cleanse the lepers, raise the dead, cast out demons. Freely you have received, freely give."
                              - Matthew 10:7-8 NKJV

We always speak as God wants us to, because he has judged us worthy to be entrusted with the Good News.
                              - 1 Thessalonians 2:4 GNT

"I consider my life worth nothing to me; my only aim is to finish the race and complete the task the Lord Jesus has given me – the task of testifying to the good news of God's grace."
                              - Acts 20:24 TNIV

When they had prayed, the place where they had gathered together was shaken, and they were all filled with the Holy Spirit and began to speak the word of God with boldness.
                              - Acts 4:31 NASB

I am not ashamed of the gospel of Christ.
                              - Romans 1:16 KJV

"Behold, I send you out as sheep in the midst of wolves. Therefore be wise as serpents and harmless as doves."
- Matthew 10:16 NKJV

Also I heard the voice of the Lord, saying:
"Whom shall I send,
And who will go for Us?"
Then I said, "Here am I! Send me."
- Isaiah 6:8 NKJV

"Go into all the world and preach the gospel to all creation."
- Mark 16:15 NASB

The Lord stood by me and strengthened me, so that through me the [Gospel] message might be fully proclaimed.
- 2 Timothy 4:17 AMP

It has always been my ambition to preach the gospel where Christ was not known, so that I would not be building on someone else's foundation. Rather, as it is written:
"Those who were not told about him will
see,
and those who have not heard will
understand."
- Romans 15:20-21 TNIV

"The harvest is plentiful, but the workers are few. Ask the Lord of the harvest, therefore, to send out workers into his harvest field. Go! I am sending you out like lambs among wolves."
- Luke 10:2-3 NIV

"As You sent Me into the world, I also have sent them into the world."
> - John 17:18 NKJV

Because of the service by which you have proved yourselves, people will praise God for the obedience that accompanies your confession of the gospel of Christ, and for your generosity in sharing with them and with everyone else. And in their prayers for you their hearts will go out to you, because of the surpassing grace God has given you. Thanks be to God for his indescribable gift!
> - 2 Corinthians 9:13-15 TNIV

"For it is not you who speak, but it is the Spirit of your Father who speaks in you."
> - Matthew 10:20 NASB

See also **Church, Confessing Christ, Giving, Helping Others, Works**

Praise

I will bless the LORD at all times: his praise shall continually be in my mouth.
　　　　　　　　　　　　- Psalm 34:1 KJV

I will praise You, for I am fearfully
　　　and wonderfully made;
Marvelous are Your works,
And that my soul knows very well.
　　　　　　　　　　　　- Psalm 139:14 NKJV

Let us greet him with a song of praise,
　　joyfully sing out our psalms.
　　　　　　　　　　　　- Psalm 95:2 NAB

For great is the LORD and most worthy of praise.
　　　　　　　　　　　　- 1 Chronicles 16:25 NIV

You are a chosen generation, a royal priesthood, a holy nation, His own special people, that you may proclaim the praises of Him who called you out of darkness into His marvelous light.
　　　　　　　　　　　　- 1 Peter 2:9 NKJV

"All the earth shall worship You
And sing praises to You;
They shall sing praises to Your name."
　　　　　　　　　　　　- Psalm 66:4 NKJV

Let everything that has breath
    praise the LORD.
             - Psalm 150:6 NASB

Let us lift up our hearts and our hands
  to God in heaven.
             - Lamentations 3:41 TNIV

O come, let us worship and bow down,
  let us kneel before the LORD, our Maker!
             - Psalm 95:6 NRSV

It is good to give thanks to the LORD,
  to sing praises to your name,
    O Most High;
to declare your steadfast love in
  the morning,
  and your faithfulness by night.
             - Psalm 92:1-2 NRSV

Be filled with the Spirit, speaking to one another in
psalms and hymns and spiritual songs, singing and
making melody in your heart to the Lord.
             - Ephesians 5:18-19 NKJV

Glorify the LORD with me;
  let us exalt his name together.
             - Psalm 34:3 TNIV

O LORD, you are my God;
  I will exalt you and praise your name,
for in perfect faithfulness
  you have done marvelous things,
  things planned long ago.
             - Isaiah 25:1 NIV

O Lord, our Lord, how excellent (majestic and glorious) is Your name in all the earth! You have set Your glory on [or above] the heavens.

                              - Psalm 8:1 AMP

"Stand up and bless the LORD
        your God
Forever and ever!
Blessed be Your glorious name,
Which is exalted above all blessing
        and praise!"

                        - Nehemiah 9:5 NKJV

Praise be to the God and Father of our Lord Jesus Christ, the Father of compassion and the God of all comfort.

                      - 2 Corinthians 1:3 TNIV

Let us offer God an unending sacrifice of praise, a verbal sacrifice that is offered every time we acknowledge his name.

                      - Hebrews 13:15 JB

Praise the LORD, my soul,
    and forget not all his benefits –
who forgives all your sins
    and heals all your diseases,
who redeems your life from the pit
    and crowns you with love and compassion,
who satisfies your desires with good things
    so that your youth is renewed like the eagle's.
                              - Psalm 103:2-5 TNIV

I will sing unto the LORD as long as I live: I will sing praise to my God while I have my being.
                              - Psalm 104:33 KJV

Let them praise his name with dancing
   and make music to him with
      tambourine and harp.
                - Psalm 149:3 NIV

Rejoice in the LORD, O you righteous!
For praise from the upright is
      beautiful.
Praise the LORD with the harp;
Make melody to Him with an
       instrument of ten strings.
Sing to Him a new song;
Play skillfully with a shout of joy.
             - Psalm 33:1-3 NKJV

I will praise You, O Lord, with my whole heart.
              - Psalm 9:1 AMP

"The LORD lives!
Blessed by my Rock!
Let God be exalted,
The Rock of my salvation!"
            - 2 Samuel 22:47 NKJV

I will sing of the LORD's great love forever;
   with my mouth I will make your faithfulness
      known through all generations.
              - Psalm 89:1 NIV

"Our God's hand of protection is on all who worship
him."
              - Ezra 8:22 NLT

Sing to the LORD, all the earth;
    proclaim his salvation day after day.
                           - 1 Chronicles 16:23 TNIV

Enter into His gates with thanksgiving,
And into His courts with praise.
Be thankful to Him, and bless His name.
                           - Psalm 100:4 NKJV

O Lord, open my lips,
    and my mouth will declare your praise.
                           - Psalm 51:15 NRSV

My mouth will speak your praises,
        LORD;
    all flesh will bless your holy name
        forever.
                           - Psalm 145:21 NAB

"He is your praise and He is your God, who has done
these great and awesome things for you which your
eyes have seen."
                           - Deuteronomy 10:21 NASB

My mouth is filled with your praise,
    declaring your splendor all day long.
                           - Psalm 71:8 TNIV

It is good to sing praises to our God;
For it is pleasant, and praise is beautiful.
                           - Psalm 147:1 NKJV

Accept one another, then, just as Christ accepted you,
in order to bring praise to God.
- Romans 15:7 NIV

Sing to God, sing praises to his name;
lift up a song to him who rides upon the clouds.
- Psalm 68:4 NRSV

Praise the LORD!
Sing to the LORD a new song,
And His praise in the assembly of
saints.
- Psalm 149:1 NKJV

From the rising of the sun to the place
where it sets,
the name of the LORD is to be praised.
- Psalm 113:3 NIV

Praise him for his mighty deeds;
praise him according to his surpassing greatness!
- Psalm 150:2 NRSV

Make a joyful shout to God, all the
earth!
Sing out the honor of His name;
Make His praise glorious.
- Psalm 66:1-2 NKJV

"The LORD gave and the LORD has
taken away.
Blessed be the name of the LORD."
- Job 1:21 NASB

Let the high praises of God be in
    their mouth,
And a two-edged sword in their hand.
                    - Psalm 149:6 NASB

See also **Glory, Happiness, Rejoice, Speaking Boldly**

Prayer

"All the things you pray and ask for – believe that you have received them, and you will have them."
                    - Mark 11:24 HCSB

Don't worry about anything; instead, pray about everything. Tell God what you need, and thank him for all he has done.
                    - Philippians 4:6 NLT

'If you have faith, everything you ask for in prayer you will receive.'
                    - Matthew 21:22 JB

We have confidence in God and receive from him whatever we ask, because we keep his commandments and do what pleases him.
                    - 1 John 3:21-22 NAB

"For the eyes of the Lord are on the
        righteous
    and his ears are attentive to their
        prayer."
                            - 1 Peter 3:12 NIV

"I have prayed for you, that your faith should not fail."
                            - Luke 22:32 NKJV

Pray for the peace of Jerusalem:
    "May they prosper who love you."
                            - Psalm 122:6 NRSV

"Watch and pray so that you will not fall into temptation. The spirit is willing, but the body is weak."
                            - Mark 14:38 NIV

"Love your enemies, bless those who curse you, do
good to those who hate you, and pray for those who
spitefully use you and persecute you."
                            - Matthew 5:44 NKJV

Devote yourselves to prayer; stay alert in it with
thanksgiving.
                            - Colossians 4:2 HCSB

You faithfully answer our prayers with
        awesome deeds,
    O God our savior.
                            - Psalm 65:5 NLT

When they had prayed, the place in which they were gathered together was shaken; and they were all filled with the Holy Spirit and spoke the word of God with boldness.

- Acts 4:31 NRSV

This is the confidence that we have in Him, that if we ask anything according to His will, He hears us. And if we know that He hears us, whatever we ask, we know that we have the petitions that we have asked of Him.

- 1 John 5:14-15 NKJV

The prayer of a righteous person is powerful and effective.

- James 5:16 TNIV

"I assure you: Anything you ask the Father in My name, He will give you."

- John 16:23 HCSB

The end of all things is at hand; therefore be serious and watchful in your prayers.

- 1 Peter 4:7 NKJV

He answered their prayers because they trusted in Him.

- 1 Chronicles 5:20 NASB

Pray for us. We are sure that we have a clear conscience and desire to live honorably in every way.

- Hebrews 13:18 TNIV

Pray without ceasing.

- 1 Thessalonians 5:17 KJV

Elijah was a human being like us, and he prayed fervently that it might not rain, and for three years and six months it did not rain on the earth. Then he prayed again, and the heaven gave rain and the earth yielded its harvest.

- James 5:17-18 NRSV

Pray also for me, that whenever I speak, words may be given me so that I will fearlessly make known the mystery of the gospel.

- Ephesians 6:19 TNIV

I want men everywhere to lift up holy hands in prayer.

- 1 Timothy 2:8 NIV

Evening and morning and at noon
I will pray, and cry aloud,
And He shall hear my voice.

- Psalm 55:17 NKJV

" ' "I have heard your prayer, I have seen your tears; surely I will heal you." ' "

- 2 Kings 20:5 NKJV

As my life was fading away,
I remembered the LORD.
My prayer came to You,
to Your holy temple.

- Jonah 2:7 HCSB

With all prayer and supplication, pray at every opportunity in the Spirit.
- Ephesians 6:18 NAB

"Ask and it will be given to you; seek and you will find; knock and the door will be opened to you. For everyone who asks, receives; and the one who seeks, finds; and to the one who knocks, the door will be opened."
- Matthew 7:7-8 NAB

The prayer of faith will save the sick, and the Lord will raise them up.
- James 5:15 NRSV

"Whatever you ask in My name, that I will do, that the Father may be glorified in the Son. If you ask anything in My name, I will do it."
- John 14:13-14 NKJV

See also **Faith**

Prophesy

Pursue love and strive for the spiritual gifts, and especially that you may prophesy.
- 1 Corinthians 14:1 NRSV

No prophecy of Scripture is of any private interpretation, for prophecy never came by the will of man, but holy men of God spoke as they were moved by the Holy Spirit.
- 2 Peter 1:20-21 NKJV

Therefore, my brothers and sisters, be eager to prophesy.
- 1 Corinthians 14:39 TNIV

The testimony of Jesus is the spirit of prophecy.
- Revelation 19:10 KJV

One who speaks in a tongue edifies himself; but one who prophesies edifies the church.
- 1 Corinthians 14:4 NASB

We also have the prophetic message as something completely reliable, and you will do well to pay attention to it, as to a light shining in a dark place, until the day dawns and the morning star rises in your hearts.
- 2 Peter 1:19 TNIV

" 'In the last days, God says,
   I will pour out my Spirit on all people.
Your sons and daughters will prophesy,
   your young men will see visions,
   your old men will dream dreams.
Even on my servants, both men and women,
   I will pour out my Spirit in those days,
   and they will prophesy.' "
                              - Acts 2:17-18 NIV

Everyone who prophesies speaks to men for their strengthening, encouragement and comfort.
                              - 1 Corinthians 14:3 NIV

See also **Purpose**

Prosper

"Keep this Book of the Law always on your lips; meditate on it day and night, so that you may be careful to do everything written in it. Then you will be prosperous and successful."
                              - Joshua 1:8 TNIV

"The God of heaven Himself will prosper us."
                              - Nehemiah 2:20 NKJV

If they obey and serve Him, they shall spend their days in prosperity and their years in pleasantness and joy.
                              - Job 36:11 AMP

The righteous shall flourish like a
    palm tree,
He shall grow like a cedar in
    Lebanon.
Those who are planted in the house
    of the LORD
Shall flourish in the courts of our
    God.
They shall still bear fruit in old age;
They shall be fresh and flourishing,
To declare that the LORD is upright;
He is my rock, and there is no
    unrighteousness in Him.
                    - Psalm 92:12-15 NKJV

As long as he sought the LORD, God made him prosper.
                    - 2 Chronicles 26:5 NRSV

The one who looks intently into the perfect law of freedom and perseveres in it, and is not a forgetful hearer
but a doer who acts – this person will be blessed in
what he does.
                    - James 1:25 HCSB

A generous man will prosper;
    he who refreshes others will himself
        be refreshed.
                    - Proverbs 11:25 NIV

"I am the vine, you are the branches. He who abides in
Me, and I in him, bears much fruit; for without Me
you can do nothing."
                    - John 15:5 NKJV

The reward given by wisdom is success.
                    - Ecclesiastes 10:10 JB

His delight is in the law of the LORD,
    And in His law he meditates day and
        night.
He shall be like a tree
    Planted by the rivers of water,
    That brings forth its fruit in its
        season,
    Whose leaf also shall not wither;
And whatever he does shall prosper.
                    - Psalm 1:2-3 NKJV

I pray that you may prosper in every way and be in
good health, just as your soul prospers.
                    - 3 John 2 HCSB

"I know the plans I have for you," declares the LORD,
"plans to prosper you and not to harm you, plans to
give you hope and a future."
                    - Jeremiah 29:11 TNIV

Pray for the peace of Jerusalem: they shall prosper
that love thee.
                    - Psalm 122:6 KJV

"Keep the charge of the LORD your God: to walk in His
ways, to keep His statutes, His commandments, His
judgments, and His testimonies, ...that you may prosper in all that you do and wherever you turn."
                    - 1 Kings 2:3 NKJV

"Submit to God and be at peace with him;
in this way prosperity will come to you."
- Job 22:21 NIV

Give generously...and do so without a grudging heart;
then because of this the LORD your God will bless you
in all your work and in everything you put your hand
to.
- Deuteronomy 15:10 TNIV

"Believe in the LORD your God, and you will be established; believe in His prophets, and you will succeed."
- 2 Chronicles 20:20 HCSB

In everything he did he had great success, because the
LORD was with him.
- 1 Samuel 18:14 TNIV

An arrogant man stirs up strife,
But he who trusts in the LORD will prosper.
- Proverbs 28:25 NASB

See also **Blessing, Victory**

Receiving

Every good and perfect gift is from above, coming down from the Father of the heavenly lights.
                              - James 1:17 TNIV

"All that you ask for in prayer, believe that you will receive it and it shall be yours."
                              - Mark 11:24 NAB

"Behold, I am coming quickly, and My reward is with Me, to render to every man according to what he has done."
                              - Revelation 22:12 NASB

"If you remain in me and my words remain in you, ask for whatever you want and it will be done for you."
                              - John 15:7 NAB

What I received I passed on to you as of first importance: that Christ died for our sins according to the Scriptures, that he was buried, that he was raised on the third day according to the Scriptures.
                              - 1 Corinthians 15:3-4 TNIV

I will send forth upon you what My Father has promised; but remain in the city [Jerusalem] until you are clothed with power from on high.
                              - Luke 24:49 AMP

"Everyone who has given up houses or brothers or
sisters or father or mother or children or lands for the
sake of my name will receive a hundred times more,
and will inherit eternal life."

- Matthew 19:29 NAB

For the LORD God is a sun and shield;
The LORD gives grace and glory;
No good thing does He withhold from those who
        walk uprightly.

- Psalm 84:11 NASB

"Bring all the tithes into the
        storehouse,
That there may be food in My house,
And try Me now in this,"
Says the LORD of hosts,
"If I will not open for you the windows
        of heaven
And pour out for you such blessing
That there will not be room enough
        to receive it."

- Malachi 3:10 NKJV

"I have given you authority to tread on snakes and
scorpions, and over all the power of the enemy; and
nothing will hurt you."

- Luke 10:19 NRSV

Did you receive the Spirit from works of the law, or
from faith in what you heard? Does, then, the one who
supplies the Spirit to you and works mighty deeds
among you do so from works of the law or from faith
in what you heard?

- Galatians 3:2,5 NAB

Yet to all who received him, to those who believed in his name, he gave the right to become children of God.
- John 1:12 NIV

Although you have not seen him, you love him; and even though you do not see him now, you believe in him and rejoice with an indescribable and glorious joy, for you are receiving the outcome of your faith, the salvation of your souls.
- 1 Peter 1:8-9 NRSV

Whatever we ask we receive from Him, because we keep His commandments and do those things that are pleasing in His sight.
- 1 John 3:22 NKJV

"Whoever drinks of the water that I shall give him will never thirst. But the water that I shall give him will become in him a fountain of water springing up into everlasting life."
- John 4:14 NKJV

The man who plants and the man who waters have one purpose, and each will be rewarded according to his own labor.
- 1 Corinthians 3:8 NIV

When the chief Shepherd is revealed, you will receive the unfading crown of glory.
- 1 Peter 5:4 NAB

"If you believe, you will receive whatever you ask for in prayer."
- Matthew 21:22 TNIV

"Do not labor for the food which perishes, but for the food which endures to everlasting life, which the Son of Man will give you, because God the Father has set His seal on Him."
                                    - John 6:27 NKJV

We have different gifts, according to the grace given us. If a man's gift is prophesying, let him use it in proportion to his faith. If it is serving, let him serve; if it is teaching, let him teach; if it is encouraging, let him encourage; if it is contributing to the needs of others, let him give generously; if it is leadership, let him govern diligently; if it is showing mercy, let him do it cheerfully.
                                    - Romans 12:6-8 NIV

Remember the LORD your God, for it is he who gives you the ability to produce wealth.
                                    - Deuteronomy 8:18 TNIV

We who live by the Spirit eagerly wait to receive by faith the righteousness God has promised to us.
                                    - Galatians 5:5 NLT

By grace you have been saved through faith, and this is not from you; it is the gift of God.
                                    - Ephesians 2:8 NAB

We must all appear before the judgment seat of Christ, so that each may be repaid for what he has done in the body, whether good or bad.
                                    - 2 Corinthians 5:10 HCSB

Judge nothing before the appointed time; wait till the Lord comes. He will bring to light what is hidden in darkness and will expose the motives of people's hearts. At that time each will receive their praise from God.
                                    - 1 Corinthians 4:5 TNIV

Let us not grow tired of doing good, for in due time we shall reap our harvest, if we do not give up.
                                    - Galatians 6:9 NAB

"Ask and it will be given to you; seek and you will find; knock and the door will be opened to you. For everyone who asks receives; he who seeks finds; and to him who knocks, the door will be opened."
                                    - Matthew 7:7-8 NIV

"Riches and honor come from You, and You are the ruler of everything. In Your hand are power and might, and it is in Your hand to make great and to give strength to all."
                                    - 1 Chronicles 29:12 HCSB

Find your delight in the LORD
   who will give you your heart's desire.
                                    - Psalm 37:4 NAB

"Come out from among them
And be separate, says the Lord.
Do not touch what is unclean,
And I will receive you."
                                    - 2 Corinthians 6:17 NKJV

"You will receive power when the Holy Spirit has come upon you."

> \- Acts 1:8 NRSV

You have need of endurance, so that when you have done the will of God, you may receive what was promised.

> \- Hebrews 10:36 NASB

The Spirit himself testifies with our spirit that we are God's children. Now if we are children, then we are heirs – heirs of God and co-heirs with Christ, if indeed we share in his sufferings in order that we may also share in his glory.

> \- Romans 8:16-17 TNIV

"From everyone to whom much has been given, much will be required; and from the one to whom much has been entrusted, even more will be demanded."

> \- Luke 12:48 NRSV

" 'Look, the LORD your God has set the land before you; go up and possess it, as the LORD God of your fathers has spoken to you; do not fear or be discouraged.' "

> \- Deuteronomy 1:21 NKJV

For the LORD gives wisdom;
   from his mouth come knowledge and
      understanding.

> \- Proverbs 2:6 TNIV

Whatever you do, do from the heart, as for the Lord and not for others, knowing that you will receive from the Lord the due payment of the inheritance.

- Colossians 3:23-24 NAB

"Whoever receives one child like this in My name receives Me; and whoever receives Me does not receive Me, but Him who sent Me."

- Mark 9:37 NASB

"Peace I leave with you; my peace I give to you. Not as the world gives do I give it to you. Do not let your hearts be troubled or afraid."

- John 14:27 NAB

"To him who is thirsty I will give to drink without cost from the spring of the water of life. He who overcomes will inherit all this, and I will be his God and he will be my son."

- Revelation 21:6-7 NIV

"A man can receive nothing unless it has been given to him from heaven."

- John 3:27 NKJV

Instruct those who are rich in this present world not to be conceited or to fix their hope on the uncertainty of riches, but on God, who richly supplies us with all things to enjoy.

- 1 Timothy 6:17 NASB

Each of you has your own gift from God; one has this gift, another has that.

- 1 Corinthians 7:7 TNIV

Do you not know that those who run in a race all run, but only one receives the prize? Run in such a way that you may win.
> - 1 Corinthians 9:24 NASB

If any of you is lacking in wisdom, ask God, who gives to all generously and ungrudgingly, and it will be given you.
> - James 1:5 NRSV

This is the confidence we have in approaching God: that if we ask anything according to his will, he hears us. And if we know that he hears us – whatever we ask – we know that we have what we asked of him.
> - 1 John 5:14-15 TNIV

"Peace be with you; as the Father has sent Me, I also send you." And when He had said this, He breathed on them and said to them, "Receive the Holy Spirit."
> - John 20:21-22 NASB

"As you go, preach this message: 'The kingdom of heaven is near.' Heal the sick, raise the dead, cleanse those who have leprosy, drive out demons. Freely you have received, freely give."
> - Matthew 10:7-8 NIV

For unto us a Child is born,
Unto us a Son is given;
And the government will be upon
      His shoulder.
And His name will be called
Wonderful, Counselor, Mighty God,
Everlasting Father, Prince of Peace.
> - Isaiah 9:6 NKJV

"I assure you: Anything you ask the Father in My name, He will give you. Until now you have asked for nothing in My name. Ask and you will receive, that your joy may be complete."

                            - John 16:23-24 HCSB

See also **Generosity, Humility**

Rejoice

Although you have not seen him, you love him; and even though you do not see him now, you believe in him and rejoice with an indescribable and glorious joy, for you are receiving the outcome of your faith, the salvation of your souls.

                            - 1 Peter 1:8-9 NRSV

I rejoiced when they said to me,
    "Let us go to the house of the LORD."

                            - Psalm 122:1 NAB

Rejoice always.

                            - 1 Thessalonians 5:16 TNIV

"Behold our God, to whom we looked
        to save us!
    This is the LORD for whom we looked;
        let us rejoice and be glad that he has
            saved us!"

                            - Isaiah 25:9 NAB

Rejoice in the LORD, O you righteous!
For praise from the upright is
        beautiful.
Praise the LORD with the harp;
Make melody to Him with an
        instrument of ten strings.
Sing to Him a new song;
Play skillfully with a shout of joy.
                        - Psalm 33:1-3 NKJV

Rejoice in the Lord always [delight, gladden yourselves
in Him]; again I say, Rejoice!
                        - Philippians 4:4 AMP

Rejoice, be made complete, be comforted, be like-
minded, live in peace; and the God of love and peace
will be with you.
                        - 2 Corinthians 13:11 NASB

We also rejoice in God through our Lord Jesus Christ,
through whom we have now received reconciliation.
                        - Romans 5:11 NIV

The LORD says, "Shout and rejoice, O beautiful Jerusalem, for I am coming to live among you."
                        - Zechariah 2:10 NLT

The humble will be filled with fresh joy
        from the LORD.
    The poor will rejoice in the Holy One
        of Israel.
                        - Isaiah 29:19 NLT

O clap your hands, all ye people; shout unto God with the voice of triumph.

> \- Psalm 47:1 KJV

Rejoice with those who rejoice, and weep with those who weep.

> \- Romans 12:15 NASB

"My heart rejoices in the LORD;
　in the LORD my horn is lifted high.
My mouth boasts over my enemies,
　for I delight in your deliverance."

> \- 1 Samuel 2:1 TNIV

I rejoice in your promise,
　like someone on finding a vast treasure.

> \- Psalm 119:162 JB

Be glad and rejoice with all your
　　　heart,
The LORD has taken away your
　　　judgments,
He has cast out your enemy.
The King of Israel, the LORD, is in
　　　your midst;
You shall see disaster no more.

> \- Zephaniah 3:14-15 NKJV

Let all who seek You rejoice and be
　　　glad in You;
And let those who love Your salvation
　　　say continually,
"Let God be magnified."

> \- Psalm 70:4 NASB

We rejoice in the hope of the glory of God.
                              - Romans 5:2 NIV

I will greatly rejoice in the LORD,
    my whole being shall exult in my God;
for he has clothed me with the garments of salvation,
    he has covered me with the robe of righteousness.
                              - Isaiah 61:10 NRSV

"The LORD your God is with you,
    he is mighty to save.
He will take great delight in you,
    he will quiet you with his love,
    he will rejoice over you with singing."
                              - Zephaniah 3:17 NIV

And my soul shall be joyful in the LORD;
It shall rejoice in His salvation.
                              - Psalm 35:9 NKJV

I rejoiced greatly to find some of your children walking
in the truth just as we were commanded by the Father.
                              - 2 John 4 NAB

For though the fig tree blossom not
    nor fruit be on the vines,
Though the yield of the olive fail
    and the terraces produce no nourishment,
Though the flocks disappear from the fold
    and there be no herd in the stalls,
Yet will I rejoice in the LORD
    and exult in my saving God.
                              - Habakkuk 3:17-18 NAB

"You now have sorrow; but I will see you again and your heart will rejoice, and your joy no one will take from you."
- John 16:22 NKJV

This is the day that the LORD has made;
let us rejoice and be glad in it.
- Psalm 118:24 NRSV

See also **Happiness, Joy, Praise**

Repentance

"There will be more joy in heaven over one sinner who repents than over ninety-nine righteous persons who need no repentance."
- Luke 15:7 NASB

"Those who are well have no need of a physician, but those who are sick. I did not come to call the righteous, but sinners, to repentance."
- Mark 2:17 NKJV

When God saw what they did and how they turned from their evil ways, he had compassion and did not bring upon them the destruction he had threatened.
- Jonah 3:10 NIV

For Your name's sake, O Lord, pardon my iniquity and my guilt, for [they are] great.
                              - Psalm 25:11 AMP

"Repent and be baptized, every one of you, in the name of Jesus Christ for the forgiveness of your sins. And you will receive the gift of the Holy Spirit."
                              - Acts 2:38 TNIV

"If the wicked person turns from all the sins he has committed, keeps all My statutes, and does what is just and right, he will certainly live; he will not die."
                              - Ezekiel 18:21 HCSB

You were continually straying like sheep, but now you have returned to the Shepherd and Guardian of your souls.
                              - 1 Peter 2:25 NASB

For the sorrow that is according to the will of God produces a repentance without regret, leading to salvation, but the sorrow of the world produces death.
                              - 2 Corinthians 7:10 NASB

"If your brother sins against you, rebuke him; and if he repents, forgive him. And if he sins against you seven times in a day, and seven times in a day returns to you, saying, 'I repent,' you shall forgive him."
                              - Luke 17:3-4 NKJV

Wash me thoroughly from my iniquity,
    and cleanse me from my sin.
                              - Psalm 51:2 NRSV

Let the wicked forsake his way,
And the unrighteous man his
        thoughts;
Let him return to the LORD,
And He will have mercy on him;
And to our God,
For He will abundantly pardon.
                          - Isaiah 55:7 NKJV

" 'Return to me,' declares the LORD Almighty, 'and I will return to you.' "
                          - Zechariah 1:3 TNIV

Be not wise in thine own eyes: fear the LORD, and depart from evil.
                          - Proverbs 3:7 KJV

"For the LORD your God is gracious and compassionate, and will not turn His face away from you if you return to Him."
                          - 2 Chronicles 30:9 NASB

I will declare my iniquity;
I will be in anguish over my sin.
                          - Psalm 38:18 NKJV

My sacrifice [the sacrifice acceptable] to God is a broken spirit; a broken and a contrite heart [broken down with sorrow for sin and humbly and thoroughly penitent], such, O God, You will not despise.
                          - Psalm 51:17 AMP

"Repent, then, and turn to God, so that your sins may be wiped out, that times of refreshing may come from the Lord."

- Acts 3:19 NIV

For You, Lord, are good, and ready
        to forgive,
And abundant in mercy to all those
        who call upon You.

- Psalm 86:5 NKJV

"Come now, and let us reason
        together,"
Says the LORD,
"Though your sins are as scarlet,
They will be as white as snow;
Though they are red like crimson,
They will be like wool."

- Isaiah 1:18 NASB

"If my people, who are called by my name, will humble themselves and pray and seek my face and turn from their wicked ways, then I will hear from heaven, and I will forgive their sin and will heal their land."

- 2 Chronicles 7:14 TNIV

See also **Forgiveness, Mercy, Reconciliation,
    Salvation**

Sacrifice

"Whoever desires to come after Me, let him deny himself, and take up his cross, and follow Me. For whoever desires to save his life will lose it, but whoever loses his life for My sake and the gospel's will save it."
                                        - Mark 8:34-35 NKJV

Let us offer God an unending sacrifice of praise, a verbal sacrifice that is offered every time we acknowledge his name.
                                        - Hebrews 13:15 JB

I regard everything as loss because of the surpassing value of knowing Christ Jesus my Lord. For his sake I have suffered the loss of all things, and I regard them as rubbish, in order that I may gain Christ.
                                        - Philippians 3:8 NRSV

Greater love hath no man than this, that a man lay down his life for his friends.
                                        - John 15:13 KJV

By faith Moses, when he became of age, refused to be called the son of Pharaoh's daughter, choosing rather to suffer affliction with the people of God than to enjoy the passing pleasures of sin.
                                        - Hebrews 11:24-25 NKJV

If I give all my possessions to feed the poor, and if I surrender my body to be burned, but do not have love, it profits me nothing.
                                        - 1 Corinthians 13:3 NASB

This is how we know what love is: Jesus Christ laid down his life for us. And we ought to lay down our lives for one another.

- 1 John 3:16 TNIV

Do not forget to do good and to share with others, for with such sacrifices God is pleased.

- Hebrews 13:16 NIV

My sacrifice [the sacrifice acceptable] to God is a broken spirit; a broken and a contrite heart [broken down with sorrow for sin and humbly and thoroughly penitent], such, O God, You will not despise.

- Psalm 51:17 AMP

"For even the Son of Man did not come to be served, but to serve, and to give his life as a ransom for many."

- Mark 10:45 NIV

Jesus said to Simon, "Do not be afraid. From now on you will catch men." So when they had brought their boats to land, they forsook all and followed Him.

- Luke 5:10-11 NKJV

I am willing to endure anything if it will bring salvation and eternal glory in Christ Jesus to those God has chosen.

- 2 Timothy 2:10 NLT

I will sacrifice to You with the voice of thanksgiving; I will pay that which I have vowed. Salvation and deliverance belong to the Lord!

- Jonah 2:9 AMP

"Everyone who has given up houses or brothers or sisters or father or mother or children or lands for the sake of my name will receive a hundred times more, and will inherit eternal life."
- Matthew 19:29 NAB

See also **Live in Christ, Longsuffering**

Seek God

"I am the bread of life; he who comes to Me will not hunger, and he who believes in Me will never thirst."
- John 6:35 NASB

You will seek Me and find Me, when you search for Me with all your heart.
- Jeremiah 29:13 NKJV

Seek the LORD while He may be found;
call to Him while He is near.
- Isaiah 55:6 HCSB

I sought the LORD, and he answered me;
he delivered me from all my fears.
- Psalm 34:4 NIV

"Whoever calls on the name of the LORD
Shall be saved."
- Joel 2:32 NKJV

He will give eternal life to those who keep on doing
good, seeking after the glory and honor and immortality that God offers.

- Romans 2:7 NLT

The LORD is near to all who call on him,
to all who call on him in truth.

- Psalm 145:18 NRSV

"Whoever does not carry his own cross and come after
Me cannot be My disciple."

- Luke 14:27 NASB

"Now acquaint yourself with Him,
and be at peace;
Thereby good will come to you."

- Job 22:21 NKJV

But as for me, I will look to the LORD,
I will put my trust in God my savior.

- Micah 7:7 NAB

It is good for me to draw near to God; I have put my
trust in the Lord God and made Him my refuge, that I
may tell of all Your works.

- Psalm 73:28 AMP

"The hand of our God is gracious to all who seek Him."

- Ezra 8:22 HCSB

Lord, you are kind and forgiving,
most loving to all who call on you.

- Psalm 86:5 NAB

You drew near on the day I
    called on You,
And said, "Do not fear!"
          - Lamentations 3:57 NKJV

"Sow for yourselves righteousness,
    reap the fruit of unfailing love,
and break up your unplowed ground;
    for it is time to seek the LORD,
until he comes
    and showers righteousness on you."
          - Hosea 10:12 NIV

Seek the LORD and His strength;
Seek His face evermore!
          - 1 Chronicles 16:11 NKJV

The lions may grow weak and hungry,
    but those who seek the LORD lack no
        good thing.
          - Psalm 34:10 TNIV

Those who know your name will
        trust in you,
    for you, LORD, have never forsaken
        those who seek you.
          - Psalm 9:10 NIV

"We sought the LORD our God, and he has given us
peace on every side."
          - 2 Chronicles 14:7 NLT

"Come to Me, all of you who are weary and burdened,
and I will give you rest."
          - Matthew 11:28 HCSB

When You said, "Seek My face,"
My heart said to You, "Your face,
    LORD, I will seek."
               - Psalm 27:8 NKJV

As long as he sought the LORD, God made him prosper.
               - 2 Chronicles 26:5 NAB

Call on Me in the day of trouble; I will deliver you, and you shall honor and glorify Me.
               - Psalm 50:15 AMP

"If you seek Him, He will be found by you."
               - 2 Chronicles 15:2 HCSB

" 'Call to Me, and I will answer you, and show you great and mighty things, which you do not know.' "
               - Jeremiah 33:3 NKJV

In the day of my trouble I will call on You, for You will answer me.
               - Psalm 86:7 AMP

As the deer pants for streams of water,
    so my soul pants for you, O God.
My soul thirsts for God, for the living God.
               - Psalm 42:1-2 NIV

Evil men do not understand justice,
but those who seek the LORD understand
    everything.
               - Proverbs 28:5 HCSB

You who seek God, your hearts
    shall live.
                - Psalm 69:32 NKJV

"Now set your heart and your soul to seek the LORD
your God."
                - 1 Chronicles 22:19 NASB

The LORD is good to those who wait
    for Him,
To the soul who seeks Him.
                - Lamentations 3:25 NKJV

"May you be richly rewarded by the LORD, the God of
Israel, under whose wings you have come to take refuge."
                - Ruth 2:12 TNIV

Let all who seek You rejoice and be
    glad in You;
And let those who love Your salvation
    say continually,
"Let God be magnified."
                - Psalm 70:4 NASB

Draw near to God, and He will draw near to you.
                - James 4:8 HCSB

My soul longs, yes, even faints
For the courts of the LORD;
My heart and my flesh cry out for
    the living God.
                - Psalm 84:2 NKJV

O God, you are my God,
　　earnestly I seek you;
my soul thirsts for you,
　　my body longs for you,
in a dry and weary land
　　where there is no water.
　　　　　　　　- Psalm 63:1 NIV

"I am the door; if anyone enters through Me, he will be
saved, and will go in and out and find pasture."
　　　　　　　　- John 10:9 NASB

Because He has inclined His ear to me,
Therefore I shall call upon Him as long
　　　　　as I live.
　　　　　　　　- Psalm 116:2 NASB

"Therefore do not worry, saying, 'What shall we eat?'
or 'What shall we drink?' or 'What shall we wear?' For
your heavenly Father knows that you need all these
things. But seek first the kingdom of God and His
righteousness, and all these things shall be added to
you."
　　　　　　　　- Matthew 6:31-33 NKJV

"Come, follow me," Jesus said, "and I will make you
fishers of men."
　　　　　　　　- Mark 1:17 NIV

" 'Behold, I stand at the door and knock; if anyone
hears My voice and opens the door, I will come in to
him and will dine with him, and he with Me.' "
　　　　　　　　- Revelation 3:20 NASB

See also **Live in Christ, Walk in Christ**

Speaking Boldly

Pray on my behalf, that utterance may be given to me in the opening of my mouth, to make known with boldness the mystery of the gospel, for which I am an ambassador in chains; that in proclaiming it I may speak boldly, as I ought to speak.
- Ephesians 6:19-20 NASB

Then said I:
   "Ah, Lord GOD!
   Behold, I cannot speak, for I am a youth."
But the LORD said to me:
   "Do not say, 'I am a youth,'
   For you shall go to all to whom I send you,
   And whatever I command you, you shall speak."
- Jeremiah 1:6-7 NKJV

The Lord stood by me and strengthened me, so that through me the [Gospel] message might be fully proclaimed.
- 2 Timothy 4:17 AMP

"I consider my life worth nothing to me; my only aim is to finish the race and complete the task the Lord Jesus has given me – the task of testifying to the good news of God's grace."
- Acts 20:24 TNIV

Let the redeemed of the LORD say so, whom he hath redeemed from the hand of the enemy.
- Psalm 107:2 KJV

Preach the Word; be prepared in season and out of season; correct, rebuke and encourage – with great patience and careful instruction.

- 2 Timothy 4:2 NIV

"Now go! I will be with you as you speak, and I will instruct you in what to say."

- Exodus 4:12 NLT

Let your speech always be with grace, as though seasoned with salt, so that you will know how you should respond to each person.

- Colossians 4:6 NASB

"I must speak only what God puts in my mouth."

- Numbers 22:38 TNIV

His word was in my heart like a burning fire
Shut up in my bones;
I was weary of holding it back,
And I could not.

- Jeremiah 20:9 NKJV

No one should despise your youth; instead, you should be an example to the believers in speech, in conduct, in love, in faith, in purity.

- 1 Timothy 4:12 HCSB

The might of your awesome deeds shall be proclaimed,
and I will declare your greatness.

- Psalm 145:6 NRSV

As shoes for your feet put on whatever will make you ready to proclaim the gospel of peace.

- Ephesians 6:15 NRSV

You shall speak My words to them whether they will hear or refuse to hear.

- Ezekiel 2:7 AMP

"Do not be afraid, but speak, and do not keep silent; for I am with you."

- Acts 18:9-10 NKJV

I will sing of the LORD's great love forever;
   with my mouth I will make your faithfulness
     known through all generations.

- Psalm 89:1 NIV

Declare His glory among the nations, His marvelous works among all peoples.

- 1 Chronicles 16:24 AMP

For I am not ashamed of the gospel of Christ, for it is the power of God to salvation for everyone who believes.

- Romans 1:16 NKJV

We speak as those approved by God to be entrusted with the gospel. We are not trying to please people but God, who tests our hearts.

- 1 Thessalonians 2:4 TNIV

We do not use words that come from human wisdom. Instead, we speak words given to us by the Spirit, using the Spirit's words to explain spiritual truths.
                                    - 1 Corinthians 2:13 NLT

"Lord, consider their threats and enable your servants to speak your word with great boldness." After they prayed, the place where they were meeting was shaken. And they were all filled with the Holy Spirit and spoke the word of God boldly.
                                    - Acts 4:29,31 NIV

"Whatever the LORD says to me, that I will speak."
                                    - 1 Kings 22:14 NRSV

Having such a hope, we use great boldness in our speech.
                                    - 2 Corinthians 3:12 NASB

"When they deliver you up, do not worry about how or what you should speak. For it will be given to you in that hour what you should speak; for it is not you who speak, but the Spirit of your Father who speaks in you."
                                    - Matthew 10:19-20 NKJV

I shall not die but live
    and declare the deeds of the LORD.
                                    - Psalm 118:17 NAB

I thought it good to declare the signs and wonders that the Most High God has worked for me.
                                    - Daniel 4:2 NKJV

My mouth will speak the praise of the
> LORD,
> and all flesh will bless his holy name
> > forever and ever.
> > > - Psalm 145:21 NRSV

"I myself shall give you a wisdom in speaking that all your adversaries will be powerless to resist or refute."
> - Luke 21:15 NAB

Do not allow what you consider good to be spoken of as evil.
> - Romans 14:16 NIV

"What I tell you in the darkness, speak in the light; and what you hear whispered in your ear, proclaim upon the housetops."
> - Matthew 10:27 NASB

See also **Confessing Christ, Courage, Ministry, Praise**

Thanksgiving

Be filled with the Spirit, speaking to one another with psalms, hymns and songs from the Spirit. Sing and make music from your heart to the Lord, always giving thanks to God the Father for everything, in the name of our Lord Jesus Christ.

- Ephesians 5:18-20 TNIV

Thanks be to God who gives us the victory through our Lord Jesus Christ.

- 1 Corinthians 15:57 NAB

Enter into His gates with thanksgiving,
And into His courts with praise.
Be thankful to Him, and bless His name.

- Psalm 100:4 NKJV

Let us thank God for his priceless gift!

- 2 Corinthians 9:15 GNT

I will give thanks to the LORD with my
        whole heart;
    I will tell of all your wonderful deeds.

- Psalm 9:1 NRSV

I thank Christ Jesus our Lord, who has given me strength, and who judged me faithful enough to call me into his service.

- 1 Timothy 1:12 JB

I will sacrifice to You with the voice of thanksgiving.

- Jonah 2:9 AMP

Thanks be to God who always leads us in triumph in Christ, and through us diffuses the fragrance of His knowledge in every place.
                              - 2 Corinthians 2:14 NKJV

Devote yourselves to prayer, keeping alert in it with an attitude of thanksgiving.
                              - Colossians 4:2 NASB

"We give You thanks, O Lord
        God Almighty,
The One who is and who was
        and who is to come,
Because You have taken Your
        great power and reigned."
                              - Revelation 11:17 NKJV

It is good to give thanks to the LORD,
        to sing praises to your name,
        O Most High;
to declare your steadfast love in
        the morning,
        and your faithfulness by night.
                              - Psalm 92:1-2 NRSV

Give thanks whatever happens. That is what God wants for you in Christ Jesus.
                              - 1 Thessalonians 5:18 NCV

Don't worry about anything; instead, pray about everything. Tell God what you need, and thank him for all he has done.
                              - Philippians 4:6 NLT

So we Your people and the sheep
       of Your pasture
Will give thanks to You forever;
To all generations we will tell of
       Your praise.

                - Psalm 79:13 NASB

Oh, give thanks to the LORD, for He
       is good!
For His mercy endures forever.

              - 1 Chronicles 16:34 NKJV

We give thanks to You, O God, we
       give thanks!
For Your wondrous works declare
       that Your name is near.

                - Psalm 75:1 NKJV

In all your ways acknowledge Him,
And He will make your paths straight.

                - Proverbs 3:6 NASB

Let us enter His presence with thanksgiving;
let us shout triumphantly to Him in song.

                - Psalm 95:2 HCSB

Whatever you do in word or deed, do all in the name of
the Lord Jesus, giving thanks through Him to God the
Father.

                - Colossians 3:17 NASB

See also **Humility, Joy, Praise**

Trust

The LORD is my rock and my fortress
    and my deliverer;
My God, my strength, in whom I will
    trust;
My shield and the horn of my
    salvation, my stronghold.
                  - Psalm 18:2 NKJV

Trust in the LORD with all your heart
    and lean not on your own understanding.
                  - Proverbs 3:5 NIV

O LORD my God, in You I put my
    trust;
Save me from all those who
    persecute me;
And deliver me.
                  - Psalm 7:1 NKJV

Vindicate me, O LORD, for I have
    walked in my integrity,
And I have trusted in the LORD without
    wavering.
                  - Psalm 26:1 NASB

Keep and protect me, O God, for in You I have found
refuge, and in You do I put my trust and hide myself.
                  - Psalm 16:1 AMP

Whenever I am afraid,
I will trust in You.
                  - Psalm 56:3 NKJV

Trust in the Lord forever!
    For the Lord is an eternal Rock.
                     - Isaiah 26:4 NAB

"Blessed is the man who trusts in
        the Lord,
    whose confidence is in him.
He will be like a tree planted by the water
    that sends out its roots by the stream.
It does not fear when heat comes;
    its leaves are always green.
It has no worries in a year of drought
    and never fails to bear fruit."
                  - Jeremiah 17:7-8 NIV

" 'Because you trusted me, I will give you your life as a reward. I will rescue you and keep you safe. I , the Lord, have spoken!' "
                  - Jeremiah 39:18 NLT

The Lord is good,
    a refuge in times of trouble.
He cares for those who trust in him.
                  - Nahum 1:7 TNIV

In God I trust; I will not be afraid.
    What can man do to me?
                  - Psalm 56:11 NIV

"We are powerless before this great multitude who are coming against us; nor do we know what to do, but our eyes are on You."
                  - 2 Chronicles 20:12 NASB

As for God, His way is perfect;
The word of the LORD is proven;
He is a shield to all who trust in
      Him.
- Psalm 18:30 NKJV

At dawn let me hear of your kindness,
    for in you I trust.
Show me the path I should walk,
    for to you I entrust my life.
- Psalm 143:8 NAB

Command those who are rich in this present age not
to be haughty, nor to trust in uncertain riches but in
the living God, who gives us richly all things to enjoy.
- 1 Timothy 6:17 NKJV

Those who know your name trust
    in you,
  for you, LORD, have never forsaken
    those who seek you.
- Psalm 9:10 TNIV

By waiting and by calm you
    shall be saved,
  in quiet and in trust your
    strength lies.
- Isaiah 30:15 NAB

Some trust in chariots and some
    in horses,
  but we trust in the name of the LORD
    our God.
- Psalm 20:7 NIV

Christ will make his home in your hearts as you trust
in him. Your roots will grow down into God's love and
keep you strong.

- Ephesians 3:17 NLT

"You will keep him in perfect
      peace,
Whose mind is stayed on You,
Because he trusts in You."

- Isaiah 26:3 NKJV

It is better to trust in the LORD than to put confidence
in man. It is better to trust in the LORD than to put
confidence in princes.

- Psalm 118:8-9 KJV

In You, O LORD, I put my trust;
Let me never be put to shame.

- Psalm 71:1 NKJV

The LORD's unfailing love
   surrounds those who trust in him.

- Psalm 32:10 TNIV

May the God of hope fill you with all joy and peace as
you trust in him, so that you may overflow with hope
by the power of the Holy Spirit.

- Romans 15:13 NIV

He answered their prayers, because they trusted in
him.

- 1 Chronicles 5:20 NIV

Oh, taste and see that the LORD is
        good;
Blessed is the man who trusts in
        Him!
                                - Psalm 34:8 NKJV

Submit yourselves therefore to God. Resist the devil,
and he will flee from you.
                                - James 4:7 NRSV

He who trusts in the LORD will prosper.
                                - Proverbs 28:25 NAB

It is good for me to draw near to God; I have put my
trust in the Lord God and made Him my refuge, that I
may tell of all Your works.
                                - Psalm 73:28 AMP

And the LORD shall help them and
        deliver them;
He shall deliver them from the
        wicked,
And save them,
Because they trust in Him.
                                - Psalm 37:40 NKJV

See also **Promise, Truth**

Victory

Everyone born of God overcomes the world. This is the victory that has overcome the world, even our faith. Who is it that overcomes the world? Only the one who believes that Jesus is the Son of God.

- 1 John 5:4-5 TNIV

Thanks be to God, who gives us the victory through our Lord Jesus Christ.

- 1 Corinthians 15:57 NASB

" ' "He who overcomes shall be clothed in white garments, and I will not blot out his name from the Book of Life; but I will confess his name before My Father and before His angels." ' "

- Revelation 3:5 NKJV

Yet in all these things we are more than conquerors through Him who loved us.

- Romans 8:37 NKJV

"The LORD your God you shall fear; and He will deliver you from the hand of all your enemies."

- 2 Kings 17:39 NASB

You, dear children, are from God and have overcome them [false prophets], because the one who is in you is greater than the one who is in the world.

- 1 John 4:4 NIV

"To those who are victorious, I will give the right to eat from the tree of life, which is in the paradise of God."
                                        - Revelation 2:7 TNIV

The God of peace will soon crush Satan under your feet.
                                        - Romans 16:20 HCSB

"These things I have spoken to you, so that in Me you may have peace. In the world you have tribulation, but take courage; I have overcome the world."
                                        - John 16:33 NASB

"He who overcomes shall inherit all things, and I will be his God and he shall be My son."
                                        - Revelation 21:7 NKJV

"All who are victorious will become pillars in the Temple of my God, and they will never have to leave it."
                                        - Revelation 3:12 NLT

"Fear not! Stand your ground, and you will see the victory the LORD will win for you today."
                                        - Exodus 14:13 NAB

"He who overcomes will not be hurt at all by the second death."
                                        - Revelation 2:11 NIV

The LORD, your God, is in your midst,
    a warrior who gives victory;
he will rejoice over you with gladness,
    he will renew you in his love.
                                        - Zephaniah 3:17 NRSV

Thanks be to God who always leads us in triumph in Christ, and through us diffuses the fragrance of His knowledge in every place.

- 2 Corinthians 2:14 NKJV

" 'He who overcomes, I will grant to him to sit down with Me on My throne, as I also overcame and sat down with My Father on His throne.' "

- Revelation 3:21 NASB

See also **Perseverance, Prosper, Soldier of God**

Walk in Christ

"I am the vine, you are the branches. He who abides in Me, and I in him, bears much fruit; for without Me you can do nothing."

- John 15:5 NKJV

Walk in the Spirit, and you shall not fulfill the lust of the flesh.

- Galatians 5:16 NKJV

If you abide in My word [hold fast to My teachings and live in accordance with them], you are truly My disciples.

- John 8:31 AMP

Those who belong to Christ Jesus have crucified the sinful nature with its passions and desires. Since we live by the Spirit, let us keep in step with the Spirit.
- Galatians 5:24-25 NIV

"Whoever serves me must follow me, and where I am, there also will my servant be. The Father will honor whoever serves me."
- John 12:26 NAB

There is therefore now no condemnation to those who are in Christ Jesus, who do not walk according to the flesh, but according to the Spirit.
- Romans 8:1 NKJV

"If you abide in Me, and My words abide in you, ask whatever you wish, and it will be done for you."
- John 15:7 NASB

Happy are all who fear the LORD,
   who walk in the ways of God.
- Psalm 128:1 NAB

For you were once darkness, but now you are light in the Lord. Walk as children of light.
- Ephesians 5:8 NKJV

As you have received Christ Jesus the Lord, walk in Him, rooted and built up in Him and established in the faith, just as you were taught, and overflowing with thankfulness.
- Colossians 2:6-7 HCSB

"I am the Light of the world; he who follows Me will not walk in the darkness, but will have the Light of life."
                    - John 8:12 NASB

Whoever acknowledges that Jesus is the Son of God, God remains in him and he in God.
                    - 1 John 4:15 NAB

If we walk in the light as He is in the light, we have fellowship with one another, and the blood of Jesus Christ His Son cleanses us from all sin.
                    - 1 John 1:7 NKJV

"You shall follow the LORD your God and fear Him; and you shall keep His commandments, listen to His voice, serve Him, and cling to Him."
                    - Deuteronomy 13:4 NASB

Let the same mind be in you that was in Christ Jesus.
                    - Philippians 2:5 NRSV

This is love: that we walk in obedience to his commands. As you have heard from the beginning, his command is that you walk in love.
                    - 2 John 6 TNIV

If anyone obeys his word, God's love is truly made complete in him. This is how we know we are in him: Whoever claims to live in him must walk as Jesus did.
                    - 1 John 2:5-6 NIV

See also **Live in Christ, Obedience, Seek God**

Works

You see that his faith and his actions were working together, and his faith was made complete by what he did.
- James 2:22 NIV

"All who have faith in me will do the works I have been doing, and they will do even greater things than these, because I am going to the Father."
- John 14:12 TNIV

It is the will of God that by doing good you may silence the ignorance of foolish people.
- 1 Peter 2:15 NAB

For as the body without the spirit is dead, so faith without works is dead also.
- James 2:26 NKJV

We must all appear before the judgment seat of Christ, so that each may be repaid for what he has done in the body, whether good or bad.
- 2 Corinthians 5:10 HCSB

He will give eternal life to those who keep on doing good, seeking after the glory and honor and immortality that God offers.
- Romans 2:7 NLT

Whatever you do, whether in word or deed, do it all in the name of the Lord Jesus, giving thanks to God the Father through him.

- Colossians 3:17 TNIV

Don't be deceived: God is not mocked. For whatever a man sows he will also reap, because the one who sows to his flesh will reap corruption from the flesh, but the one who sows to the Spirit will reap eternal life from the Spirit.

- Galatians 6:7-8 HCSB

The man who plants and the man who waters have one purpose, and each will be rewarded according to his own labor.

- 1 Corinthians 3:8 NIV

"I, the LORD, search the heart,
I test the mind,
Even to give every man according to
        his ways,
According to the fruit of his doings."

- Jeremiah 17:10 NKJV

Whatever you do, work at it with all your heart, as working for the Lord, not for men, since you know that you will receive an inheritance from the Lord as a reward. It is the Lord Christ you are serving.

- Colossians 3:23-24 NIV

Whoever sows sparingly will also reap sparingly, and whoever sows bountifully will also reap bountifully.

- 2 Corinthians 9:6 NAB

Say to the righteous that it shall be well with them, for they shall eat the fruit of their deeds.
                                        - Isaiah 3:10 AMP

Your every act should be done with love.
                                        - 1 Corinthians 16:14 NAB

God poured out the Holy Spirit abundantly on us through Jesus Christ our Savior, so that by his grace we might be put right with God and come into possession of the eternal life we hope for. This is a true saying. I want you to give special emphasis to these matters, so that those who believe in God may be concerned with giving their time to doing good deeds, which are good and useful for everyone.
                                        - Titus 3:6-8 GNT

As for you, brothers, never tire of doing what is right.
                                        - 2 Thessalonians 3:13 NIV

You see that a person is justified by works and not by faith alone.
                                        - James 2:24 NRSV

We constantly pray for you, that our God may make you worthy of his calling, and that by his power he may bring to fruition your every desire for goodness and your every deed prompted by faith.
                                        - 2 Thessalonians 1:11 TNIV

We are God's workmanship, created in Christ Jesus to do good works, which God prepared in advance for us to do.
                                        - Ephesians 2:10 NIV

"The Son of Man will come in the glory of His Father with His angels, and then He will reward each according to his works."
> - Matthew 16:27 NKJV

Observe what is right, do what is just;
  for my salvation is about to come.
> - Isaiah 56:1 NAB

It is not the hearers of the law who are righteous in God's sight, but the doers of the law who will be justified.
> - Romans 2:13 NRSV

God is able to provide you with every blessing in abundance, so that by always having enough of everything, you may share abundantly in every good work.
> - 2 Corinthians 9:8 NRSV

He who looks into the perfect law of liberty and continues in it, and is not a forgetful hearer but a doer of the work, this one will be blessed in what he does.
> - James 1:25 NKJV

Beloved, do not imitate evil but imitate good. Whoever does what is good is of God; whoever does what is evil has never seen God.
> - 3 John 11 NAB

Let us not love with words or tongue but with actions and in truth.
> - 1 John 3:18 TNIV

"Behold, I am coming soon! My reward is with me, and I will give to everyone according to what he has done."
- Revelation 22:12 NIV

Prove yourselves doers of the word, and not merely hearers who delude themselves.
- James 1:22 NASB

"Whatever you want men to do to you, do also to them, for this is the Law and the Prophets."
- Matthew 7:12 NKJV

Be firm, steadfast, always fully devoted to the work of the Lord, knowing that in the Lord your labor is not in vain.
- 1 Corinthians 15:58 NAB

Do not neglect doing good and sharing, for with such sacrifices God is pleased.
- Hebrews 13:16 NASB

So whether you eat or drink, or whatever you do, do everything for the glory of God.
- 1 Corinthians 10:31 NAB

"Choose for yourselves this day whom you will serve.... As for me and my household, we will serve the LORD."
- Joshua 24:15 NIV

The Lord will reward each one of you for whatever good you do, whether you are slave or free.
- Ephesians 6:8 TNIV

Even a young man is known by his actions –
by whether his behavior is pure and upright.
                              - Proverbs 20:11 HCSB

Let us not grow tired of doing good, for in due time we
shall reap our harvest, if we do not give up. So then,
while we have the opportunity, let us do good to all,
but especially to those who belong to the family of the
faith.
                              - Galatians 6:9-10 NAB

"You are the light of the world. A city that is set on a
hill cannot be hidden. Nor do they light a lamp and
put it under a basket, but on a lampstand, and it
gives light to all who are in the house. Let your light
so shine before men, that they may see your good
works and glorify your Father in heaven."
                              - Matthew 5:14-16 NKJV

Remind them to be subject to rulers and authorities,
to be obedient, to be ready for every good work.
                              - Titus 3:1 NRSV

They are to do good, to be rich in good works, generous, and ready to share, thus storing up for themselves the treasure of a good foundation for the future,
so that they may take hold of the life that really is life.
                              - 1 Timothy 6:18-19 NRSV

I know that there is nothing better for people than to
be happy and to do good while they live.
                              - Ecclesiastes 3:12 TNIV

"Then the King will say to those on His right hand, 'Come, you blessed of My Father, inherit the kingdom prepared for you from the foundation of the world: for I was hungry and you gave Me food; I was thirsty and you gave Me drink; I was a stranger and you took Me in; I was naked and you clothed Me; I was sick and you visited Me; I was in prison and you came to Me.'

"Then the righteous will answer Him, saying, 'Lord, when did we see You hungry and feed You, or thirsty and give You drink? When did we see You a stranger and take You in, or naked and clothe You? Or when did we see You sick, or in prison, and come to You?' And the King will answer and say to them, 'Assuredly, I say to you, inasmuch as you did it to one of the least of these My brethren, you did it to Me.' "

- Matthew 25:34-40 NKJV

See also **Faith, Generosity, Helping Others, Ministry**

Overcoming
Problems

3

Doubt

But let him ask in faith, with no doubting, for he who doubts is like a wave of the sea driven and tossed by the wind.

- James 1:6 NKJV

Do not throw away your confidence, which has a great reward.

- Hebrews 10:35 NASB

" 'If you do not stand firm in your faith,
    you will not stand at all.' "

- Isaiah 7:9 TNIV

"Why are you troubled, and why do doubts arise in your hearts?"

- Luke 24:38 NASB

Whoever doubts stands condemned if he eats, because his eating is not from faith, and everything that is not from faith is sin.

- Romans 14:23 HCSB

"You of little faith, why did you doubt?"

- Matthew 14:31 NRSV

You must show mercy to those whose faith is wavering.

- Jude 22 NLT

"If anyone says to this mountain, 'Go, throw yourself into the sea,' and does not doubt in his heart but believes that what he says will happen, it will be done for him."

         - Mark 11:23 NIV

See also **Confidence, Faith, Fear, Worry**

Earthly Possessions

"Do not store up for yourselves treasures on earth, where moth and rust destroy, and where thieves break in and steal. But store up for yourselves treasures in heaven, where moth and rust do not destroy, and where thieves do not break in and steal. For where your treasure is, there your heart will be also."

         - Matthew 6:19-21 NIV

Put to death the sinful, earthly things lurking within you.

         - Colossians 3:5 NLT

"Others are those sown among the thorns: these are the ones who hear the word, but the cares of the world, and the lure of wealth, and the desire for other things come in and choke the word, and it yields nothing."

         - Mark 4:18-19 NRSV

Their end is destruction; their god is their stomach; their glory is in their shame. They are focused on earthly things.
- Philippians 3:19 HCSB

Do not love the world or the things in the world. The love of the Father is not in those who love the world; for all that is in the world – the desire of the flesh, the desire of the eyes, the pride in riches – comes not from the Father but from the world. And the world and its desire are passing away, but those who do the will of God live forever.
- 1 John 2:15-17 NRSV

Set your minds on things above, not on earthly things.
- Colossians 3:2 NIV

See also **Treasure, Wisdom of Men**

Fear

"Do not be afraid or discouraged, for the LORD your God is with you wherever you go."
- Joshua 1:9 HCSB

In God I trust; I will not be afraid.
    What can man do to me?
- Psalm 56:11 NIV

For God has not given us a spirit of fearfulness, but one of power, love, and sound judgment.

>   - 2 Timothy 1:7 HCSB

There is no fear in love; instead, perfect love drives out fear, because fear involves punishment. So the one who fears has not reached perfection in love.

>   - 1 John 4:18 HCSB

" 'Fear not, for I am with you;
  Be not dismayed, for I am your God.
  I will strengthen you,
  Yes, I will help you,
  I will uphold you with My righteous
       right hand.' "

>   - Isaiah 41:10 NKJV

"Hear me, you who know what is right,
   you people who have my law in your hearts:
Do not fear the reproach of men
   or be terrified by their insults."

>   - Isaiah 51:7 NIV

Whenever I am afraid,
I will trust in You.

>   - Psalm 56:3 NKJV

"Do not be afraid of anything that you are going to suffer. Indeed, the devil will throw some of you into prison, that you may be tested, and you will face an ordeal for ten days. Remain faithful until death, and I will give you the crown of life."

>   - Revelation 2:10 NAB

"Why are you so fearful? How is it that you have no faith?"

> \- Mark 4:40 NKJV

Even if you should suffer for what is right, you are blessed. "Do not fear their threats; do not be frightened."

> \- 1 Peter 3:14 TNIV

I sought the LORD, and he answered me;
    he delivered me from all my fears.

> \- Psalm 34:4 NIV

"You shall not be terrified of them; for the LORD your God, the great and awesome God, is among you."

> \- Deuteronomy 7:21 NKJV

With the LORD on my side I do not fear.
    What can mortals do to me?

> \- Psalm 118:6 NRSV

"Fear not, for I have redeemed you;
I have called you by your name;
You are Mine.
When you pass through the waters,
    I will be with you;
And through the rivers, they shall
    not overflow you.
When you walk through the fire, you
    shall not be burned,
Nor shall the flame scorch you."

> \- Isaiah 43:1-2 NKJV

"Do not be afraid of their faces,
For I am with you to deliver you,"
    says the LORD.
                    - Jeremiah 1:8 NKJV

"Do not fear! Stand by and see the salvation of the
LORD which He will accomplish for you today."
                    - Exodus 14:13 NASB

"Be strong and courageous. Do not be afraid or terrified because of them, for the LORD your God goes with
you; he will never leave you nor forsake you."
                    - Deuteronomy 31:6 TNIV

Yea, though I walk through the valley of the shadow of
death, I will fear no evil: for thou art with me; thy rod
and thy staff they comfort me.
                    - Psalm 23:4 KJV

"Do not be afraid any longer, only believe."
                    - Mark 5:36 NASB

The LORD is my light and my salvation –
    whom shall I fear?
The LORD is the stronghold of my life –
    of whom shall I be afraid?
                    - Psalm 27:1 TNIV

"Do not be afraid; I am the First and the Last. I am He
who lives, and was dead, and behold, I am alive forevermore."
                    - Revelation 1:17-18 NKJV

Say to those with fearful hearts,
   "Be strong, do not fear;
your God will come,
   he will come with vengeance;
with divine retribution
   he will come to save you."
- Isaiah 35:4 TNIV

When you lie down, you will not be
    afraid;
Yes, you will lie down and your sleep
    will be sweet.
- Proverbs 3:24 NKJV

"I, yes I, am the one who comforts you.
   So why are you afraid of mere humans,
   who wither like the grass and disappear?"
- Isaiah 51:12 NLT

"Peace I leave with you; my peace I give to you. Not as the world gives do I give it to you. Do not let your hearts be troubled or afraid."
- John 14:27 NAB

"Do not fear those who kill the body but are unable to kill the soul; but rather fear Him who is able to destroy both soul and body in hell."
- Matthew 10:28 NASB

See also **Courage, Doubt, Faith, Worry**

Letting Go of the Past

Brethren, I do not count myself to have apprehended; but one thing I do, forgetting those things which are behind and reaching forward to those things which are ahead, I press toward the goal for the prize of the upward call of God in Christ Jesus.

- Philippians 3:13-14 NKJV

"Behold, I will create
new heavens and a new earth.
The former things will not be remembered,
nor will they come to mind."

- Isaiah 65:17 NIV

Put off your old self, which is being corrupted by its deceitful desires; to be made new in the attitude of your minds; and to put on the new self, created to be like God in true righteousness and holiness.

- Ephesians 4:22-24 NIV

So if anyone is in Christ, there is a new creation: everything old has passed away; see, everything has become new!

- 2 Corinthians 5:17 NRSV

Just as Christ was raised from the dead by the glory of the Father, even so we also should walk in newness of life.

- Romans 6:4 NKJV

"I have been crucified with Christ; and it is no longer I who live, but Christ lives in me; and the life which I now live in the flesh I live by faith in the Son of God, who loved me and gave Himself up for me."

- Galatians 2:20 NASB

"Forget the former things;
    do not dwell on the past.
See, I am doing a new thing!"

- Isaiah 43:18-19 TNIV

Then He who sat on the throne said, "Behold, I make all things new."

- Revelation 21:5 NKJV

See also **Forgiveness, Reconciliation, Repentance**

Mourning

Praise be to the God and Father of our Lord Jesus Christ, the Father of compassion and the God of all comfort, who comforts us in all our troubles, so that we can comfort those in any trouble with the comfort we ourselves receive from God.

- 2 Corinthians 1:3-4 TNIV

You have turned my mourning into dancing;
    you have taken off my sackcloth
    and clothed me with joy.

- Psalm 30:11 NRSV

"God will wipe away every tear from their eyes; there shall be no more death, nor sorrow, nor crying. There shall be no more pain, for the former things have passed away."

- Revelation 21:4 NKJV

Those who sow with tears
    will reap with songs of joy.

- Psalm 126:5 TNIV

Rejoice with those who rejoice, weep with those who weep.

- Romans 12:15 NAB

For the sorrow that is according to the will of God produces a repentance without regret, leading to salvation, but the sorrow of the world produces death.

- 2 Corinthians 7:10 NASB

"He sets on high those who are lowly,
    and those who mourn are lifted to safety."

- Job 5:11 NRSV

The LORD is near to those who have a
        broken heart,
And saves such as have a contrite spirit.

- Psalm 34:18 NKJV

"Blessed are they who mourn,
    for they will be comforted."

- Matthew 5:4 NAB

"I will turn their mourning into gladness;
  I will give them comfort and joy instead of sorrow."
                              - Jeremiah 31:13 NIV

For we know that if the earthly tent which is our house is torn down, we have a building from God, a house not made with hands, eternal in the heavens.
                              - 2 Corinthians 5:1 NASB

Is anyone among you suffering? Let him pray. The prayer of faith will save the sick, and the Lord will raise him up.
                              - James 5:13,15 NKJV

"Do not grieve, for the joy of the LORD is your strength."
                              - Nehemiah 8:10 NIV

"Very truly, I tell you, you will weep and mourn, but the world will rejoice; you will have pain, but your pain will turn into joy."
                              - John 16:20 NRSV

" ' "I have heard your prayer, I have seen your tears; surely I will heal you." ' "
                              - 2 Kings 20:5 NKJV

He will destroy death forever.
The Lord GOD will wipe away the tears
from every face
and remove His people's disgrace
from the whole earth.
                              - Isaiah 25:8 HCSB

"This sickness is not to end in death, but for the glory of God, so that the Son of God may be glorified by it."
                              - John 11:4 NASB

Weeping may last for the night,
But a shout of joy comes in the morning.
                              - Psalm 30:5 NASB

I refresh the wearied soul and satisfy every sorrowing soul.
                              - Jeremiah 31:25 JB

"Your sun shall no longer go down,
Nor shall your moon withdraw itself;
For the LORD will be your everlasting light,
And the days of your mourning shall be ended."
                              - Isaiah 60:20 NKJV

He heals the brokenhearted
    and binds up their wounds.
                              - Psalm 147:3 NIV

"So you have pain now; but I will see you again, and your hearts will rejoice, and no one will take your joy from you."
                              - John 16:22 NRSV

See also **Happiness, Joy, Rejoice**

Persecution

We are hard-pressed on every side, yet not crushed; we are perplexed, but not in despair; persecuted, but not forsaken; struck down, but not destroyed.
- 2 Corinthians 4:8-9 NKJV

I want you to know, beloved, that what has happened to me has actually helped to spread the gospel.
- Philippians 1:12 NRSV

Bless those who persecute you; bless and do not curse.
- Romans 12:14 NIV

"Love your enemies, bless those who curse you, do good to those who hate you, and pray for those who spitefully use you and persecute you."
- Matthew 5:44 NKJV

Do not be ashamed of your testimony to our Lord, nor of me, a prisoner for his sake; but bear your share of hardship for the gospel with the strength that comes from God.
- 2 Timothy 1:8 NAB

Therefore I take pleasure in infirmities, in reproaches, in needs, in persecutions, in distresses, for Christ's sake. For when I am weak, then I am strong.
- 2 Corinthians 12:10 NKJV

What persecutions I endured, and out of them all the Lord rescued me! Indeed, all who desire to live godly in Christ Jesus will be persecuted.

- 2 Timothy 3:11-12 NASB

It is better, if it is God's will, to suffer for doing good than for doing evil.

- 1 Peter 3:17 NIV

"Do not be afraid of anything that you are going to suffer. Indeed, the devil will throw some of you into prison, that you may be tested, and you will face an ordeal for ten days. Remain faithful until death, and I will give you the crown of life."

- Revelation 2:10 NAB

"Blessed are you when they insult you and persecute you and falsely say every kind of evil against you because of Me. Be glad and rejoice, because your reward is great in heaven. For that is how they persecuted the prophets who were before you."

- Matthew 5:11-12 HCSB

Therefore, since Christ suffered in his body, arm yourselves also with the same attitude, because those who have suffered in their bodies are done with sin.

- 1 Peter 4:1 TNIV

When they had called for the apostles and beaten them, they commanded that they should not speak in the name of Jesus, and let them go. So they departed from the presence of the council, rejoicing that they were counted worthy to suffer shame for His name.

- Acts 5:40-41 NKJV

"If the world hates you, understand that it hated Me before it hated you."
- John 15:18 HCSB

"Blessed are those who are persecuted for righteousness' sake, for theirs is the kingdom of heaven."
- Matthew 5:10 NRSV

The heathen are surprised when you do not join them in the same wild and reckless living, and so they insult you. But they will have to give an account of themselves to God, who is ready to judge the living and the dead.
- 1 Peter 4:4-5 GNT

"We must go through many hardships to enter the kingdom of God."
- Acts 14:22 TNIV

O LORD my God, in You I put my
        trust;
Save me from all those who
        persecute me;
And deliver me.
- Psalm 7:1 NKJV

When we are reviled, we bless; when we are persecuted, we endure.
- 1 Corinthians 4:12 NASB

As a good soldier of Christ Jesus you must endure your share of suffering.
- 2 Timothy 2:3 CEV

Dear friends, do not be surprised at the painful trial you are suffering, as though something strange were happening to you. But rejoice that you participate in the sufferings of Christ, so that you may be overjoyed when his glory is revealed.

- 1 Peter 4:12-13 NIV

See also **Longsuffering, Perseverance**

Temptation

No temptation has overtaken you except what is common to us all. And God is faithful; he will not let you be tempted beyond what you can bear. But when you are tempted, he will also provide a way out so that you can endure it.

- 1 Corinthians 10:13 TNIV

Blessed are those who persevere under trial, because when they have stood the test, they will receive the crown of life that God has promised to those who love him.

- James 1:12 TNIV

Even Satan disguises himself as an angel of light.

- 2 Corinthians 11:14 NRSV

Since He Himself was tested and has suffered, He is able to help those who are tested.

- Hebrews 2:18 HCSB

Lead us not into temptation, but deliver us from evil.
- Matthew 6:13 KJV

These trials will show that your faith is genuine. It is being tested as fire tests and purifies gold – though your faith is far more precious than mere gold. So when your faith remains strong through many trials, it will bring you much praise and glory and honor on the day when Jesus Christ is revealed to the whole world.
- 1 Peter 1:7 NLT

Consider it all joy, my brethren, when you encounter various trials, knowing that the testing of your faith produces endurance.
- James 1:2-3 NASB

The Lord knows how to deliver the godly out of temptations and to reserve the unjust under punishment for the day of judgment.
- 2 Peter 2:9 NKJV

Let no one say when he is tempted, "I am tempted by God"; for God cannot be tempted by evil, nor does He Himself tempt anyone. But each one is tempted when he is drawn away by his own desires and enticed.
- James 1:13-14 NKJV

"Watch and pray so that you will not fall into temptation. The spirit is willing, but the body is weak."
- Mark 14:38 NIV

"Do not be afraid of anything that you are going to suffer. Indeed, the devil will throw some of you into prison, that you may be tested, and you will face an ordeal for ten days. Remain faithful until death, and I will give you the crown of life."

- Revelation 2:10 NAB

Submit yourselves therefore to God. Resist the devil, and he will flee from you.

- James 4:7 KJV

See also **Perseverance, Victory**

Troubles

Then they cried out to the LORD in
    their trouble;
He saved them out of their distresses.
He sent His word and healed them,
And delivered them from their
    destructions.

- Psalm 107:19-20 NASB

"I have told you this so that you might have peace in me. In the world you will have trouble, but take courage, I have conquered the world."

- John 16:33 NAB

The LORD is good,
    a refuge in times of trouble.
He cares for those who trust in him.

- Nahum 1:7 NIV

"Call upon Me in the day of trouble;
I will deliver you, and you shall
  glorify Me."
                          - Psalm 50:15 NKJV

The righteous cry out, and the LORD hears them;
  he delivers them from all their troubles.
                          - Psalm 34:17 TNIV

But I will sing of Your power;
Yes, I will sing aloud of Your mercy
  in the morning;
For You have been my defense
And refuge in the day of my trouble.
                          - Psalm 59:16 NKJV

The salvation of the just is from
      the LORD,
    their refuge in time of distress.
                          - Psalm 37:39 NAB

"Come to Me, all of you who are weary and burdened,
and I will give you rest."
                          - Matthew 11:28 HCSB

Turn to me and be gracious to me,
  for I am lonely and afflicted.
Relieve the troubles of my heart,
    and bring me out of my distress.
                          - Psalm 25:16-17 NRSV

The righteous is delivered from trouble,
And it comes to the wicked instead.
                          - Proverbs 11:8 NKJV

Our light and momentary troubles are achieving for us an eternal glory that far outweighs them all. So we fix our eyes not on what is seen, but on what is unseen. For what is seen is temporary, but what is unseen is eternal.

         - 2 Corinthians 4:17-18 NIV

Cast your burden upon the LORD and
      He will sustain you;
He will never allow the righteous to
      be shaken.

         - Psalm 55:22 NASB

Praise be to the God and Father of our Lord Jesus Christ, the Father of compassion and the God of all comfort, who comforts us in all our troubles, so that we can comfort those in any trouble with the comfort we ourselves receive from God.

         - 2 Corinthians 1:3-4 TNIV

In the day of my trouble I will call on You, for You will answer me.

         - Psalm 86:7 AMP

From now on let no person trouble me [by making it necessary for me to vindicate my apostolic authority and the divine truth of my Gospel], for I bear on my body the [brand] marks of the Lord Jesus [the wounds, scars, and other outward evidence of persecutions – these testify to His ownership of me]!

         - Galatians 6:17 AMP

God is our refuge and strength,
      an ever-present help in trouble.

         - Psalm 46:1 TNIV

How blessed is he who considers the
 helpless;
The LORD will deliver him in a day of
 trouble.
      - Psalm 41:1 NASB

Though I walk in the midst of trouble,
 You will revive me;
You will stretch forth Your hand against
 the wrath of my enemies,
And Your right hand will save me.
      - Psalm 138:7 NASB

"Do not let your hearts be troubled. Trust in God;
trust also in me. In my Father's house are many
rooms; if it were not so, I would have told you. I am
going there to prepare a place for you. And if I go and
prepare a place for you, I will come back and take you
to be with me that you also may be where I am. You
know the way to the place where I am going."
      - John 14:1-4 NIV

See also **Protection**

Unbelief

Jesus said to him, "If you can believe, all things are possible to him who believes." Immediately the father of the child cried out and said with tears, "Lord, I believe; help my unbelief!"

- Mark 9:23-24 NKJV

The fool says in his heart,
  "God does not exist."

- Psalm 14:1 HCSB

Take care, brethren, that there not be in any one of you an evil, unbelieving heart that falls away from the living God.

- Hebrews 3:12 NASB

They stumble because they disobey and disbelieve [God's] Word.

- 1 Peter 2:8 AMP

"Because you have so little faith. I tell you the truth, if you have faith as small as a mustard seed, you can say to this mountain, 'Move from here to there' and it will move. Nothing will be impossible for you."

- Matthew 17:20 NIV

He did not do many miracles there because of their unbelief.

- Matthew 13:58 NASB

"Decide today whom you will serve.... As for me and my household, we will serve the LORD."
                                    - Joshua 24:15 NAB

" 'If you do not stand firm in your faith,
    you will not stand at all.' "
                                    - Isaiah 7:9 TNIV

So we see they were not allowed to enter and have God's rest, because they did not believe.
                                    - Hebrews 3:19 NCV

See also **Believing, Faith, Foolishness**

Weakness

God hath chosen the foolish things of the world to confound the wise; and God hath chosen the weak things of the world to confound the things which are mighty.
                                    - 1 Corinthians 1:27 KJV

He gives power to the weak,
And to those who have no might He
        increases strength.
                                    - Isaiah 40:29 NKJV

If you faint in the day of adversity, your strength is small.
                                    - Proverbs 24:10 AMP

And He said to me, "My grace is sufficient for you, for My strength is made perfect in weakness." Therefore most gladly I will rather boast in my infirmities, that the power of Christ may rest upon me. Therefore I take pleasure in infirmities, in reproaches, in needs, in persecutions, in distresses, for Christ's sake. For when I am weak, then I am strong.
                    - 2 Corinthians 12:9-10 NKJV

The Spirit helps us in our weakness.
                    - Romans 8:26 TNIV

Proclaim this among the nations:
"Prepare for war!
Wake up the mighty men,
Let all the men of war draw near,
Let them come up.
Beat your plowshares into swords
And your pruning hooks into spears;
Let the weak say, 'I am strong.'"
                    - Joel 3:9-10 NKJV

See also **Strength**

Worry

"Do not worry about tomorrow, for tomorrow will worry about itself. Each day has enough trouble of its own."
                                    - Matthew 6:34 NIV

Do not fret because of evildoers,
Nor be envious of the workers of
        iniquity.
For they shall soon be cut down
        like the grass,
And wither as the green herb.
                                    - Psalm 37:1-2 NKJV

"Observe how the lilies of the field grow; they do not toil nor do they spin, yet I say to you that not even Solomon in all his glory clothed himself like one of these. But if God so clothes the grass of the field, which is alive today and tomorrow is thrown into the furnace, will He not much more clothe you?"
                                    - Matthew 6:28-30 NASB

Don't worry about anything, but pray about everything.
                                    - Philippians 4:6 CEV

"Do not worry about your life, what you will eat or drink; or about your body, what you will wear. Is not life more important than food, and the body more important than clothes?"
                                    - Matthew 6:25 NIV

When my anxious thoughts multiply
    within me,
Your consolations delight my soul.
                - Psalm 94:19 NASB

Cease from anger, and forsake
    wrath;
Do not fret – it only causes harm.
                - Psalm 37:8 NKJV

"When they hand you over, do not worry about how you are to speak or what you are to say. You will be given at that moment what you are to say. For it will not be you who speak but the Spirit of your Father speaking through you."
                - Matthew 10:19-20 NAB

"Which of you by worrying can add one cubit to his stature?"
                - Matthew 6:27 NKJV

Cast all your worries upon him because he cares for you.
                - 1 Peter 5:7 NAB

"Therefore do not worry, saying, 'What will we eat?' or 'What will we drink?' or 'What will we wear?' ...Indeed your heavenly Father knows that you need all these things. But strive first for the kingdom of God and his righteousness, and all these things will be given to you as well."
                - Matthew 6:31-33 NRSV

See also **Doubt, Fear, Peace of Mind**

Vices to Avoid

4

Anger

Everyone must be quick to hear, slow to speak and slow to anger; for the anger of man does not achieve the righteousness of God.

- James 1:19-20 NASB

"In your anger do not sin": Do not let the sun go down while you are still angry, and do not give the devil a foothold.

- Ephesians 4:26-27 NIV

A fool gives full vent to anger,
but the wise quietly holds it back.

- Proverbs 29:11 NRSV

You must also put away all the following: anger, wrath, malice, slander, and filthy language from your mouth.

- Colossians 3:8 HCSB

Give up your anger, abandon
your wrath;
do not be provoked; it brings
only harm.

- Psalm 37:8 NAB

Do not be quickly provoked in your spirit,
for anger resides in the lap of fools.

- Ecclesiastes 7:9 TNIV

I want men everywhere to lift up holy hands in prayer, without anger or disputing.

> \- 1 Timothy 2:8 NIV

Get rid of all bitterness, rage and anger, brawling and slander, along with every form of malice. Be kind and compassionate to one another, forgiving each other, just as in Christ God forgave you.

> \- Ephesians 4:31-32 TNIV

Be angry, and do not sin.
Meditate within your heart on
    your bed, and be still.

> \- Psalm 4:4 NKJV

See also **Compassion, Hatred, Kindness, Love, Quick-Tempered, Self-Control**

Boasting

May I never boast about anything except the cross of our Lord Jesus Christ. Because of that cross, my interest in this world has been crucified, and the world's interest in me has also died.

> \- Galatians 6:14 NLT

If I must boast, I will boast of the things that show my weakness.

> \- 2 Corinthians 11:30 TNIV

Come now, you who say, "Today or tomorrow we will go to such and such a city, spend a year there, buy and sell, and make a profit"; whereas you do not know what will happen tomorrow. For what is your life? It is even a vapor that appears for a little time and then vanishes away. Instead you ought to say, "If the Lord wills, we shall live and do this or that."
- James 4:13-15 NKJV

"Let not the wise man boast of his wisdom
   or the strong man boast of his strength
   or the rich man boast of his riches,
but let him who boasts boast about this:
   that he understands and knows me,
that I am the LORD, who exercises kindness,
   justice and righteousness on earth,
   for in these I delight," declares the LORD.
- Jeremiah 9:23-24 NIV

Let another praise you, and not your
   own mouth –
a stranger, and not your own lips.
- Proverbs 27:2 NRSV

"Talk no more so very proudly;
Let no arrogance come from your mouth,
For the LORD is the God of knowledge;
And by Him actions are weighed."
- 1 Samuel 2:3 NKJV

But as it is, you boast [falsely] in your presumption and your self-conceit. All such boasting is wrong.
- James 4:16 AMP

So the one who boasts must boast in the Lord. For it is not the one commending himself who is approved, but the one the Lord commends.

- 2 Corinthians 10:17-18 HCSB

Do not boast about tomorrow,
For you do not know what a day
     may bring forth.

- Proverbs 27:1 NASB

See also **Humility, Pride, Wisdom of Men**

Complaining

Do everything without complaining or arguing, so that you may become blameless and pure, children of God without fault in a crooked and depraved generation, in which you shine like stars in the universe.

- Philippians 2:14-15 NIV

Eat whatever is sold in the meat market, asking no questions for conscience' sake; for "the earth is the LORD's, and all its fullness."

- 1 Corinthians 10:25-26 NKJV

Be hospitable to one another without complaining.

- 1 Peter 4:9 NRSV

Why should any living man complain
    when punished for his sins?

- Lamentations 3:39 NIV

I have learned how to be content with whatever I have.
- Philippians 4:11 NLT

Do not complain, brethren, against one another, so that you yourselves may not be judged; behold, the Judge is standing right at the door.
- James 5:9 NASB

See also **Obedience**

Denying God

"Everyone who will acknowledge Me before men, I will also acknowledge him before My Father in heaven. But whoever denies Me before men, I will also deny him before My Father in heaven."
- Matthew 10:32-33 HCSB

The fool has said in his heart, "There is no God."
- Psalm 53:1 NASB

If we endure, we shall also reign with Him. If we deny and disown and reject Him, He will also deny and disown and reject us.
- 2 Timothy 2:12 AMP

"For whoever is ashamed of Me and My words, the Son of Man will be ashamed of him when He comes in His glory and that of the Father and the holy angels."
- Luke 9:26 HCSB

"You shall not make for yourself an idol, or any likeness of what is in heaven above or on the earth beneath or in the water under the earth. You shall not
worship them or serve them."

- Exodus 20:4-5 NASB

Who is the liar but the one who denies that Jesus is
the Christ? This is the antichrist, the one who denies
the Father and the Son. No one who denies the Son
has the Father; everyone who confesses the Son has
the Father also.

- 1 John 2:22-23 NRSV

God also has highly exalted Him and given Him the
name which is above every name, that at the name of
Jesus every knee should bow, of those in heaven, and
of those on earth, and of those under the earth, and
that every tongue should confess that Jesus Christ is
Lord, to the glory of God the Father.

- Philippians 2:9-11 NKJV

See also **Confessing Christ**

Disobedience

Let no one deceive you with empty words, for because of such things God's wrath comes on those who are disobedient. Therefore do not be partners with them.
                    - Ephesians 5:6-7 TNIV

By this we know that we have come to know Him, if we keep His commandments. The one who says, "I have come to know Him," and does not keep His commandments, is a liar, and the truth is not in him.
                    - 1 John 2:3-4 NASB

After you have become fully obedient, we will punish everyone who remains disobedient.
                    - 2 Corinthians 10:6 NLT

"If you are willing and obedient,
    you will eat the best from the land;
but if you resist and rebel,
    you will be devoured by the sword."
                    - Isaiah 1:19-20 TNIV

"He who does not love Me does not keep My words."
                    - John 14:24 NASB

It is time for judgment to begin with the family of God; and if it begins with us, what will the outcome be for those who do not obey the gospel of God?
                    - 1 Peter 4:17 NIV

They stumble because they disobey and disbelieve [God's] Word.

- 1 Peter 2:8 AMP

The wrath of God cometh on the children of disobedience.

- Colossians 3:6 KJV

See also **Obedience**

Drunkenness

For the drunkard and the glutton shall come to poverty: and drowsiness shall clothe a man with rags.

- Proverbs 23:21 KJV

So then let us not sleep as others do, but let us be alert and sober. For those who sleep do their sleeping at night, and those who get drunk get drunk at night. But since we are of the day, let us be sober, having put on the breastplate of faith and love, and as a helmet, the hope of salvation.

- 1 Thessalonians 5:6-8 NASB

Let us walk properly, as in the day, not in revelry and drunkenness, not in lewdness and lust, not in strife and envy. But put on the Lord Jesus Christ, and make no provision for the flesh, to fulfill its lusts.

- Romans 13:13-14 NKJV

Who has woe? Who has sorrow?
  Who has strife? Who has complaints?
  Who has needless bruises? Who has
    bloodshot eyes?
Those who linger over wine,
  who go to sample bowls of mixed wine.
In the end it bites like a snake
  and poisons like a viper.
                              - Proverbs 23:29-30,32 TNIV

The end of all things is near. Therefore be alert and of sober mind so that you may pray.
                              - 1 Peter 4:7 TNIV

Your eyes will see strange things,
And your heart will utter perverse things.
Yes, you will be like one who lies
    down in the midst of the sea,
Or like one who lies at the top of the
    mast, saying:
"They have struck me, but I was not hurt;
They have beaten me, but I did not feel it.
When shall I awake, that I may seek
    another drink?"
                              - Proverbs 23:33-35 NKJV

Wine is a mocker and beer a brawler;
  whoever is led astray by them is not wise.
                              - Proverbs 20:1 NIV

Do not get drunk with wine, which will only ruin you; instead, be filled with the Spirit.
                              - Ephesians 5:18 GNT

Be sober, be vigilant; because your adversary the devil walks about like a roaring lion, seeking whom he may devour. Resist him.
> - 1 Peter 5:8-9 NKJV

See also **Holiness, Righteousness, Sin**

Evil

Do not be overcome by evil, but overcome evil with good.
> - Romans 12:21 TNIV

For the love of money is the root of all evils, and some people in their desire for it have strayed from the faith and have pierced themselves with many pains.
> - 1 Timothy 6:10 NAB

"Drive out the wicked person from among you."
> - 1 Corinthians 5:13 NRSV

Do not be provoked by evildoers;
   do not envy those who do wrong.
Like grass they wither quickly;
   like green plants they wilt away.
> - Psalm 37:1-2 NAB

Beloved, do not imitate what is evil but imitate what is good. Whoever does good is from God; whoever does evil has not seen God.

- 3 John 11 NRSV

"Wash yourselves, make yourselves clean;
Remove the evil of your deeds from My sight.
Cease to do evil."

- Isaiah 1:16 NASB

Be not wise in your own eyes,
    fear the LORD and turn away from evil.

- Proverbs 3:7 NAB

Hate evil, love good;
    maintain justice in the courts.

- Amos 5:15 TNIV

Do not be deceived: "Evil company corrupts good habits."

- 1 Corinthians 15:33 NKJV

Do not repay anyone evil for evil; be concerned for what is noble in the sight of all.

- Romans 12:17 NAB

Once you were alienated from God and were enemies in your minds because of your evil behavior. But now he has reconciled you by Christ's physical body through death to present you holy in his sight, without blemish and free from accusation.

- Colossians 1:21-22 NIV

The evil will bow down before the good,
And the wicked at the gates of the righteous.
                    - Proverbs 14:19 NASB

"The LORD shall repay the evildoer according to his
wickedness."
                    - 2 Samuel 3:39 NKJV

"Let everyone who calls upon the name of the Lord
avoid evil."
                    - 2 Timothy 2:19 NAB

Take care, brothers, that none of you may have an evil
and unfaithful heart, so as to forsake the living God.
                    - Hebrews 3:12 NAB

Deliver us from evil.
                    - Matthew 6:13 KJV

"For the eyes of the Lord are on the
        righteous
    and his ears are attentive to their
        prayer,
but the face of the Lord is against
    those who do evil."
                    - 1 Peter 3:12 NIV

They will cry out to the LORD,
    but he will not answer them.
At that time he will hide his face from them
    because of the evil they have done.
                    - Micah 3:4 TNIV

Evil men understand nothing of justice,
   but those who seek the LORD understand all.
                  - Proverbs 28:5 NAB

Abstain from every form of evil.
              - 1 Thessalonians 5:22 NASB

As righteousness leads to life,
So he who pursues evil pursues it
     to his own death.
              - Proverbs 11:19 NKJV

Be wise about what is good, and innocent about what
is evil.
              - Romans 16:19 TNIV

"But your evil has kept away both rain
     and harvest.
  Your sins have kept you from enjoying
     good things."
              - Jeremiah 5:25 NCV

"Let them turn away from evil and do good;
  let them seek peace and pursue it."
              - 1 Peter 3:11 NRSV

Seek good, not evil,
  that you may live.
Then the LORD God Almighty will be
  with you.
              - Amos 5:14 NIV

The face of the LORD is against those
        who do evil,
To cut off the remembrance of them
        from the earth.
                        - Psalm 34:16 NKJV

See also **Repentance, Sin**

Foolishness

Do not be foolish, but understand what the will of the
Lord is.
                        - Ephesians 5:17 NASB

The mind of the intelligent man seeks knowledge,
    but the mouth of fools feeds on folly.
                        - Proverbs 15:14 NAB

Claiming to be wise, they became fools.
                        - Romans 1:22 HCSB

The fear of the LORD is the beginning
        of knowledge,
    but fools despise wisdom and instruction.
                        - Proverbs 1:7 TNIV

The message of the cross is foolishness to those who
are perishing, but to us who are being saved it is the
power of God.
                        - 1 Corinthians 1:18 NAB

Wine is reckless, strong drink quarrelsome;
   unwise is he whom it seduces.
                              - Proverbs 20:1 JB

Wisdom excels folly as light excels darkness.
                         - Ecclesiastes 2:13 NASB

The wise inherit honor,
   but fools get only shame.
                         - Proverbs 3:35 TNIV

Keep away from profane and foolish discussions,
which only drive people farther away from God. Such
teaching is like an open sore that eats away the flesh.
                    - 2 Timothy 2:16-17 GNT

The fool folds his hands
   and ruins himself.
                         - Ecclesiastes 4:5 NIV

"The quiet words of the wise are
         better heeded
than the shout of a ruler of fools."
                         - Ecclesiastes 9:17 NAB

He who is slow to wrath has great
         understanding,
But he who is impulsive exalts folly.
                    - Proverbs 14:29 NKJV

Many words mark the speech of a fool.
                         - Ecclesiastes 5:3 TNIV

The fool says in his heart,
"There is no God."
- Psalm 14:1 NIV

A fool despises his father's instruction,
but a person who heeds correction is sensible.
- Proverbs 15:5 HCSB

See also **Wisdom, Wisdom of Men**

Greed

Set your mind on the things above, not on the things
that are on earth.
- Colossians 3:2 NASB

Those who want to get rich fall into temptation and a
trap and into many foolish and harmful desires that
plunge people into ruin and destruction.
- 1 Timothy 6:9 TNIV

"Take heed and beware of covetousness, for one's life
does not consist in the abundance of the things he
possesses."
- Luke 12:15 NKJV

Keep your lives free from the love of money and be
content with what you have.
- Hebrews 13:5 TNIV

One person gives freely,
yet gains more;
another withholds what is right,
only to become poor.
- Proverbs 11:24 HCSB

Whoever shuts his ears to the cry
          of the poor
Will also cry himself and not be heard.
- Proverbs 21:13 NKJV

If anyone has this world's goods and sees his brother
in need but shuts off his compassion from him – how
can God's love reside in him?
- 1 John 3:17 HCSB

Do not withhold good from those to
          whom it is due,
     when it is in your power to act.
Do not say to your neighbor,
     "Come back tomorrow and I'll give it to you" –
     when you already have it with you.
- Proverbs 3:27-28 TNIV

Command those who are rich in this present world not
to be arrogant nor to put their hope in wealth, which
is so uncertain, but to put their hope in God, who
richly provides us with everything for our enjoyment.
Command them to do good, to be rich in good deeds,
and to be generous and willing to share. In this way
they will lay up treasure for themselves as a firm
foundation for the coming age, so that they may take
hold of the life that is truly life.
- 1 Timothy 6:17-19 NIV

Do nothing from selfish ambition or conceit, but in humility regard others as better than yourselves.
- Philippians 2:3 NRSV

He who oppresses the poor blasphemes
    his Maker,
  but he who is kind to the needy glorifies
    him.
- Proverbs 14:31 NAB

For the love of money is a root of all sorts of evil, and some by longing for it have wandered away from the faith and pierced themselves with many griefs.
- 1 Timothy 6:10 NASB

See also **Generosity, Giving, Selflessness**

Hatred

Whoever hates his brother is in the darkness and walks around in the darkness; he does not know where he is going, because the darkness has blinded him.
- 1 John 2:11 NIV

"You have heard that it was said, 'You shall love your neighbor and hate your enemy.' But I say to you, love your enemies, bless those who curse you, do good to those who hate you, and pray for those who spitefully use you and persecute you."
- Matthew 5:43-44 NKJV

Hatred stirs up strife,
  but love covers all offenses.
                    - Proverbs 10:12 NRSV

Get rid of all bitterness, rage and anger, brawling and slander, along with every form of malice. Be kind and compassionate to one another, forgiving each other, just as in Christ God forgave you.
                    - Ephesians 4:31-32 TNIV

If someone says, "I love God," and hates his brother, he is a liar; for he who does not love his brother whom he has seen, how can he love God whom he has not seen? And this commandment we have from Him: that he who loves God must love his brother also.
                    - 1 John 4:20-21 NKJV

Anyone who hates (abominates, detests) his brother [in Christ] is [at heart] a murderer, and you know that no murderer has eternal life abiding (persevering) within him.
                    - 1 John 3:15 AMP

See also **Anger, Compassion, Kindness, Love**

Jealousy

Let your conduct be without covetousness; be content with such things as you have.
>   - Hebrews 13:5 NKJV

We must not be proud or irritate one another or be jealous of one another.
>   - Galatians 5:26 GNT

A heart at peace gives life to the body,
    but envy rots the bones.
>   - Proverbs 14:30 TNIV

Let us walk properly, as in the day, not in revelry and drunkenness, not in lewdness and lust, not in strife and envy. But put on the Lord Jesus Christ, and make no provision for the flesh, to fulfill its lusts.
>   - Romans 13:13-14 NKJV

Incline my heart to Your testimonies,
And not to covetousness.
>   - Psalm 119:36 NKJV

Where there is envy and selfish ambition, there will also be disorder and wickedness of every kind.
>   - James 3:16 NRSV

He that hateth covetousness shall prolong his days.
>   - Proverbs 28:16 KJV

"Take heed and beware of covetousness, for one's life does not consist in the abundance of the things he possesses."

- Luke 12:15 NKJV

You shall not covet your neighbor's house; you shall not covet your neighbor's wife, or male or female slave, or ox, or donkey, or anything that belongs to your neighbor.

- Exodus 20:17 NRSV

See also **Happiness, Love**

Judging Others

Judge nothing before the appointed time; wait till the Lord comes. He will bring to light what is hidden in darkness and will expose the motives of people's hearts. At that time each will receive their praise from God.

- 1 Corinthians 4:5 TNIV

Who are you to judge the servant of another? To his own master he stands or falls; and he will stand, for the Lord is able to make him stand.

- Romans 14:4 NASB

"May the LORD judge between you and me. And may the LORD avenge the wrongs you have done to me, but my hand will not touch you."

- 1 Samuel 24:12 TNIV

"Judge not, that you be not judged. For with what judgment you judge, you will be judged; and with the measure you use, it will be measured back to you."
                    - Matthew 7:1-2 NKJV

He who speaks evil of a brother and judges his brother, speaks evil of the law and judges the law. But if you judge the law, you are not a doer of the law but a judge.
                    - James 4:11 NKJV

You, therefore, have no excuse, you who pass judgment on someone else, for at whatever point you judge another, you are condemning yourself, because you who pass judgment do the same things.
                    - Romans 2:1 TNIV

Let us not judge one another anymore, but rather determine this – not to put an obstacle or a stumbling block in a brother's way.
                    - Romans 14:13 NASB

I care very little if I am judged by you or by any human court; indeed, I do not even judge myself. My conscience is clear, but that does not make me innocent. It is the Lord who judges me.
                    - 1 Corinthians 4:3-4 NIV

Do not lay hands on anyone hastily, nor share in other people's sins; keep yourself pure.
                    - 1 Timothy 5:22 NKJV

Why do you judge your brother? Or why do you look down on your brother? For we will all stand before God's judgment seat.

- Romans 14:10 NIV

There is only one Lawgiver and Judge, the one who is able to save and destroy. But you – who are you to judge your neighbor?

- James 4:12 TNIV

"The LORD does not see as man sees; for man looks at the outward appearance, but the LORD looks at the heart."

- 1 Samuel 16:7 NKJV

"Stop judging according to outward appearances; rather judge according to righteous judgment."

- John 7:24 HCSB

"Why do you look at the speck in your brother's eye, but do not consider the plank in your own eye? Or how can you say to your brother, 'Let me remove the speck from your eye'; and look, a plank is in your own eye? Hypocrite! First remove the plank from your own eye, and then you will see clearly to remove the speck from your brother's eye."

- Matthew 7:3-5 NKJV

See also **Judgment, Justice**

Laziness

If anyone will not work, neither shall he eat.
              - 2 Thessalonians 3:10 NKJV

The lazy man will not plow because
        of winter;
He will beg during harvest and have
        nothing.
                    - Proverbs 20:4 NKJV

The appetite of the lazy craves, and
        gets nothing,
   while the appetite of the diligent is
        richly supplied.
                    - Proverbs 13:4 NRSV

To one who knows the right thing to do and does not
do it, to him it is sin.
                    - James 4:17 NASB

The hand of the diligent will rule,
   while the lazy will be put to forced labor.
                    - Proverbs 12:24 NRSV

As vinegar to the teeth and smoke
        to the eyes,
So is the lazy man to those who
        send him.
                    - Proverbs 10:26 NKJV

Drowsiness shall clothe a man with rags.
                    - Proverbs 23:21 KJV

In all labor there is profit, but idle talk leads only to poverty.
                    - Proverbs 14:23 AMP

He who is slothful in his work
Is a brother to him who is a great
          destroyer.
                    - Proverbs 18:9 NKJV

The fool folds his hands
     and ruins himself.
                    - Ecclesiastes 4:5 NIV

Do not love sleep, or you will become poor;
Open your eyes, and you will be satisfied
          with food.
                    - Proverbs 20:13 NASB

See also **Obedience, Works**

Lying

Each of you must put off falsehood and speak truthfully to your neighbor, for we are all members of one body.
- Ephesians 4:25 TNIV

A false witness shall not be unpunished, and he who breathes out lies shall not escape.
- Proverbs 19:5 AMP

"You shall not bear false witness against your neighbor."
- Exodus 20:16 NASB

A false balance is an abomination
   to the LORD,
But a just weight is His delight.
- Proverbs 11:1 NASB

Do not lie to each other, since you have taken off your old self with its practices and have put on the new self, which is being renewed in knowledge in the image of its Creator.
- Colossians 3:9-10 NIV

Making a fortune through a lying tongue
is a vanishing mist, a pursuit of death.
- Proverbs 21:6 HCSB

The integrity of the upright guides them,
   but the unfaithful are destroyed by their duplicity.
- Proverbs 11:3 TNIV

"Do not cheat anyone by using false measures of length, weight, or quantity. Use honest scales, honest weights, and honest measures."
                              - Leviticus 19:35-36 GNT

Lying lips are an abomination to the
      LORD,
But those who deal truthfully are
      His delight.
                              - Proverbs 12:22 NKJV

So long as I still have life in me
      and the breath of God is in my nostrils,
My lips shall not speak falsehood,
      nor my tongue utter deceit!
                              - Job 27:3-4 NAB

If anyone says, "I love God," but hates his brother, he is a liar; for whoever does not love a brother whom he has seen cannot love God whom he has not seen.
                              - 1 John 4:20 NAB

Whoever of you loves life
      and desires to see many good days,
keep your tongue from evil
      and your lips from telling lies.
                              - Psalm 34:12-13 TNIV

Bread gained by deceit is sweet,
      but afterward the mouth will be
            full of gravel.
                              - Proverbs 20:17 NRSV

See also **Truth**

Pride

"The pride of your heart has deceived you,
  you who live in the clefts of the rocks
  and make your home on the heights,
you who say to yourself,
  'Who can bring me down to the ground?'
Though you soar like the eagle
  and make your nest among the stars,
  from there I will bring you down,"
    declares the LORD.
>   - Obadiah 3-4 NIV

Rise up, O Judge of the earth;
Render punishment to the proud.
>   - Psalm 94:2 NKJV

An arrogant man stirs up strife,
But he who trusts in the LORD will prosper.
>   - Proverbs 28:25 NASB

Every proud man is an abomination
    to the LORD;
  I assure you that he will not go
    unpunished.
>   - Proverbs 16:5 NAB

"God opposes the proud
  but favors the humble."
>   - James 4:6 NLT

The patient in spirit is better than the proud in spirit.
>   - Ecclesiastes 7:8 KJV

For [it is] not [the man] who praises and commends himself who is approved and accepted, but [it is the person] whom the Lord accredits and commends.
                              - 2 Corinthians 10:18 AMP

Do not be wise in your own eyes;
Fear the LORD and turn away from evil.
                              - Proverbs 3:7 NASB

Woe unto them that are wise in their own eyes, and prudent in their own sight!
                              - Isaiah 5:21 KJV

Do nothing from selfish ambition or conceit, but in humility regard others as better than yourselves.
                              - Philippians 2:3 NRSV

Man's pride causes his humiliation,
    but he who is humble of spirit obtains honor.
                              - Proverbs 29:23 NAB

Do not think of yourself more highly than you ought, but rather think of yourself with sober judgment, in accordance with the measure of faith God has given you.
                              - Romans 12:3 NIV

You rescue the humble,
    but you humiliate the proud.
                              - Psalm 18:27 NLT

We must not become conceited, provoking one another, envying one another.

- Galatians 5:26 HCSB

"Behold the proud,
His soul is not upright in him."

- Habakkuk 2:4 NKJV

The LORD tears down the house of the proud,
    but maintains the widow's boundaries.

- Proverbs 15:25 NRSV

"For everyone who exalts himself will be humbled, but
the one who humbles himself will be exalted."

- Luke 14:11 NAB

Do not be wise in your own estimation.

- Romans 12:16 NASB

Trust in the LORD with all your heart
    and lean not on your own understanding.

- Proverbs 3:5 NIV

"Behold, I am against you,
O most haughty one!" says the
        Lord GOD of hosts;
"For your day has come,
The time that I will punish you.
The most proud shall stumble
        and fall,
And no one will raise him up."

- Jeremiah 50:31-32 NKJV

Professing themselves to be wise, they became fools.
- Romans 1:22 KJV

When pride comes, disgrace follows,
but with humility comes wisdom.
- Proverbs 11:2 HCSB

Let anyone who thinks he stands [who feels sure that he has a steadfast mind and is standing firm], take heed lest he fall [into sin].
- 1 Corinthians 10:12 AMP

Pride goeth before destruction.
- Proverbs 16:18 KJV

See also **Boasting, Humility**

Quick-Tempered

One who is quick-tempered acts foolishly.
- Proverbs 14:17 NRSV

It is honorable for a man to stop
    striving,
Since any fool can start a quarrel.
- Proverbs 20:3 NKJV

A fool gives full vent to his anger,
    but a wise man keeps himself under control.
- Proverbs 29:11 NIV

The beginning of strife is as when water first trickles
[from a crack in a dam]; therefore stop contention before it becomes worse and quarreling breaks out.
                              - Proverbs 17:14 AMP

Don't let your spirit rush to be angry,
for anger abides in the heart of fools.
                              - Ecclesiastes 7:9 HCSB

Like a city that is broken into and without walls
Is a man who has no control over his spirit.
                              - Proverbs 25:28 NASB

Everyone should be quick to listen, slow to speak and
slow to become angry.
                              - James 1:19 NIV

He who is slow to anger has great understanding,
But he who is quick-tempered exalts folly.
                              - Proverbs 14:29 NASB

See also **Anger, Compassion, Kindness,
    Self-Control**

Revenge

Never take your own revenge, beloved, but leave room for the wrath of God, for it is written, "Vengeance is Mine, I will repay," says the Lord.
- Romans 12:19 NASB

Don't say, "I'll pay you back for the wrong
    you did."
Wait for the LORD, and he will make
    things right.
- Proverbs 20:22 NCV

Do not be conquered by evil, but conquer evil with good.
- Romans 12:21 HCSB

When He was reviled and insulted, He did not revile or offer insult in return; [when] He was abused and suffered, He made no threats [of vengeance]; but He trusted [Himself and everything] to Him Who judges fairly.
- 1 Peter 2:23 AMP

When ridiculed, we bless; when persecuted, we endure; when slandered, we respond gently.
- 1 Corinthians 4:12-13 NAB

Do not repay evil for evil or abuse for abuse; but, on the contrary, repay with a blessing. It is for this that you were called – that you might inherit a blessing.
- 1 Peter 3:9 NRSV

Make sure that nobody pays back wrong for wrong, but always strive to do what is good for each other and for everyone else.

> \- 1 Thessalonians 5:15 TNIV

Do not repay anyone evil for evil, but take thought for what is noble in the sight of all.

> \- Romans 12:17 NRSV

"May the LORD judge between you and me. And may the LORD avenge the wrongs you have done to me, but my hand will not touch you."

> \- 1 Samuel 24:12 TNIV

Do not say, "I'll do to him as he has
> done to me;
> I'll pay that man back for what he did."

> \- Proverbs 24:29 NIV

" 'Do not seek revenge or bear a grudge against anyone among your people, but love your neighbor as yourself.' "

> \- Leviticus 19:18 TNIV

See also **Forgiving, Judging Others, Self-Control**

Sin

For the wages of sin is death; but the gift of God is eternal life through Jesus Christ our Lord.
                              - Romans 6:23 KJV

Even Satan masquerades as an angel of light.
                              - 2 Corinthians 11:14 NAB

Let us walk properly, as in the day, not in revelry and drunkenness, not in lewdness and lust, not in strife and envy. But put on the Lord Jesus Christ, and make no provision for the flesh, to fulfill its lusts.
                              - Romans 13:13-14 NKJV

Each person is tempted when he is drawn away and enticed by his own evil desires. Then after desire has conceived, it gives birth to sin, and when sin is fully grown, it gives birth to death.
                              - James 1:14-15 HCSB

Whoever doubts stands condemned if he eats, because his eating is not from faith, and everything that is not from faith is sin.
                              - Romans 14:23 HCSB

Live by the Spirit and you will certainly not gratify the desire of the flesh.
                              - Galatians 5:16 NAB

"Let everyone who names the name of Christ depart from iniquity."

— 2 Timothy 2:19 NKJV

Put to death the sinful, earthly things lurking within you.

— Colossians 3:5 NLT

Your iniquities have separated
　you from your God;
your sins have hidden his face from you,
　so that he will not hear.

— Isaiah 59:2 TNIV

Let us lay aside every weight, and the sin which so easily ensnares us, and let us run with endurance the race that is set before us, looking unto Jesus, the author and finisher of our faith.

— Hebrews 12:1-2 NKJV

For the law of the spirit of life in Christ Jesus has freed you from the law of sin and death.

— Romans 8:2 NAB

Those who belong to Christ Jesus have crucified the sinful nature with its passions and desires. Since we live by the Spirit, let us keep in step with the Spirit.

— Galatians 5:24-25 NIV

Those who live according to the sinful nature have their minds set on what that nature desires; but those who live in accordance with the Spirit have their minds set on what the Spirit desires.

— Romans 8:5 TNIV

Awake to righteousness, and do not sin; for some do not have the knowledge of God.

- 1 Corinthians 15:34 NKJV

Consider yourselves to be dead to sin but alive for God in Christ Jesus.

- Romans 6:11 JB

"But your evil has kept away both rain
    and harvest.
  Your sins have kept you from enjoying
    good things."

- Jeremiah 5:25 NCV

He Himself bore our sins in His body on the cross, so that we might die to sin and live to righteousness; for by His wounds you were healed.

- 1 Peter 2:24 NASB

Now the works of the flesh are evident, which are: adultery, fornication, uncleanness, lewdness, idolatry, sorcery, hatred, contentions, jealousies, outbursts of wrath, selfish ambitions, dissensions, heresies, envy, murders, drunkenness, revelries, and the like; of which I tell you beforehand, just as I also told you in time past, that those who practice such things will not inherit the kingdom of God.

- Galatians 5:19-21 NKJV

God did not call us to live in immorality, but in holiness.

- 1 Thessalonians 4:7 GNT

Beloved, I urge you as aliens and strangers to abstain from fleshly lusts which wage war against the soul.
- 1 Peter 2:11 NASB

For our transgressions have multiplied
before You,
and our sins testify against us.
- Isaiah 59:12 HCSB

"Break off your sins by being righteous, and your iniquities by showing mercy to the poor."
- Daniel 4:27 NKJV

"I did not come to call the righteous, but sinners, to repentance."
- Mark 2:17 NKJV

This is a faithful saying, and worthy of all acceptation, that Christ Jesus came into the world to save sinners; of whom I am chief.
- 1 Timothy 1:15 KJV

"Everyone who sins is a slave to sin. Now a slave has no permanent place in the family, but a son belongs to it forever. So if the Son sets you free, you will be free indeed."
- John 8:34-36 TNIV

See also **Obedience, Repentance**

Speaking Foolishly

"I tell you, on the day of judgment you will have to give an account for every careless word you utter; for by your words you will be justified, and by your words you will be condemned."
                              - Matthew 12:36-37 NRSV

Everyone should be quick to listen, slow to speak and slow to become angry.
                              - James 1:19 TNIV

But these people, like irrational animals – creatures of instinct born to be caught and destroyed – speak blasphemies about things they don't understand, and in their destruction they too will be destroyed.
                              - 2 Peter 2:12 HCSB

Look at the ships also, though they are so great and are driven by strong winds, are still directed by a very small rudder wherever the inclination of the pilot desires. So also the tongue is a small part of the body, and yet it boasts of great things.
                              - James 3:4-5 NASB

Whoever of you loves life
    and desires to see many good days,
keep your tongue from evil
    and your lips from telling lies.
                              - Psalm 34:12-13 TNIV

Keep your tongue from evil and your lips from speaking deceit.
                              - Psalm 34:13 AMP

Set a guard over my mouth, O LORD;
　　keep watch over the door of my lips.
　　　　　　　　　　　　　- Psalm 141:3 NIV

Do you see a man who is hasty in his words?
There is more hope for a fool than for him.
　　　　　　　　　　　　　- Proverbs 29:20 NASB

How great a forest is set ablaze by a small fire! And
the tongue is a fire.
　　　　　　　　　　　　　- James 3:5-6 NRSV

Do not be hasty to speak, and do not be impulsive to
make a speech before God. God is in heaven and you
are on earth, so let your words be few.
　　　　　　　　　　　　　- Ecclesiastes 5:2 HCSB

When there are many words, transgression
　　　　is unavoidable,
But he who restrains his lips is wise.
　　　　　　　　　　　　　- Proverbs 10:19 NASB

Keep away from profane and foolish discussions,
which only drive people farther away from God. Such
teaching is like an open sore that eats away the flesh.
　　　　　　　　　　　　　- 2 Timothy 2:16-17 GNT

"Talk no more so very proudly;
Let no arrogance come from your mouth,
For the LORD is the God of knowledge;
And by Him actions are weighed."
　　　　　　　　　　　　　- 1 Samuel 2:3 NKJV

Those who guard their mouths preserve
      their lives;
   those who open wide their lips come
      to ruin.
                          - Proverbs 13:3 NRSV

Brothers, do not slander one another. Anyone who
speaks against his brother or judges him speaks
against the law and judges it. When you judge the law,
you are not keeping it, but sitting in judgment on it.
                          - James 4:11 NIV

Many words mark the speech of a fool.
                          - Ecclesiastes 5:3 TNIV

"It is not what goes into the mouth that defiles a person, but it is what comes out of the mouth that defiles."
                          - Matthew 15:11 NRSV

See also **Boasting, Swearing, Wisdom, Wisdom of
      Men**

Swearing

Bless those who persecute you; bless and do not curse.

- Romans 12:14 NASB

Above all, my brothers and sisters, do not swear – not by heaven or by earth or by anything else. All you need to say is a simple "Yes" or "No." Otherwise you will be condemned.

- James 5:12 TNIV

When He was reviled and insulted, He did not revile or offer insult in return.

- 1 Peter 2:23 AMP

As he loved cursing, so let it come
    to him;
As he did not delight in blessing,
    so let it be far from him.
As he clothed himself with cursing
    as with his garment,
So let it enter his body like water,
And like oil into his bones.

- Psalm 109:17-18 NKJV

You must also put away all the following: anger, wrath, malice, slander, and filthy language from your mouth.

- Colossians 3:8 HCSB

Do not revile the king even in your thoughts,
   or curse the rich in your bedroom,
because a bird of the air may carry your words,
   and a bird on the wing may report what you
     say.
                 - Ecclesiastes 10:20 NIV

"You shall not take the name of the LORD your God in vain, for the LORD will not leave him unpunished who takes His name in vain."
                 - Exodus 20:7 NASB

Keep your tongue from evil and your lips from speaking deceit.
                 - Psalm 34:13 AMP

Let no foul or polluting language, nor evil word nor unwholesome or worthless talk [ever] come out of your mouth, but only such [speech] as is good and beneficial to the spiritual progress of others, as is fitting to the need and the occasion, that it may be a blessing and give grace (God's favor) to those who hear it.
                 - Ephesians 4:29 AMP

Get rid of all bitterness, rage and anger, brawling and slander, along with every form of malice. Be kind and compassionate to one another, forgiving each other, just as in Christ God forgave you.
                 - Ephesians 4:31-32 TNIV

May the words of my mouth and the
       meditation of my heart
   be pleasing in your sight,
   O LORD, my Rock and my Redeemer.
                 - Psalm 19:14 NIV

Set a guard over my mouth, O LORD;
    keep watch over the door of my lips.
                              - Psalm 141:3 NIV

"You have heard that it was said to those of old, 'You shall not swear falsely, but shall perform your oaths to the Lord.' But I say to you, do not swear at all: neither by heaven, for it is God's throne; nor by the earth, for it is His footstool; nor by Jerusalem, for it is the city of the great King. Nor shall you swear by your head, because you cannot make one hair white or black. But let your 'Yes' be 'Yes,' and your 'No,' 'No.' For whatever is more than these is from the evil one."
                              - Matthew 5:33-37 NKJV

See also **Self-Control, Speaking Foolishly**

Unrighteousness

God sends upon them a misleading influence, a working of error and a strong delusion to make them believe what is false, in order that all may be judged and condemned who did not believe in [who refused to adhere to, trust in, and rely on] the Truth, but [instead] took pleasure in unrighteousness.
                              - 2 Thessalonians 2:11-12 AMP

Do you not know that the unrighteous will not inherit the kingdom of God?
                              - 1 Corinthians 6:9 NASB

All unrighteousness is sin.

- 1 John 5:17 NASB

"Whoever is faithful in very little is also faithful in much, and whoever is unrighteous in very little is also unrighteous in much."

- Luke 16:10 HCSB

The Lord knows how to deliver the godly out of temptations and to reserve the unjust under punishment for the day of judgment.

- 2 Peter 2:9 NKJV

"Woe to him who builds his palace by
        unrighteousness,
    his upper rooms by injustice,
making his countrymen work for nothing,
    not paying them for their labor."

- Jeremiah 22:13 NIV

The wrath of God is revealed from heaven against all ungodliness and unrighteousness of men, who suppress the truth in unrighteousness.

- Romans 1:18 NKJV

God did not call us to impurity but to holiness.

- 1 Thessalonians 4:7 NAB

"See, the Lord is coming with thousands upon thousands of his holy ones to judge everyone, and to convict all the ungodly of all the ungodly acts they have done in an ungodly way, and of all the defiant words ungodly sinners have spoken against him."

- Jude 14-15 TNIV

Do you not know that you are the temple of God and that the Spirit of God dwells in you? If anyone defiles the temple of God, God will destroy him. For the temple of God is holy, which temple you are.

- 1 Corinthians 3:16-17 NKJV

Let the wicked forsake their way,
    and the unrighteous their thoughts;
let them return to the LORD, that he
        may have mercy on them,
    and to our God, for he will abundantly
        pardon.

- Isaiah 55:7 NRSV

See also **Righteousness, Wickedness**

Wickedness

Get rid of every filthy habit and all wicked conduct. Submit to God and accept the word that he plants in your hearts, which is able to save you.

- James 1:21 GNT

" 'As I live,' says the Lord GOD, 'I have no pleasure in the death of the wicked, but that the wicked turn from his way and live. Turn, turn from your evil ways!' "

- Ezekiel 33:11 NKJV

Salvation is far from the wicked
because they do not seek Your statutes.

- Psalm 119:155 HCSB

Do not be yoked together with unbelievers. For what do righteousness and wickedness have in common? Or what fellowship can light have with darkness?
- 2 Corinthians 6:14 NIV

"The LORD shall repay the evildoer according to his wickedness."
- 2 Samuel 3:39 NKJV

Many are the woes of the wicked,
　　but the LORD's unfailing love
　　surrounds those who trust in him.
- Psalm 32:10 TNIV

When the whirlwind passes, the wicked
　　　is no more,
But the righteous has an everlasting
　　　foundation.
- Proverbs 10:25 NASB

"There is no peace," says the LORD, "for the
　　　wicked."
- Isaiah 48:22 NRSV

The wicked man borrows without meaning to repay,
but a virtuous man is generous and open-handed.
- Psalm 37:21 JB

The evil will bow down before the good,
And the wicked at the gates of the righteous.
- Proverbs 14:19 NASB

Where there is envy and selfish ambition, there will
also be disorder and wickedness of every kind.
- James 3:16 NRSV

The righteousness of the blameless makes
    a straight way for them,
  but the wicked are brought down by
    their own wickedness.
- Proverbs 11:5 NIV

"The light of the wicked indeed goes out,
And the flame of his fire does not shine."
- Job 18:5 NKJV

Better is the little of the righteous
Than the abundance of many wicked.
- Psalm 37:16 NASB

Turn from youthful desires and pursue righteousness,
faith, love, and peace, along with those who call on the
Lord with purity of heart.
- 2 Timothy 2:22 NAB

The LORD sustains the humble
  but casts the wicked to the ground.
- Psalm 147:6 TNIV

The way of the wicked is like deep darkness;
  they do not know what they stumble over.
- Proverbs 4:19 NRSV

Let the wicked forsake his way,
And the unrighteous man his
        thoughts;
Let him return to the LORD,
And He will have mercy on him;
And to our God,
For He will abundantly pardon.
                    - Isaiah 55:7 NKJV

The LORD is far from the wicked,
But He hears the prayer of the righteous.
                    - Proverbs 15:29 NASB

The wicked flee when no one is
        pursuing them,
but the righteous are as bold as a lion.
                    - Proverbs 28:1 HCSB

Woe to the wicked! Disaster is upon them!
They will be paid back for what their hands
        have done.
                    - Isaiah 3:11 NIV

"Everyone who confesses the name of the Lord must
turn away from wickedness."
                    - 2 Timothy 2:19 TNIV

The LORD watches over all who love him,
        but all the wicked he will destroy.
                    - Psalm 145:20 NRSV

God did not call us to impurity but to holiness.
                    - 1 Thessalonians 4:7 NAB

The righteous is delivered from trouble,
And it comes to the wicked instead.
                              - Proverbs 11:8 NKJV

"Drive out the wicked person from among you."
                              - 1 Corinthians 5:13 NRSV

Better is one day in your courts
    than a thousand elsewhere;
I would rather be a doorkeeper in the
        house of my God
    than dwell in the tents of the wicked.
                              - Psalm 84:10 NIV

If the wicked man turns away from all the sins he
committed, if he keeps all my statutes and does what
is right and just, he shall surely live, he shall not die.
                              - Ezekiel 18:21 NAB

The fear of the LORD prolongs life,
but the years of the wicked are cut short.
                              - Proverbs 10:27 HCSB

See also **Righteousness, Unrighteousness**

Wisdom of Men

The foolishness of God is wiser than human wisdom, and the weakness of God is stronger than human strength.
                    - 1 Corinthians 1:25 NAB

Your faith should not be in the wisdom of men but in the power of God.
                    - 1 Corinthians 2:5 NKJV

Cease from your own [human] wisdom.
                    - Proverbs 23:4 AMP

We do not use words that come from human wisdom. Instead, we speak words given to us by the Spirit, using the Spirit's words to explain spiritual truths.
                    - 1 Corinthians 2:13 NLT

Christ did not send me to baptize, but to preach the gospel – not with words of human wisdom, lest the cross of Christ be emptied of its power.
                    - 1 Corinthians 1:17 NIV

We have conducted ourselves in the world...with integrity and godly sincerity. We have done so, relying not on worldly wisdom but on God's grace.
                    - 2 Corinthians 1:12 TNIV

God hath chosen the foolish things of the world to confound the wise; and God hath chosen the weak things of the world to confound the things which are mighty.

- 1 Corinthians 1:27 KJV

If any man among you thinks that he is wise in this age, he must become foolish, so that he may become wise. For the wisdom of this world is foolishness before God. For it is written, "He is the one who catches the wise in their craftiness"; and again, "The LORD knows the reasonings of the wise, that they are useless." So then let no one boast in men.

- 1 Corinthians 3:18-21 NASB

See also **Foolishness, Wisdom**

Concepts of the Faith

5

All Things Are Possible

"If you can believe, all things are possible to him who believes."
                                        - Mark 9:23 NKJV

"I know that You can do all things,
And that no purpose of Yours can
          be thwarted."
                                        - Job 42:2 NASB

"Nothing will be impossible with God."
                                        - Luke 1:37 NRSV

" 'Ah, Lord GOD! Behold, You have made the heavens and the earth by Your great power and outstretched arm. There is nothing too hard for You.' "
                                        - Jeremiah 32:17 NKJV

"The things that are impossible with people are possible with God."
                                        - Luke 18:27 NASB

I can do all things through Christ who strengthens me.
                                        - Philippians 4:13 NKJV

With God's power working in us, God can do much, much more than anything we can ask or imagine.
                                        - Ephesians 3:20 NCV

"With men it is impossible, but not with God; for with God all things are possible."
                    - Mark 10:27 NKJV

"Behold, I am the LORD, the God of all flesh; is anything too difficult for Me?"
                    - Jeremiah 32:27 NASB

"If you have faith as small as a mustard seed, you can say to this mountain, 'Move from here to there' and it will move. Nothing will be impossible for you."
                    - Matthew 17:20 NIV

"Is anything too hard for the LORD?"
                    - Genesis 18:14 TNIV

See also **Believing, Faith, Hope**

Church

There are diversities of gifts, but the same Spirit. There are differences of ministries, but the same Lord. And there are diversities of activities, but it is the same God who works all in all.
                    - 1 Corinthians 12:4-6 NKJV

For My house will be called a house of prayer for all peoples.
                    - Isaiah 56:7 AMP

The church of the living God...is the pillar and foundation of the truth.

- 1 Timothy 3:15 NLT

No one can lay any foundation other than the one we already have – Jesus Christ.

- 1 Corinthians 3:11 NLT

You are no longer strangers and foreigners, but fellow citizens with the saints and members of the household of God, having been built on the foundation of the apostles and prophets, Jesus Christ Himself being the chief cornerstone.

- Ephesians 2:19-20 NKJV

Day after day the churches grew stronger in faith and increased in number.

- Acts 16:5 NAB

He is also the head of the body, the church;
He is the beginning, the firstborn from the dead,
so that He might come to have first place in
      everything.

- Colossians 1:18 HCSB

"I tell you, you are Peter, and on this rock I will build my church, and the gates of Hades will not prevail against it."

- Matthew 16:18 NRSV

See also **Ministry**

Creation

"Let Us make man in Our image, according to Our likeness; let them have dominion over the fish of the sea, over the birds of the air, and over the cattle, over all the earth and over every creeping thing that creeps on the earth."
                              - Genesis 1:26 NKJV

By Him all things were created, both in the heavens and on earth, visible and invisible, whether thrones or dominions or rulers or authorities – all things have been created through Him and for Him. He is before all things, and in Him all things hold together.
                              - Colossians 1:16-17 NASB

"In the beginning, O Lord, you laid the foundations
        of the earth,
    and the heavens are the work of your hands."
                              - Hebrews 1:10 NIV

"The Spirit of God has made me;
    the breath of the Almighty gives me life."
                              - Job 33:4 TNIV

"You are worthy, our Lord and God,
    to receive glory and honor and power,
for you created all things,
    and by your will they existed and
        were created."
                              - Revelation 4:11 NRSV

From the creation of the world His invisible attributes, that is, His eternal power and divine nature, have been clearly seen, being understood through what He has made.
- Romans 1:20 HCSB

By the word of the LORD the heavens were made,
    their starry host by the breath of his mouth.
- Psalm 33:6 TNIV

The heavens are Yours, the earth also is Yours; the world and all that is in it, You have founded them.
- Psalm 89:11 AMP

Every house is built by someone, but the One who built everything is God.
- Hebrews 3:4 HCSB

"Fear God and give him glory, for his time has come to sit in judgment. Worship him who made heaven and earth and sea and springs of water."
- Revelation 14:7 NAB

Have we not all one Father? Has not one God created us?
- Malachi 2:10 AMP

"You alone are the LORD.
You have made the heavens,
The heaven of heavens with all their host,
The earth and all that is on it,
The seas and all that is in them.
You give life to all of them
And the heavenly host bows down before You."
- Nehemiah 9:6 NASB

How many are your works, O LORD!
In wisdom you made them all.
                    - Psalm 104:24 NIV

I will praise You, for I am fearfully
          and wonderfully made;
Marvelous are Your works,
And that my soul knows very well.
                    - Psalm 139:14 NKJV

"It is I who made the earth
    and created mankind upon it.
My own hands stretched out the heavens;
    I marshaled their starry hosts."
                    - Isaiah 45:12 NIV

So God created man in His own image, in the image
and likeness of God He created him; male and female
He created them.
                    - Genesis 1:27 AMP

By faith we understand that the universe was ordered
by the word of God, so that what is visible came into
being through the invisible.
                    - Hebrews 11:3 NAB

In the beginning God created the heavens and the
earth.
                    - Genesis 1:1 NIV

But now, O LORD, You are our Father,
We are the clay, and You our potter;
And all of us are the work of Your hand.
                    - Isaiah 64:8 NASB

He who forms the mountains,
   creates the wind,
   and reveals his thoughts to man,
he who turns dawn to darkness,
   and treads the high places of the earth –
   the LORD God Almighty is his name.

- Amos 4:13 NIV

And the LORD God formed man of the dust of the ground, and breathed into his nostrils the breath of life; and man became a living being.

- Genesis 2:7 NKJV

It is He who made the earth by His power,
Who established the world by His wisdom;
And by His understanding He has stretched
   out the heavens.

- Jeremiah 10:12 NASB

Know that the LORD Himself is God;
It is He who has made us, and not
   we ourselves;
We are His people and the sheep of
   His pasture.

- Psalm 100:3 NASB

All things came into being through him, and without him not one thing came into being.

- John 1:3 NRSV

By wisdom the LORD laid the earth's foundations,
   by understanding he set the heavens in place.

- Proverbs 3:19 NIV

We are God's masterpiece. He has created us anew in Christ Jesus, so we can do the good things he planned for us long ago.

- Ephesians 2:10 NLT

"See, I will create
   new heavens and a new earth.
The former things will not be remembered,
   nor will they come to mind."

- Isaiah 65:17 TNIV

" 'Ah, Lord GOD! Behold, You have made the heavens and the earth by Your great power and outstretched arm. There is nothing too hard for You.' "

- Jeremiah 32:17 NKJV

The rich and the poor have this in common:
   the LORD is the maker of them all.

- Proverbs 22:2 NRSV

See also **Power of God, Wonders of God**

Eternal Life

"I am the resurrection and the life. He who believes in me will live, even though he dies; and whoever lives and believes in me will never die."
                                    - John 11:25-26 NIV

This is the promise which He Himself made to us: eternal life.
                                    - 1 John 2:25 NASB

For the wages of sin is death, but the gift of God is eternal life in Christ Jesus our Lord.
                                    - Romans 6:23 HCSB

Everyone who competes in the games goes into strict training. They do it to get a crown that will not last, but we do it to get a crown that will last forever.
                                    - 1 Corinthians 9:25 TNIV

Blessed are those who persevere under trial, because when they have stood the test, they will receive the crown of life that God has promised to those who love him.
                                    - James 1:12 TNIV

Let them do good, that they be rich in good works, ready to give, willing to share, storing up for themselves a good foundation for the time to come, that they may lay hold on eternal life.
                                    - 1 Timothy 6:18-19 NKJV

We also know that the Son of God has come and has given us discernment to know the one who is true. And we are in the one who is true, in his Son Jesus Christ. He is the true God and eternal life.

- 1 John 5:20 NAB

He who believes in Me [who adheres to, trusts in, relies on, and has faith in Me] has (now possesses) eternal life.

- John 6:47 AMP

God poured out the Holy Spirit abundantly on us through Jesus Christ our Savior, so that by his grace we might be put right with God and come into possession of the eternal life we hope for.

- Titus 3:6-7 GNT

The one who sows to please his sinful nature, from that nature will reap destruction; the one who sows to please the Spirit, from the Spirit will reap eternal life.

- Galatians 6:8 NIV

Keep yourselves in the love of God and wait for the mercy of our Lord Jesus Christ that leads to eternal life.

- Jude 21 NAB

Now if we have died with Christ, we believe that we shall also live with Him, knowing that Christ, having been raised from the dead, is never to die again.

- Romans 6:8-9 NASB

Our Savior Jesus Christ...has abolished death and brought life and immortality to light through the gospel.

- 2 Timothy 1:10 NKJV

God raised the Lord and will also raise us by his power.

- 1 Corinthians 6:14 NAB

We believe that Jesus died and rose again, and so we believe that God will take back with Jesus those who have died believing in him.

- 1 Thessalonians 4:14 GNT

The world and its desires pass away, but whoever does the will of God lives forever.

- 1 John 2:17 TNIV

For if we have died with Him,
    we will also live with Him.

- 2 Timothy 2:11 HCSB

"Most assuredly, I say to you, he who hears My word and believes in Him who sent Me has everlasting life, and shall not come into judgment, but has passed from death into life."

- John 5:24 NKJV

Christ has indeed been raised from the dead, the firstfruits of those who have fallen asleep. For since death came through a man, the resurrection of the dead comes also through a man. For as in Adam all die, so in Christ all will be made alive.

- 1 Corinthians 15:20-22 NIV

"Did I not tell you that if you believe you will see the glory of God?"
- John 11:40 NAB

Fight the good fight of the faith. Take hold of the eternal life to which you were called when you made your good confession in the presence of many witnesses.
- 1 Timothy 6:12 TNIV

"Whoever wishes to come after me must deny himself, take up his cross, and follow me. For whoever wishes to save his life will lose it, but whoever loses his life for my sake and that of the gospel will save it."
- Mark 8:34-35 NAB

" ' "He who overcomes shall be clothed in white garments, and I will not blot out his name from the Book of Life; but I will confess his name before My Father and before His angels." ' "
- Revelation 3:5 NKJV

Now that you have been set free from sin and have become slaves to God, the benefit you reap leads to holiness, and the result is eternal life.
- Romans 6:22 NIV

"Do not labor for the food which perishes, but for the food which endures to everlasting life, which the Son of Man will give you, because God the Father has set His seal on Him."
- John 6:27 NKJV

When the chief Shepherd is revealed, you will receive the unfading crown of glory.
- 1 Peter 5:4 NAB

He will give eternal life to those who keep on doing good, seeking after the glory and honor and immortality that God offers.

- Romans 2:7 NLT

"For I know that my Redeemer lives,
    and that at the last he will stand upon
        the earth;
and after my skin has been thus destroyed,
    then in my flesh I shall see God."

- Job 19:25-26 NRSV

God has given us eternal life, and this life is in his Son. Whoever has the Son has life; whoever does not have the Son of God does not have life. I write these things to you who believe in the name of the Son of God so that you may know that you have eternal life.

- 1 John 5:11-13 TNIV

Then Jesus, looking at him, loved him, and said to him, "One thing you lack: Go your way, sell whatever you have and give to the poor, and you will have treasure in heaven; and come, take up the cross, and follow Me."

- Mark 10:21 NKJV

"For God so loved the world that he gave his one and only Son, that whoever believes in him shall not perish but have eternal life."

- John 3:16 NIV

You have been born again, but not to a life that will quickly end. Your new life will last forever because it comes from the eternal, living word of God.

- 1 Peter 1:23 NLT

"Let not your heart be troubled; you believe in God, believe also in Me. In My Father's house are many mansions; if it were not so, I would have told you. I go to prepare a place for you. And if I go and prepare a place for you, I will come again and receive you to Myself; that where I am, there you may be also. And where I go you know, and the way you know."

- John 14:1-4 NKJV

"He who overcomes will not be hurt at all by the second death."

- Revelation 2:11 NIV

"Whoever drinks of the water that I shall give him will never thirst. But the water that I shall give him will become in him a fountain of water springing up into everlasting life."

- John 4:14 NKJV

He saved us, not because of righteous things we had done, but because of his mercy. He saved us through the washing of rebirth and renewal by the Holy Spirit, whom he poured out on us generously through Jesus Christ our Savior, so that, having been justified by his grace, we might become heirs having the hope of eternal life.

- Titus 3:5-7 TNIV

We know that if the earthly tent we live in is destroyed, we have a building from God, an eternal house in heaven, not built by human hands.

- 2 Corinthians 5:1 NIV

"Lord, to whom shall we go? You have the words of eternal life."

- John 6:68 NIV

For the Lord Himself will descend from heaven with a shout, with the voice of the archangel and with the trumpet of God, and the dead in Christ will rise first. Then we who are alive and remain will be caught up together with them in the clouds to meet the Lord in the air, and so we shall always be with the Lord. Therefore comfort one another with these words.

- 1 Thessalonians 4:16-18 NASB

"To those who are victorious, I will give the right to eat from the tree of life, which is in the paradise of God."

- Revelation 2:7 TNIV

One thing I ask of the LORD;
   this I seek:
To dwell in the LORD's house
   all the days of my life,
To gaze on the LORD's beauty,
   to visit his temple.

- Psalm 27:4 NAB

"I am the living bread that came down from heaven. Whoever eats of this bread will live forever; and the bread that I will give for the life of the world is my flesh."

- John 6:51 NRSV

"My sheep hear My voice, and I know them, and they follow Me. And I give them eternal life, and they shall never perish; neither shall anyone snatch them out of My hand."

- John 10:27-28 NKJV

I have fought the good fight, I have finished the race, I have kept the faith. Now there is in store for me the crown of righteousness, which the Lord, the righteous Judge, will award to me on that day – and not only to me, but also to all who have longed for his appearing.

- 2 Timothy 4:7-8 TNIV

"Everyone who has left houses or brothers or sisters or father or mother or children or fields for my sake will receive a hundred times as much and will inherit eternal life."

- Matthew 19:29 NIV

See also **Kingdom of Heaven, Life, Salvation**

Favor of God

For his anger lasts only a moment,
    but his favor lasts a lifetime;
weeping may remain for a night,
    but rejoicing comes in the morning.

- Psalm 30:5 TNIV

" 'I will look on you favorably and make you fruitful, multiply you and confirm My covenant with you.' "

- Leviticus 26:9 NKJV

The favors of the LORD are not exhausted,
    his mercies are not spent;
They are renewed each morning,
    so great is his faithfulness.

- Lamentations 3:22-23 NAB

He mocks proud mockers
    but shows favor to the humble and oppressed.
                        - Proverbs 3:34 TNIV

Whoever finds me [Wisdom] finds life and draws forth
and obtains favor from the Lord.
                        - Proverbs 8:35 AMP

LORD, when You showed Your favor,
You made me stand like a strong mountain.
                        - Psalm 30:7 HCSB

He who finds a [true] wife finds a good thing and obtains favor from the Lord.
                        - Proverbs 18:22 AMP

" 'You have granted me life and
        favor,
And Your care has preserved my
        spirit.' "
                        - Job 10:12 NKJV

Never let loyalty and faithfulness leave you.
Tie them around your neck;
    write them on the tablet of your heart.
Then you will find favor and high regard
in the sight of God and man.
                        - Proverbs 3:3-4 HCSB

The good obtain favor from the LORD.
                        - Proverbs 12:2 NRSV

For You, O LORD, will bless the righteous;
With favor You will surround him as with
    a shield.
                - Psalm 5:12 NKJV

See also **Blessing, Grace**

Freedom

For the law of the Spirit of life in Christ Jesus has
made me free from the law of sin and death.
                - Romans 8:2 NKJV

"You will know the truth, and the truth will set you
free."
                - John 8:32 HCSB

"Now I will break their yoke from your neck
    and tear your shackles away."
                - Nahum 1:13 TNIV

You were called for freedom, brothers. But do not use
this freedom as an opportunity for the flesh; rather,
serve one another through love.
                - Galatians 5:13 NAB

You have been set free from sin and have become
slaves to righteousness.
                - Romans 6:18 NIV

Now the Lord is the Spirit, and where the Spirit of the Lord is, there is liberty.

- 2 Corinthians 3:17 NASB

Stand fast therefore in the liberty by which Christ has made us free, and do not be entangled again with a yoke of bondage.

- Galatians 5:1 NKJV

Now that you have been set free from sin and have becomes slaves of God, the benefit you reap leads to holiness, and the result is eternal life.

- Romans 6:22 TNIV

Although I am free in regard to all, I have made myself a slave to all so as to win over as many as possible.

- 1 Corinthians 9:19 NAB

The LORD gives freedom to the
        prisoners.

- Psalm 146:7 NKJV

"If the Son sets you free, you will be free indeed."
- John 8:36 NIV

See also **Eternal Life, Passion of Jesus, Salvation**

Healing

"To you who fear My name
The Sun of Righteousness shall arise
With healing in His wings."
                         - Malachi 4:2 NKJV

"For He bruises, but He binds up;
He wounds, but His hands make whole."
                         - Job 5:18 NKJV

"This sickness is not to end in death, but for the glory
of God, so that the Son of God may be glorified by it."
                         - John 11:4 NASB

Praise the LORD, my soul,
    and forget not all his benefits –
who forgives all your sins
    and heals all your diseases,
who redeems your life from the pit
    and crowns you with love and compassion,
who satisfies your desires with good things
    so that your youth is renewed like the eagle's.
                         - Psalm 103:2-5 TNIV

Heal me, O LORD, and I shall be healed;
    save me, and I shall be saved.
                         - Jeremiah 17:14 NRSV

" 'For I will restore you to health
And I will heal you of your wounds,'
    declares the LORD."
                         - Jeremiah 30:17 NASB

"By faith in the name of Jesus, this man whom you see and know was made strong. It is Jesus' name and the faith that comes through him that has given this complete healing to him, as you can all see."
- Acts 3:16 NIV

The prayer of faith will save the sick person, and the Lord will raise him up.
- James 5:15 NAB

O LORD my God, I called to you for help
    and you healed me.
O LORD, you brought me up from the grave;
    you spared me from going down into the pit.
- Psalm 30:2-3 NIV

Jesus said to him, "Go your way; your faith has made you well." And immediately he received his sight and followed Jesus on the road.
- Mark 10:52 NKJV

He Himself bore our sins in His body on the cross, so that we might die to sin and live to righteousness; for by His wounds you were healed.
- 1 Peter 2:24 NASB

"I am the LORD who heals you."
- Exodus 15:26 NLT

I will seek that which was lost and bring back that which has strayed, and I will bandage the hurt and the crippled and will strengthen the weak and the sick.
- Ezekiel 34:16 AMP

He sent His word and healed them,
And delivered them from their destructions.
                                    - Psalm 107:20 NASB

The whole crowd was trying to touch Him, because
power was coming out from Him and healing them all.
                                    - Luke 6:19 HCSB

He was pierced for our transgressions,
    he was crushed for our iniquities;
the punishment that brought us peace was
        upon him,
    and by his wounds we are healed.
                                    - Isaiah 53:5 NIV

"Stand up and go; your faith has made you well."
                                    - Luke 17:19 NASB

" ' "I have heard your prayer, I have seen your tears;
surely I will heal you." ' "
                                    - 2 Kings 20:5 NKJV

He heals the brokenhearted and binds up their
wounds [curing their pains and their sorrows].
                                    - Psalm 147:3 AMP

See also **Passion of Jesus, Salvation**

Holy Spirit

'You will receive power when the Holy Spirit comes on you.'
- Acts 1:8 JB

"Peace be with you; as the Father has sent Me, I also send you." And when He had said this, He breathed on them and said to them, "Receive the Holy Spirit."
- John 20:21-22 NASB

Now hope does not disappoint, because the love of God has been poured out in our hearts by the Holy Spirit who was given to us.
- Romans 5:5 NKJV

They saw what seemed to be tongues of fire that separated and came to rest on each of them. All of them were filled with the Holy Spirit and began to speak in other tongues as the Spirit enabled them.
- Acts 2:3-4 TNIV

If you are led by the Spirit, you are not subject to the law.
- Galatians 5:18 NRSV

Did you receive the Spirit from works of the law, or from faith in what you heard? Does, then, the one who supplies the Spirit to you and works mighty deeds among you do so from works of the law or from faith in what you heard?
- Galatians 3:2,5 NAB

" 'In the last days, God says,
     I will pour out my Spirit on all people.
Your sons and daughters will prophesy,
     your young men will see visions,
     your old men will dream dreams.
Even on my servants, both men and women,
     I will pour out my Spirit in those days,
     and they will prophesy.' "
                    - Acts 2:17-18 NIV

Truly I am full of power by the spirit of the LORD.
                    - Micah 3:8 KJV

"When the Spirit of truth comes, He will guide you into
all the truth."
                    - John 16:13 HCSB

"Repent, and let every one of you be baptized in the
name of Jesus Christ for the remission of sins; and
you shall receive the gift of the Holy Spirit."
                    - Acts 2:38 NKJV

May the God of hope fill you with all joy and peace in
believing, so that you may overflow with hope by the
power of the Holy Spirit.
                    - Romans 15:13 HCSB

He saved us through the washing of rebirth and renewal by the Holy Spirit, whom he poured out on us
generously through Jesus Christ our Savior, so that,
having been justified by his grace, we might become
heirs having the hope of eternal life.
                    - Titus 3:5-7 NIV

The Spirit helps us in our weakness.
- Romans 8:26 TNIV

"I have baptized you with water, but He will baptize you with the Holy Spirit."
- Mark 1:8 HCSB

The fruit of the Spirit is love, joy, peace, patience, kindness, generosity, faithfulness, gentleness, self-control. Against such there is no law.
- Galatians 5:22-23 NAB

If the Spirit of Him who raised Jesus from the dead lives in you, then He who raised Christ from the dead will also bring your mortal bodies to life through His Spirit who lives in you.
- Romans 8:11 HCSB

"Very truly I tell you, no one can enter the kingdom of God without being born of water and the Spirit. Flesh gives birth to flesh, but the Spirit gives birth to spirit."
- John 3:5-6 TNIV

This is how you can recognize the Spirit of God: Every spirit that acknowledges that Jesus Christ has come in the flesh is from God.
- 1 John 4:2 TNIV

Now it is God who makes both us and you stand firm in Christ. He anointed us, set his seal of ownership on us, and put his Spirit in our hearts as a deposit, guaranteeing what is to come.
- 2 Corinthians 1:21-22 NIV

When they had prayed, the place where they had gathered together was shaken, and they were all filled
with the Holy Spirit and began to speak the word of
God with boldness.
                        - Acts 4:31 NASB

Now the Lord is the Spirit, and where the Spirit of the
Lord is, there is freedom.
                        - 2 Corinthians 3:17 NAB

If you are reproached for the name of Christ, blessed
are you, for the Spirit of glory and of God rests upon
you. On their part He is blasphemed, but on your part
He is glorified.
                        - 1 Peter 4:14 NKJV

"We are witnesses of these things, and so is the Holy
Spirit, whom God has given to those who obey him."
                        - Acts 5:32 TNIV

Do you not know that you are the temple of God and
that the Spirit of God dwells in you?
                        - 1 Corinthians 3:16 NKJV

Be filled with the Spirit, speaking to one another in
psalms and hymns and spiritual songs, singing and
making melody with your heart to the Lord.
                        - Ephesians 5:18-19 NASB

" 'Not by might nor by power, but by my Spirit,' says
the LORD Almighty."
                        - Zechariah 4:6 NIV

See also **Power of God**

Judgment

We must all appear before the judgment seat of Christ, so that each may be repaid for what he has done in the body, whether good or bad.
- 2 Corinthians 5:10 HCSB

Every one of us shall give account of himself to God.
- Romans 14:12 KJV

"See, the Lord is coming with thousands upon thousands of his holy ones to judge everyone, and to convict all the ungodly of all the ungodly acts they have done in an ungodly way, and of all the defiant words ungodly sinners have spoken against him."
- Jude 14-15 TNIV

It is time for the judgment to begin with the household of God; if it begins with us, how will it end for those who fail to obey the gospel of God?
- 1 Peter 4:17 NAB

"Fear God and give glory to Him, for the hour of His judgment has come; and worship Him who made heaven and earth, the sea and springs of water."
- Revelation 14:7 NKJV

Why do you criticize and pass judgment on your brother? Or you, why do you look down upon or despise your brother? For we shall all stand before the judgment seat of God.
- Romans 14:10 AMP

"For the LORD is the God of knowledge;
And by Him actions are weighed."
                    - 1 Samuel 2:3 NKJV

Judgment will be merciless to one who has shown no
mercy.
                    - James 2:13 NASB

Fear God and keep his commandments,
    for this is the whole duty of man.
For God will bring every deed into judgment,
    including every hidden thing,
    whether it is good or evil.
                    - Ecclesiastes 12:13-14 NIV

"Multitudes who sleep in the dust of the earth will
awake: some to everlasting life, others to shame and
everlasting contempt."
                    - Daniel 12:2 TNIV

The heathen are surprised when you do not join them
in the same wild and reckless living, and so they insult you. But they will have to give an account of
themselves to God, who is ready to judge the living
and the dead.
                    - 1 Peter 4:4-5 GNT

I saw the dead, small and great, standing before God,
and books were opened. And another book was
opened, which is the Book of Life. And the dead were
judged according to their works, by the things which
were written in the books.
                    - Revelation 20:12 NKJV

See also **Justice, Second Coming**

Kingdom of Heaven

"The kingdom of heaven is like a treasure hidden in the field, which a man found and hid again; and from joy over it he goes and sells all that he has and buys that field."
- Matthew 13:44 NASB

"Anyone who breaks one of the least of these commandments and teaches others to do the same will be called least in the kingdom of heaven, but whoever practices and teaches these commands will be called great in the kingdom of heaven."
- Matthew 5:19 NIV

"For I say to you, among those born of women there is not a greater prophet than John the Baptist; but he who is least in the kingdom of God is greater than he."
- Luke 7:28 NKJV

Blessed are the poor in spirit: for theirs is the kingdom of heaven.
- Matthew 5:3 KJV

One thing I ask of the LORD;
   this I seek:
To dwell in the LORD's house
   all the days of my life,
To gaze on the LORD's beauty,
   to visit his temple.
- Psalm 27:4 NAB

Our citizenship is in heaven, from which we also eagerly wait for the Savior, the Lord Jesus Christ.
                              - Philippians 3:20 NKJV

" 'To him who overcomes, I will grant to eat of the tree of life which is in the Paradise of God.' "
                              - Revelation 2:7 NASB

"They are blessed who are persecuted for
        doing good,
    for the kingdom of heaven belongs to them."
                              - Matthew 5:10 NCV

"Not everyone who says to me, 'Lord, Lord,' will enter the kingdom of heaven, but only those who do the will of my Father who is in heaven."
                              - Matthew 7:21 TNIV

"God will wipe away every tear from their eyes; there shall be no more death, nor sorrow, nor crying. There shall be no more pain, for the former things have passed away."
                              - Revelation 21:4 NKJV

"All who are victorious will become pillars in the Temple of my God, and they will never have to leave it."
                              - Revelation 3:12 NLT

"For He is the living God and enduring
        forever,
And His kingdom is one which will not
        be destroyed,
And His dominion will be forever."
                              - Daniel 6:26 NASB

The Lord will rescue me from every evil threat and will bring me safe to his heavenly kingdom.
                                    - 2 Timothy 4:18 NAB

"It is necessary for us to undergo many hardships to enter the kingdom of God."
                                    - Acts 14:22 NAB

Unless a person is born again (anew, from above), he cannot ever see (know, be acquainted with, and experience) the kingdom of God.
                                    - John 3:3 AMP

How great are His signs! And how mighty His wonders! His kingdom is an everlasting kingdom, and His dominion is from generation to generation.
                                    - Daniel 4:3 AMP

The street of the city was pure gold, like transparent glass. But I saw no temple in it, for the Lord God Almighty and the Lamb are its temple. The city had no need of the sun or of the moon to shine in it, for the glory of God illuminated it. The Lamb is its light. And the nations of those who are saved shall walk in its light, and the kings of the earth bring their glory and honor into it.
                                    - Revelation 21:21-24 NKJV

"The righteous will shine like the sun in the kingdom of their Father."
                                    - Matthew 13:43 NAB

"Very truly I tell you, no one can enter the kingdom of God without being born of water and the Spirit. Flesh gives birth to flesh, but the Spirit gives birth to spirit."
- John 3:5-6 TNIV

Then the angel showed me the river of the water of life, as clear as crystal, flowing from the throne of God and of the Lamb down the middle of the great street of the city. On each side of the river stood the tree of life, bearing twelve crops of fruit, yielding its fruit every month. And the leaves of the tree are for the healing of the nations.
- Revelation 22:1-2 NIV

See also **Eternal Life, Wonders of God**

Law

Love does no wrong to a neighbor; therefore love is the fulfillment of the law.
- Romans 13:10 NASB

"A person is not justified by observing the law, but by faith in Jesus Christ. So we, too, have put our faith in Christ Jesus that we may be justified by faith in Christ and not by observing the law, because by observing the law no one will be justified."
- Galatians 2:16 TNIV

Owe no one anything, except to love one another; for the one who loves another has fulfilled the law.
- Romans 13:8 NRSV

For the law of the Spirit of life in Christ Jesus has set you free from the law of sin and of death.
- Romans 8:2 NRSV

It is not the hearers of the Law who are just before God, but the doers of the Law will be justified.
- Romans 2:13 NASB

This is the covenant that I will make with the house of Israel after those days, says the Lord: I will imprint My laws upon their minds, even upon their innermost thoughts and understanding, and engrave them upon their hearts; and I will be their God, and they shall be My people.
- Hebrews 8:10 AMP

I do not set aside the grace of God; for if righteousness comes through the law, then Christ died for nothing.
- Galatians 2:21 HCSB

Did you receive the Spirit by the works of the law or by hearing with faith? So then, does God supply you with the Spirit and work miracles among you by the works of the law or by hearing with faith?
- Galatians 3:2,5 HCSB

May Your compassion come to me
 that I may live,
For Your law is my delight.
- Psalm 119:77 NASB

If a law had been given that could impart life, then righteousness would certainly have come by the law.
- Galatians 3:21 TNIV

Christ has already accomplished the purpose for which the law was given. As a result, all who believe in him are made right with God.

- Romans 10:4 NLT

For his sake I have suffered the loss of all things, and I regard them as rubbish, in order that I may gain Christ and be found in him, not having a righteousness of my own that comes from the law, but one that comes through faith in Christ, the righteousness from God based on faith.

- Philippians 3:8-9 NRSV

The entire law is fulfilled in keeping this one command: "Love your neighbor as yourself."

- Galatians 5:14 TNIV

I delight in the law of God in my inmost self.

- Romans 7:22 NRSV

Before this faith came, we were held prisoners by the law, locked up until faith should be revealed. So the law was put in charge to lead us to Christ that we might be justified by faith. Now that faith has come, we are no longer under the supervision of the law.

- Galatians 3:23-25 NIV

Sin is not to have any power over you, since you are not under the law but under grace.

- Romans 6:14 NAB

If you are led by the Spirit, you are not subject to the law.

- Galatians 5:18 NRSV

"Whatever you want men to do to you, do also to them, for this is the Law and the Prophets."

                              - Matthew 7:12 NKJV

Through the law I died to the law, so that I might live to God.

                              - Galatians 2:19 NRSV

Bear one another's burdens, and so fulfill the law of Christ.

                              - Galatians 6:2 NKJV

His delight is in the law of the LORD,
    and on his law he meditates day and night.
He is like a tree planted by streams of water,
    which yields its fruit in season
and whose leaf does not wither.
    Whatever he does prospers.

                              - Psalm 1:2-3 NIV

The fruit of the Spirit is love, joy, peace, patience, kindness, goodness, faithfulness, gentleness, self-control; against such things there is no law.

                              - Galatians 5:22-23 NASB

See also **Obedience, Scripture**

Light

"I am the Light of the world; he who follows Me will not walk in the darkness, but will have the Light of life."
- John 8:12 NASB

If we walk in the Light as He Himself is in the Light, we have fellowship with one another, and the blood of Jesus His Son cleanses us from all sin.
- 1 John 1:7 NASB

The path of the righteous is like the first
    gleam of dawn,
  shining ever brighter till the full light
    of day.
- Proverbs 4:18 NIV

The night is far spent, the day is at hand. Therefore let us cast off the works of darkness, and let us put on the armor of light.
- Romans 13:12 NKJV

We have the prophetic message more fully confirmed. You will do well to be attentive to this as to a lamp shining in a dark place, until the day dawns and the morning star rises in your hearts.
- 2 Peter 1:19 NRSV

God is light, and in him is no darkness at all.
- 1 John 1:5 KJV

You are all sons of the light and sons of the day. We do not belong to the night or to the darkness. So then, let us not be like others, who are asleep, but let us be alert and self-controlled. For those who sleep, sleep at night, and those who get drunk, get drunk at night. But since we belong to the day, let us be self-controlled, putting on faith and love as a breastplate, and the hope of salvation as a helmet.

- 1 Thessalonians 5:5-8 NIV

The darkness is passing away and the true Light is already shining.

- 1 John 2:8 NASB

For once you were darkness, but now in the Lord you are light. Live as children of light – for the fruit of the light is found in all that is good and right and true.

- Ephesians 5:8-9 NRSV

For with You is the fountain of life;
In Your light we see light.

- Psalm 36:9 NASB

"You are the light of the world. A city set on a mountain cannot be hidden. Nor do they light a lamp and then put it under a bushel basket; it is set on a lampstand, where it gives light to all in the house. Just so, your light must shine before others, that they may see your good deeds and glorify your heavenly Father."

- Matthew 5:14-16 NAB

The city has no need of the sun or of the moon to shine on it, for the glory of God has illumined it, and its lamp is the Lamb.

- Revelation 21:23 NASB

The LORD is my light and my salvation –
   whom shall I fear?

               - Psalm 27:1 NIV

Anyone who claims to be in the light but hates his brother is still in the darkness. Whoever loves his brother lives in the light, and there is nothing in him to make him stumble.

               - 1 John 2:9-10 NIV

Arise, shine;
For your light has come!
And the glory of the LORD is risen
      upon you.

               - Isaiah 60:1 NKJV

You, LORD, keep my lamp burning;
   my God turns my darkness into light.

               - Psalm 18:28 TNIV

It is the God who said, "Let light shine out of darkness," who has shone in our hearts to give the light of the knowledge of the glory of God in the face of Jesus Christ.

               - 2 Corinthians 4:6 NRSV

"The sun will no more be your light by day,
   nor will the brightness of the moon shine
      on you,
for the LORD will be your everlasting light,
   and your God will be your glory."

               - Isaiah 60:19 TNIV

You are a chosen generation, a royal priesthood, a holy nation, His own special people, that you may proclaim the praises of Him who called you out of darkness into His marvelous light.
                                    - 1 Peter 2:9 NKJV

Send Your light and Your truth; let them
          lead me.
Let them bring me to Your holy mountain,
to Your dwelling place.
                                    - Psalm 43:3 HCSB

"I have come as Light into the world, so that everyone who believes in Me will not remain in darkness."
                                    - John 12:46 NASB

See also **Power of God**

Passion of Jesus

"For God so loved the world, that He gave His only begotten Son, that whoever believes in Him shall not perish, but have eternal life."
                                    - John 3:16 NASB

You know the grace of our Lord Jesus Christ: although He was rich, for your sake He became poor, so that by His poverty you might become rich.
                                    - 2 Corinthians 8:9 HCSB

Greater love hath no man than this, that a man lay down his life for his friends.

- John 15:13 KJV

In bringing many sons to glory, it was fitting that God, for whom and through whom everything exists, should make the author of their salvation perfect through suffering.

- Hebrews 2:10 NIV

This is how we know what love is: Jesus Christ laid down his life for us. And we ought to lay down our lives for one another.

- 1 John 3:16 TNIV

God demonstrates His own love toward us, in that while we were still sinners, Christ died for us.

- Romans 5:8 NKJV

Being found in appearance as a man, He humbled Himself by becoming obedient to the point of death, even death on a cross.

- Philippians 2:8 NASB

God's love was revealed among us in this way: God sent his only Son into the world so that we might live through him. In this is love, not that we loved God but that he loved us and sent his Son to be the atoning sacrifice for our sins.

- 1 John 4:9-10 NRSV

Christ has rescued us from the curse pronounced by the law. When he was hung on the cross, he took upon himself the curse for our wrongdoing.

- Galatians 3:13 NLT

He died for all, so that they who live might no longer live for themselves, but for Him who died and rose again on their behalf.
                                    - 2 Corinthians 5:15 NASB

"The Son of Man did not come to be served but to serve and to give his life as a ransom for many."
                                    - Mark 10:45 NAB

What I received I passed on to you as of first importance: that Christ died for our sins according to the Scriptures, that he was buried, that he was raised on the third day according to the Scriptures.
                                    - 1 Corinthians 15:3-4 TNIV

Live a life of love, just as Christ loved us and gave himself up for us as a fragrant offering and sacrifice to God.
                                    - Ephesians 5:2 NIV

He made peace with everything in heaven
        and on earth
    by means of Christ's blood on the cross.
                                    - Colossians 1:20 NLT

In Him we have redemption (deliverance and salvation) through His blood, the remission (forgiveness) of our offenses (shortcomings and trespasses), in accordance with the riches and the generosity of His gracious favor.
                                    - Ephesians 1:7 AMP

There is one God, and one mediator also between God and men, the man Christ Jesus, who gave Himself as a ransom for all.

- 1 Timothy 2:5-6 NASB

Without the shedding of blood there is no forgiveness of sins.

- Hebrews 9:22 NRSV

He Himself bore our sins in His body on the cross, so that we might die to sin and live to righteousness; for by His wounds you were healed.

- 1 Peter 2:24 NASB

Yet He Himself bore our sicknesses,
and He carried our pains;
but we in turn regarded Him stricken,
struck down by God, and afflicted.

- Isaiah 53:4 HCSB

Jesus died for us so that we can live together with him, whether we are alive or dead when he comes.

- 1 Thessalonians 5:10 NCV

For as by one man's disobedience many were made sinners, so also by one Man's obedience many will be made righteous.

- Romans 5:19 NKJV

This is a faithful saying, and worthy of all acceptation, that Christ Jesus came into the world to save sinners; of whom I am chief.

- 1 Timothy 1:15 KJV

God did not choose us to suffer his anger, but to possess salvation through our Lord Jesus Christ, who died for us in order that we might live together with him.

- 1 Thessalonians 5:9-10 GNT

He was pierced for our transgressions,
    he was crushed for our iniquities;
the punishment that brought us peace was
        on him,
    and by his wounds we are healed.

- Isaiah 53:5 TNIV

We see Jesus, who was made a little lower than the angels, now crowned with glory and honor because he suffered death, so that by the grace of God he might taste death for everyone.

- Hebrews 2:9 NIV

He was oppressed and He was
        afflicted,
Yet He opened not His mouth;
He was led as a lamb to the slaughter,
And as a sheep before its shearers
        is silent,
So He opened not His mouth.

- Isaiah 53:7 NKJV

The Son of God appeared for this purpose, to destroy the works of the devil.

- 1 John 3:8 NASB

See also **Love, Salvation**

Power of God

His divine power has given us everything required for life and godliness, through the knowledge of Him who called us by His own glory and goodness.
- 2 Peter 1:3 HCSB

The kingdom of God does not consist in words but in power.
- 1 Corinthians 4:20 NASB

"The Almighty is beyond our reach and exalted
    in power;
  in his justice and great righteousness, he
    does not oppress."
- Job 37:23 TNIV

The foolishness of God is wiser than human wisdom, and the weakness of God is stronger than human strength.
- 1 Corinthians 1:25 NAB

Great is our Lord, and abundant in power;
  his understanding is beyond measure.
- Psalm 147:5 NRSV

Oh, the depth of the riches both of the wisdom and knowledge of God! How unsearchable are His judgments and His ways past finding out!
- Romans 11:33 NKJV

" 'Ah, Lord GOD! Behold, You have made the heavens and the earth by Your great power and outstretched arm. There is nothing too hard for You.' "
- Jeremiah 32:17 NKJV

Everyone in the crowd sought to touch him because power came forth from him and healed them all.
- Luke 6:19 NAB

Who has measured the waters in
        the hollow of His hand,
Measured heaven with a span
And calculated the dust of the earth
        in a measure?
Weighed the mountains in scales
And the hills in a balance?
- Isaiah 40:12 NKJV

You formed the mountains by your power
    and armed yourself with mighty strength.
- Psalm 65:6 NLT

For the message of the cross is foolishness to those who are perishing, but to us who are being saved it is the power of God.
- 1 Corinthians 1:18 TNIV

Ever since the creation of the world, his invisible attributes of eternal power and divinity have been able to be understood and perceived in what he has made.
- Romans 1:20 NAB

You are complete in Him, who is the head of all principality and power.
- Colossians 2:10 NKJV

Join with me in suffering for the gospel according to the power of God, who has saved us and called us with a holy calling, not according to our works, but according to His own purpose and grace which was granted us in Christ Jesus from all eternity.
                                        - 2 Timothy 1:8-9 NASB

With God's power working in us, God can do much, much more than anything we can ask or imagine.
                                        - Ephesians 3:20 NCV

Be exalted, O LORD, in your strength!
    We will sing and praise your power.
                                        - Psalm 21:13 NRSV

"We give You thanks, O Lord
        God Almighty,
The One who is and who was
        and who is to come,
Because You have taken Your
        great power and reigned."
                                        - Revelation 11:17 NKJV

Your faith should not depend on human philosophy but on the power of God.
                                        - 1 Corinthians 2:5 JB

The mountains quake before him
    and the hills melt away.
The earth trembles at his presence,
    the world and all who live in it.
Who can withstand his indignation?
    Who can endure his fierce anger?
His wrath is poured out like fire;
    the rocks are shattered before him.
                                        - Nahum 1:5-6 TNIV

We have this treasure in jars of clay to show that this all-surpassing power is from God and not from us.
- 2 Corinthians 4:7 NIV

And He said to me, "My grace is sufficient for you, for My strength is made perfect in weakness." Therefore most gladly I will rather boast in my infirmities, that the power of Christ may rest upon me.
- 2 Corinthians 12:9 NKJV

I am not ashamed of the gospel, because it is the power of God for the salvation of everyone who believes.
- Romans 1:16 NIV

God has not only raised the Lord, but will also raise us up through His power.
- 1 Corinthians 6:14 NASB

"I am the Alpha and the Omega, the Beginning and the End," says the Lord, "who is and who was and who is to come, the Almighty."
- Revelation 1:8 NKJV

"Riches and honor come from You, and You are the ruler of everything. In Your hand are power and might, and it is in Your hand to make great and to give strength to all."
- 1 Chronicles 29:12 HCSB

Say to God, "How awesome are your deeds!
    So great is your power
    that your enemies cringe before you."
- Psalm 66:3 NIV

He has made the earth by His power,
He has established the world by His wisdom,
And has stretched out the heavens at His discretion.
                                - Jeremiah 10:12 NKJV

See also **Creation, Kingdom of Heaven, Wonders of
    God**

Promise

"Surely I am with you always, to the very end of the
age."
                                - Matthew 28:20 NIV

"It is I who sweep away your transgressions
for My own sake
and remember your sins no more."
                                - Isaiah 43:25 HCSB

"Be strong and of good courage; do not be afraid, nor
be dismayed, for the LORD your God is with you wherever you go."
                                - Joshua 1:9 NKJV

According to His promise we are looking for new heavens and a new earth, in which righteousness dwells.
                                - 2 Peter 3:13 NASB

The God of peace will crush Satan under your feet
shortly.
                                - Romans 16:20 NKJV

Let us hold fast the confession of our hope without wavering, for He who promised is faithful.
- Hebrews 10:23 NASB

"Each one of you must turn away from your sins and be baptized in the name of Jesus Christ, so that your sins will be forgiven; and you will receive God's gift, the Holy Spirit. For God's promise was made to you and your children, and to all who are far away – all whom the Lord our God calls to himself."
- Acts 2:38-39 GNT

"There is nothing covered that won't be uncovered, and nothing hidden that won't be made known."
- Matthew 10:26 HCSB

By his power God raised the Lord from the dead, and he will raise us also.
- 1 Corinthians 6:14 TNIV

"Honor your father and mother" – this is the first commandment with a promise: "so that it may be well with you and you may live long on the earth."
- Ephesians 6:2-3 NRSV

Having patiently waited, he obtained the promise.
- Hebrews 6:15 NASB

I rejoice in your promise,
    like someone on finding a vast treasure.
- Psalm 119:162 JB

For physical training is of some value, but godliness has value for all things, holding promise for both the present life and the life to come.

- 1 Timothy 4:8 NIV

No matter how many promises God has made, they are "Yes" in Christ. And so through him the "Amen" is spoken by us to the glory of God. Now it is God who makes both us and you stand firm in Christ. He anointed us, set his seal of ownership on us, and put his Spirit in our hearts as a deposit, guaranteeing what is to come.

- 2 Corinthians 1:20-22 NIV

Do not fear, for I am with you;
do not be afraid, for I am your God.
I will strengthen you; I will help you;
I will hold on to you with My righteous
     right hand.

- Isaiah 41:10 HCSB

Your testimonies are righteous forever.

- Psalm 119:144 NASB

This is the covenant that I will make with the house of Israel after those days, says the Lord: I will imprint My laws upon their minds, even upon their innermost thoughts and understanding, and engrave them upon their hearts; and I will be their God, and they shall be My people.

- Hebrews 8:10 AMP

"There has not failed one word of all His good promise."

- 1 Kings 8:56 NKJV

When you make a vow to God, do not delay to fulfill it. He has no pleasure in fools; fulfill your vow. It is better not to make a vow than to make one and not fulfill it.

- Ecclesiastes 5:4-5 TNIV

No temptation has overtaken you except what is common to humanity. God is faithful and He will not allow you to be tempted beyond what you are able, but with the temptation He will also provide a way of escape, so that you are able to bear it.

- 1 Corinthians 10:13 HCSB

The LORD's promises are pure,
    like silver refined in a furnace,
    purified seven times over.

- Psalm 12:6 NLT

"Though the mountains be shaken
    and the hills be removed,
yet my unfailing love for you will not be shaken
    nor my covenant of peace be removed,"
    says the LORD, who has compassion on you.

- Isaiah 54:10 NIV

Be mindful of His covenant forever, the promise which He commanded and established to a thousand generations.

- 1 Chronicles 16:15 AMP

He Himself has said, "I will never leave you nor forsake you."

- Hebrews 13:5 NKJV

Blessed are those who persevere under trial, because when they have stood the test, they will receive the crown of life that God has promised to those who love him.

- James 1:12 TNIV

"Bring the whole tithe into the storehouse, that there may be food in my house. Test me in this," says the LORD Almighty, "and see if I will not throw open the floodgates of heaven and pour out so much blessing that there will not be room enough to store it."

- Malachi 3:10 TNIV

Train yourself in godliness, for, while physical training is of some value, godliness is valuable in every way, holding promise for both the present life and the life to come.

- 1 Timothy 4:7-8 NRSV

Not one of the good promises which the LORD had made to the house of Israel failed; all came to pass.

- Joshua 21:45 NASB

"When you pass through the waters,
    I will be with you;
And through the rivers, they will
    not overflow you.
When you walk through the fire, you
    will not be scorched,
Nor will the flame burn you."

- Isaiah 43:2 NASB

"I have given my word to the LORD, and I cannot go back on it."

- Judges 11:35 NKJV

"I have set my rainbow in the clouds, and it will be the sign of the covenant between me and the earth. Whenever I bring clouds over the earth and the rainbow appears in the clouds, I will remember my covenant between me and you and all living creatures of every kind. Never again will the waters become a flood to destroy all life."

- Genesis 9:13-15 NIV

You need endurance to do the will of God and receive what he has promised.

- Hebrews 10:36 NAB

"When you make a vow to the LORD your God, do not put off doing what you promised; the LORD will hold you to your vow, and it is a sin not to keep it."

- Deuteronomy 23:21 GNT

We who live by the Spirit eagerly wait to receive by faith the righteousness God has promised to us.

- Galatians 5:5 NLT

I will send forth upon you what My Father has promised; but remain in the city [Jerusalem] until you are clothed with power from on high.

- Luke 24:49 AMP

For the LORD God is a sun and shield;
The LORD gives grace and glory;
No good thing does He withhold from those
    who walk uprightly.

- Psalm 84:11 NASB

Since we have these promises, dear friends, let us purify ourselves from everything that contaminates body and spirit, perfecting holiness out of reverence for God.

- 2 Corinthians 7:1 TNIV

This is the promise which He Himself made to us: eternal life.

- 1 John 2:25 NASB

"If you have faith the size of a mustard seed, you will say to this mountain, 'Move from here to there,' and it will move; and nothing will be impossible for you."

- Matthew 17:20 NRSV

See also **Loyalty, Peace of Mind, Trust, Truth**

Protection

The Lord is faithful; he will strengthen you and guard you from the evil one.

- 2 Thessalonians 3:3 NRSV

I lift up my eyes to the hills –
  where does my help come from?
My help comes from the LORD,
  the Maker of heaven and earth.

- Psalm 121:1-2 NIV

"I call upon the LORD, who is worthy
    to be praised,
And I am saved from my enemies."
                - 2 Samuel 22:4 NASB

We do not wrestle against flesh and blood, but against principalities, against powers, against the rulers of the darkness of this age, against spiritual hosts of wickedness in the heavenly places. Therefore take up the whole armor of God, that you may be able to withstand in the evil day.
                - Ephesians 6:12-13 NKJV

The LORD is good,
a stronghold in a day of distress;
He cares for those who take refuge in Him.
                - Nahum 1:7 HCSB

You are my hiding place;
    you will protect me from trouble
    and surround me with songs of deliverance.
                - Psalm 32:7 TNIV

"The LORD your God is with you,
    he is mighty to save."
                - Zephaniah 3:17 NIV

The LORD helps them and delivers them;
He delivers them from the wicked and
    saves them,
Because they take refuge in Him.
                - Psalm 37:40 NASB

The LORD watches over all who love him.
- Psalm 145:20 NRSV

In the fear of the LORD is a strong
defense;
even for one's children he will
be a refuge.
- Proverbs 14:26 NAB

"The LORD is my rock and my fortress and
my deliverer;
The God of my strength, in whom I will trust;
My shield and the horn of my salvation,
My stronghold and my refuge;
My Savior."
- 2 Samuel 22:2-3 NKJV

Do not, O LORD, withhold your mercy
from me;
let your steadfast love and your faithfulness
keep me safe forever.
- Psalm 40:11 NRSV

"The LORD your God you shall fear; and He will deliver
you from the hand of all your enemies."
- 2 Kings 17:39 NASB

When you pass through the waters,
I will be with you;
and through the rivers, they shall
not overwhelm you;
when you walk through fire you
shall not be burned,
and the flame shall not consume you.
- Isaiah 43:2 NRSV

"Our God's hand of protection is on all who worship him."

- Ezra 8:22 NLT

O LORD my God, in You I have
taken refuge;
Save me from all those who pursue
me, and deliver me.

- Psalm 7:1 NASB

" 'Because you trusted me, I will give you your life as a reward. I will rescue you and keep you safe. I, the LORD, have spoken!' "

- Jeremiah 39:18 NLT

The angel of the LORD encamps
around those who fear Him,
And rescues them.

- Psalm 34:7 NASB

"My sheep hear My voice, and I know them, and they follow Me. And I give them eternal life, and they shall never perish; neither shall anyone snatch them out of My hand."

- John 10:27-28 NKJV

Deliver me from my enemies, O my God;
Defend me from those who rise up against me.

- Psalm 59:1 NKJV

The Lord shall be your confidence, firm and strong, and shall keep your foot from being caught.

- Proverbs 3:26 AMP

You have preserved my life
　　from the pit of destruction,
When you cast behind your back
　　all my sins.
　　　　　　　　　　- Isaiah 38:17 NAB

Do not be a terror to me;
You are my hope in the day of doom.
　　　　　　　　　　- Jeremiah 17:17 NKJV

You satisfy the desire of those who
　　　　　fear you;
　　you hear their cry and save them.
　　　　　　　　　　- Psalm 145:19 NAB

You rescue the humble,
　　but you humiliate the proud.
　　　　　　　　　　- Psalm 18:27 NLT

I was delivered from the lion's mouth. The Lord will
rescue me from every evil attack and will bring me
safely to his heavenly kingdom.
　　　　　　　　　　- 2 Timothy 4:17-18 NIV

Call on Me in the day of trouble; I will deliver you, and
you shall honor and glorify Me.
　　　　　　　　　　- Psalm 50:15 AMP

The eyes of the LORD are on those
　　　　　who fear him,
　　on those whose hope is in his unfailing love,
to deliver them from death
　　and keep them alive in famine.
　　　　　　　　　　- Psalm 33:18-19 NIV

" 'Fear not, for I am with you;
Be not dismayed, for I am your God.
I will strengthen you,
Yes, I will help you,
I will uphold you with My righteous
right hand.' "
- Isaiah 41:10 NKJV

God is our refuge and strength,
an ever-present help in trouble.
- Psalm 46:1 TNIV

The salvation of the righteous comes
from the LORD;
he is their stronghold in time of
trouble.
- Psalm 37:39 TNIV

"No weapon that is formed against you
will prosper."
- Isaiah 54:17 NASB

As for God, His way is perfect;
The word of the LORD is proven;
He is a shield to all who trust in
Him.
- Psalm 18:30 NKJV

The LORD is my light and my salvation;
Whom shall I fear?
The LORD is the defense of my life;
Whom shall I dread?
- Psalm 27:1 NASB

"They will fight against you,
But they shall not prevail against you.
For I am with you," says the LORD,
    "to deliver you."
           - Jeremiah 1:19 NKJV

You have been a refuge for the poor,
   a refuge for the needy in his distress,
a shelter from the storm
   and a shade from the heat.
           - Isaiah 25:4 NIV

May integrity and uprightness protect
    me,
   because my hope, LORD, is in you.
           - Psalm 25:21 TNIV

"Behold, I give you the authority to trample on serpents and scorpions, and over all the power of the
enemy, and nothing shall by any means hurt you."
           - Luke 10:19 NKJV

"Your God whom you constantly serve will Himself
deliver you."
           - Daniel 6:16 NASB

Keep and protect me, O God, for in You I have found
refuge, and in You do I put my trust and hide myself.
           - Psalm 16:1 AMP

God is my shield,
   saving those whose hearts are true and right.
           - Psalm 7:10 NLT

In you, LORD, I have taken refuge;
   let me never be put to shame;
   deliver me in your righteousness.
Turn your ear to me,
   come quickly to my rescue;
be my rock of refuge,
   a strong fortress to save me.
Since you are my rock and my fortress,
   for the sake of your name lead and guide me.
                  - Psalm 31:1-3 TNIV

For he will command his angels concerning you
   to guard you in all your ways.
                  - Psalm 91:11 NRSV

When the enemy comes in like a
      flood,
The Spirit of the LORD will lift up
   a standard against him.
                  - Isaiah 59:19 NKJV

Jesus said to the woman, "Your faith has saved you;
go in peace."
                  - Luke 7:50 NIV

As for me, I call to God,
   and the LORD saves me.
Evening, morning and noon
   I cry out in distress,
   and he hears my voice.
He rescues me unharmed
   from the battle waged against me,
   even though many oppose me.
                  - Psalm 55:16-18 TNIV

The peace of God, which surpasses all comprehension, will guard your hearts and your minds in Christ Jesus.

- Philippians 4:7 NASB

Lead us not into temptation, but deliver us from evil.

- Matthew 6:13 KJV

I sought the LORD, and he answered me;
he delivered me from all my fears.

- Psalm 34:4 TNIV

Keep me as the apple of Your
eye;
Hide me under the shadow of
Your wings.

- Psalm 17:8 NKJV

Now I know that the LORD saves His anointed;
He will answer him from His holy heaven
With the saving strength of His right hand.

- Psalm 20:6 NASB

The name of the LORD is a strong tower;
the righteous run to it and are safe.

- Proverbs 18:10 NIV

The LORD shall preserve you from all evil;
He shall preserve your soul.
The LORD shall preserve your going out and
your coming in
From this time forth, and even forevermore.

- Psalm 121:7-8 NKJV

Everyone who calls on the name of the Lord will be saved.
> \- Romans 10:13 HCSB

See also **Healing, Peace of Mind, Troubles, Trust**

Purpose

There is a time for everything,
and a season for every activity under the heavens:
    a time to be born and a time to die,
    a time to plant and a time to uproot,
    a time to kill and a time to heal,
    a time to tear down and a time to build,
    a time to weep and a time to laugh,
    a time to mourn and a time to dance,
    a time to scatter stones and a time to gather them,
    a time to embrace and a time to refrain,
    a time to search and a time to give up,
    a time to keep and a time to throw away,
    a time to tear and a time to mend,
    a time to be silent and a time to speak,
    a time to love and a time to hate,
    a time for war and a time for peace.
> \- Ecclesiastes 3:1-8 TNIV

In him we were also chosen, having been predestined according to the plan of him who works out everything in conformity with the purpose of his will.
> \- Ephesians 1:11 NIV

We know that God causes all things to work together for good to those who love God, to those who are called according to His purpose.

            - Romans 8:28 NASB

The Son of God appeared for this purpose, to destroy the works of the devil.

            - 1 John 3:8 NASB

"For the LORD of hosts has purposed,
And who will annul it?
His hand is stretched out,
And who will turn it back?"

            - Isaiah 14:27 NKJV

Do not neglect the gift that is in you.

            - 1 Timothy 4:14 HCSB

We are God's workmanship, created in Christ Jesus to do good works, which God prepared in advance for us to do.

            - Ephesians 2:10 NIV

"I know the plans I have for you," declares the LORD, "plans to prosper you and not to harm you, plans to give you hope and a future."

            - Jeremiah 29:11 TNIV

You are a chosen generation, a royal priesthood, a holy nation, His own special people, that you may proclaim the praises of Him who called you out of darkness into His marvelous light.

            - 1 Peter 2:9 NKJV

Everything that was written in the past was written to teach us, so that through the endurance taught in the Scriptures and the encouragement they provide we might have hope.

- Romans 15:4 TNIV

So then do not be foolish, but understand what the will of the Lord is.

- Ephesians 5:17 NASB

God purposed that through (by the service, the intervention of) Him [the Son] all things should be completely reconciled back to Himself, whether on earth or in heaven, as through Him, [the Father] made peace by means of the blood of His cross.

- Colossians 1:20 AMP

I know that you can do all things,
   and that no purpose of yours can
     be hindered.

- Job 42:2 NAB

"As the rain and the snow
   come down from heaven,
and do not return to it
   without watering the earth
and making it bud and flourish,
   so that it yields seed for the sower and
     bread for the eater,
so is my word that goes out from my mouth:
   It will not return to me empty,
but will accomplish what I desire
   and achieve the purpose for which I sent it."

- Isaiah 55:10-11 TNIV

The man who plants and the man who waters have one purpose, and each will be rewarded according to his own labor.

- 1 Corinthians 3:8 NIV

For He says:
        "In an acceptable time I have heard you,
        And in the day of salvation I have helped
                you."
Behold, now is the accepted time; behold, now is the day of salvation.

- 2 Corinthians 6:2 NKJV

Let the morning bring me word of your
        unfailing love,
    for I have put my trust in you.
Show me the way I should go,
    for to you I lift up my soul.

- Psalm 143:8 NIV

I want you to know, beloved, that what has happened to me has actually helped to spread the gospel.

- Philippians 1:12 NRSV

Each of you has your own gift from God; one has this gift, another has that.

- 1 Corinthians 7:7 TNIV

I have spoken it, I will also bring it to pass; I have purposed it, I will also do it.

- Isaiah 46:11 KJV

Do not be ashamed of the testimony of our Lord, nor of me His prisoner, but share with me in the sufferings for the gospel according to the power of God, who has saved us and called us with a holy calling, not according to our works, but according to His own purpose and grace which was given to us in Christ Jesus before time began.

> \- 2 Timothy 1:8-9 NKJV

The LORD will fulfill His purpose for me.
LORD, Your love is eternal;
do not abandon the work of Your hands.

> \- Psalm 138:8 HCSB

"Nothing is covered up that will not be uncovered, and nothing secret that will not become known."

> \- Matthew 10:26 NRSV

See also **Ministry, Scripture, Truth**

Reconciliation

Since we have now been justified by his blood, how much more shall we be saved from God's wrath through him! For if, when we were God's enemies, we were reconciled to him through the death of his Son, how much more, having been reconciled, shall we be saved through his life! Not only is this so, but we also rejoice in God through our Lord Jesus Christ, through whom we have now received reconciliation.

- Romans 5:9-11 NIV

"If you are offering your gift on the altar, and there you remember that your brother has something against you, leave your gift there in front of the altar. First go and be reconciled with your brother, and then come and offer your gift."

- Matthew 5:23-24 HCSB

You were continually straying like sheep, but now you have returned to the Shepherd and Guardian of your souls.

- 1 Peter 2:25 NASB

If anyone is in Christ, there is a new creation: everything old has passed away; see, everything has become new! All this is from God, who reconciled us to himself through Christ, and has given us the ministry of reconciliation; that is, in Christ God was reconciling the world to himself, not counting their trespasses against them, and entrusting the message of reconciliation to us.

- 2 Corinthians 5:17-19 NRSV

Let us draw near to God with a sincere heart in full assurance of faith, having our hearts sprinkled to cleanse us from a guilty conscience and having our bodies washed with pure water.
- Hebrews 10:22 TNIV

I, I am He
who blots out your transgressions for
my own sake,
and I will not remember your sins.
- Isaiah 43:25 NRSV

It has pleased [the Father] that all the divine fullness (the sum total of the divine perfection, powers, and attributes) should dwell in Him permanently. And God purposed that through (by the service, the intervention of) Him [the Son] all things should be completely reconciled back to Himself, whether on earth or in heaven, as through Him, [the Father] made peace by means of the blood of His cross.
- Colossians 1:19-20 AMP

"Come now, and let us reason
together,"
Says the LORD,
"Though your sins are as scarlet,
They will be as white as snow;
Though they are red like crimson,
They will be like wool."
- Isaiah 1:18 NASB

We are ambassadors for Christ, as though God were making an appeal through us; we beg you on behalf of Christ, be reconciled to God.
- 2 Corinthians 5:20 NASB

If we walk in the light as He Himself is in the light, we have fellowship with one another, and the blood of Jesus His Son cleanses us from all sin.

- 1 John 1:7 HCSB

"For I will forgive their wickedness
    and will remember their sins no more."

- Jeremiah 31:34 TNIV

You were once alienated and hostile in mind because of your evil actions. But now He has reconciled you by His physical body through His death, to present you holy, faultless, and blameless before Him – if indeed you remain grounded and steadfast in the faith, and are not shifted away from the hope of the gospel that you heard.

- Colossians 1:21-23 HCSB

See also **Forgiveness, Mercy, Repentance,
    Salvation**

Salvation

Having been perfected, He became the author of eternal salvation to all who obey Him.

- Hebrews 5:9 NKJV

"Believe in the Lord Jesus, and you will be saved – you and your household."

- Acts 16:31 TNIV

"Do not fear! Stand by and see the salvation of the
LORD which He will accomplish for you today."
- Exodus 14:13 NASB

He saved us, not because of righteous things we had
done, but because of his mercy. He saved us through
the washing of rebirth and renewal by the Holy Spirit,
whom he poured out on us generously through Jesus
Christ our Savior, so that, having been justified by his
grace, we might become heirs having the hope of eternal life.
- Titus 3:5-7 TNIV

"I am the gate. Whoever enters through me will be
saved, and will come in and go out and find pasture."
- John 10:9 NAB

Take the helmet of salvation and the sword of the Spirit, which is the word of God.
- Ephesians 6:17 NAB

God did not appoint us to suffer wrath but to receive
salvation through our Lord Jesus Christ. He died for
us so that, whether we are awake or asleep, we may
live together with him.
- 1 Thessalonians 5:9-10 NIV

The salvation of the righteous comes
    from the LORD;
  he is their stronghold in time of
    trouble.
- Psalm 37:39 TNIV

"In the time of my favor I heard you,
  and in the day of salvation I helped you."
I tell you, now is the time of God's favor, now is the
day of salvation.

> \- 2 Corinthians 6:2 NIV

Heal me, O LORD, and I shall be healed;
  save me, and I shall be saved.

> \- Jeremiah 17:14 NRSV

On that day it will be said,
"Look, this is our God;
we have waited for Him, and He has saved us.
This is the LORD; we have waited for Him.
Let us rejoice and be glad in His salvation."

> \- Isaiah 25:9 HCSB

Let us put on faith and love for a breastplate, and the
hope of salvation for a helmet.

> \- 1 Thessalonians 5:8 JB

Since we have now been justified by his blood, how
much more shall we be saved from God's wrath
through him! For if, when we were God's enemies, we
were reconciled to him through the death of his Son,
how much more, having been reconciled, shall we be
saved through his life!

> \- Romans 5:9-10 NIV

Join with me in suffering for the gospel according to
the power of God, who has saved us and called us
with a holy calling, not according to our works, but
according to His own purpose and grace which was
granted us in Christ Jesus from all eternity.

> \- 2 Timothy 1:8-9 NASB

If you confess with your mouth, "Jesus is Lord," and believe in your heart that God raised Him from the dead, you will be saved. With the heart one believes, resulting in righteousness, and with the mouth one confesses, resulting in salvation.

- Romans 10:9-10 HCSB

"Maintain justice
 and do what is right,
for my salvation is close at hand
 and my righteousness will soon be revealed."

- Isaiah 56:1 TNIV

Surely his salvation is at hand for those
 who fear him,
 that his glory may dwell in our land.

- Psalm 85:9 NRSV

I am willing to endure anything if it will bring salvation and eternal glory in Christ Jesus to those God has chosen.

- 2 Timothy 2:10 NLT

"Salvation belongs to our God who is seated on the throne, and to the Lamb!"

- Revelation 7:10 NRSV

For the sorrow that is according to the will of God produces a repentance without regret, leading to salvation.

- 2 Corinthians 7:10 NASB

Though you have not seen him, you love him; and even though you do not see him now, you believe in him and are filled with an inexpressible and glorious joy, for you are receiving the goal of your faith, the salvation of your souls.

- 1 Peter 1:8-9 NIV

From childhood you have known the Holy Scriptures, which are able to make you wise for salvation through faith which is in Christ Jesus.

- 2 Timothy 3:15 NKJV

I rejoice heartily in the LORD,
    in my God is the joy of my soul;
For he has clothed me with a robe
        of salvation,
    and wrapped me in a mantle of
        justice.

- Isaiah 61:10 NAB

Restore to me the joy of Your salvation
And sustain me with a willing spirit.

- Psalm 51:12 NASB

"There is salvation in no one else; for there is no other name under heaven that has been given among men by which we must be saved."

- Acts 4:12 NASB

I am not ashamed of the gospel, because it is the power of God that brings salvation to everyone who believes.

- Romans 1:16 TNIV

For the LORD takes pleasure in His
  people;
He will beautify the humble with
  salvation.
       - Psalm 149:4 NKJV

Salvation and deliverance belong to the Lord!
       - Jonah 2:9 AMP

It is good that one should hope and
  wait quietly
For the salvation of the LORD.
       - Lamentations 3:26 NKJV

You know what [a critical] hour this is, how it is high
time now for you to wake up out of your sleep (rouse
to reality). For salvation (final deliverance) is nearer to
us now than when we first believed.
       - Romans 13:11 AMP

"Whoever calls on the name of the LORD
Shall be saved."
       - Joel 2:32 NKJV

"Lift up your eyes to the sky,
Then look to the earth beneath;
For the sky will vanish like smoke,
And the earth will wear out like a garment
And its inhabitants will die in like manner;
But My salvation will be forever."
       - Isaiah 51:6 NASB

The LORD is my strength and song,
And He has become my salvation.

> \- Psalm 118:14 NASB

My soul shall be joyful in the LORD: it shall rejoice in his salvation.

> \- Psalm 35:9 KJV

"And you will be hated by all for My name's sake. But he who endures to the end shall be saved."

> \- Mark 13:13 NKJV

You know that it was not with perishable things such as silver or gold that you were redeemed from the empty way of life handed down to you from your ancestors, but with the precious blood of Christ, a lamb without blemish or defect.

> \- 1 Peter 1:18-19 TNIV

O wretched man that I am! Who will deliver me from this body of death? I thank God – through Jesus Christ our Lord!

> \- Romans 7:24-25 NKJV

"Today salvation has come to this house.... For the Son of Man has come to seek and to save that which was lost."

> \- Luke 19:9-10 NASB

See also **Eternal Life, Passion of Jesus, Reconciliation**

Scripture

His delight is in the law of the LORD,
And in His law he meditates day and night.
He will be like a tree firmly planted by
      streams of water,
Which yields its fruit in its season
And its leaf does not wither;
And in whatever he does, he prospers.
- Psalm 1:2-3 NASB

The grass withers, the flower fades;
   but the word of our God will stand forever.
- Isaiah 40:8 NRSV

The law from your mouth is more precious to me
   than thousands of pieces of silver and gold.
- Psalm 119:72 TNIV

Faith comes from hearing the message, and the message is heard through the word of Christ.
- Romans 10:17 NIV

Those who love Your law have great peace,
And nothing causes them to stumble.
- Psalm 119:165 NASB

I delivered to you as of first importance what I also received, that Christ died for our sins according to the Scriptures, and that He was buried, and that He was raised on the third day according to the Scriptures.
- 1 Corinthians 15:3-4 NASB

Then he opened their minds so they could understand
the Scriptures.

- Luke 24:45 NIV

Oh, how I love your law!
    It is my meditation all day long.

- Psalm 119:97 NRSV

Everything that was written in the past was written to
teach us, so that through the endurance taught in the
Scriptures and the encouragement they provide we
might have hope.

- Romans 15:4 TNIV

For the message of the cross is foolishness to those
who are perishing, but to us who are being saved it is
the power of God.

- 1 Corinthians 1:18 TNIV

"Heaven and earth will pass away, but My words will
by no means pass away."

- Mark 13:31 NKJV

Let the word of Christ dwell in you richly as you teach
and admonish one another with all wisdom, and as
you sing psalms, hymns and spiritual songs with gra-
titude in your hearts to God.

- Colossians 3:16 NIV

Take the helmet of salvation and the sword of the Spirit, which is the word of God.

- Ephesians 6:17 NIV

You must continue in the things which you have learned and been assured of, knowing from whom you have learned them, and that from childhood you have known the Holy Scriptures, which are able to make you wise for salvation through faith which is in Christ Jesus.

- 2 Timothy 3:14-15 NKJV

The word of God is living and active and sharper than any two-edged sword, and piercing as far as the division of soul and spirit, of both joints and marrow, and able to judge the thoughts and intentions of the heart.

- Hebrews 4:12 NASB

Thy word is a lamp unto my feet, and a light unto my path.

- Psalm 119:105 KJV

"This Book of the Law shall not depart from your mouth, but you shall meditate in it day and night, that you may observe to do according to all that is written in it. For then you will make your way prosperous, and then you will have good success."

- Joshua 1:8 NKJV

"Is not my word like fire," declares the LORD, "and like a hammer that breaks a rock in pieces?"

- Jeremiah 23:29 TNIV

" 'Man shall not live by bread alone, but by every word that proceeds from the mouth of God.' "

- Matthew 4:4 NKJV

Your word is very pure,
Therefore Your servant loves it.
                    - Psalm 119:140 NASB

All Scripture is inspired by God and profitable for
teaching, for reproof, for correction, for training in
righteousness; so that the man of God may be ade-
quate, equipped for every good work.
                    - 2 Timothy 3:16-17 NASB

I have hidden your word in my heart
    that I might not sin against you.
                    - Psalm 119:11 TNIV

Let Your tender mercies come to me,
        that I may live;
For Your law is my delight.
                    - Psalm 119:77 NKJV

See also **Law, Obedience, Prophesy, Truth**

Second Coming

For you yourselves know perfectly that the day of the Lord so comes as a thief in the night.
                              - 1 Thessalonians 5:2 NKJV

The end of all things is near. Therefore be alert and of sober mind so that you may pray.
                              - 1 Peter 4:7 TNIV

"No one knows about that day or hour, not even the angels in heaven, nor the Son, but only the Father."
                              - Mark 13:32 NIV

"At that time Michael, the great prince who protects your people, will arise. There will be a time of distress such as has not happened from the beginning of nations until then. But at that time your people – everyone whose name is found written in the book – will be delivered. Multitudes who sleep in the dust of the earth will awake: some to everlasting life, others to shame and everlasting contempt. Those who are wise will shine like the brightness of the heavens, and those who lead many to righteousness, like the stars for ever and ever."
                              - Daniel 12:1-3 NIV

In accordance with his promise, we wait for new heavens and a new earth, where righteousness is at home.
                              - 2 Peter 3:13 NRSV

" 'Behold, I am coming quickly! Hold fast what you have, that no one may take your crown.' "
- Revelation 3:11 NKJV

You know what [a critical] hour this is, how it is high time now for you to wake up out of your sleep (rouse to reality). For salvation (final deliverance) is nearer to us now than when we first believed.
- Romans 13:11 AMP

We know that when He appears, we will be like Him, because we will see Him just as He is. And everyone who has this hope fixed on Him purifies himself, just as He is pure.
- 1 John 3:2-3 NASB

"You also must be ready, because the Son of Man will come at an hour when you do not expect him."
- Luke 12:40 NIV

"Watch! Be alert! For you don't know when the time is coming. It is like a man on a journey, who left his house, gave authority to his slaves, gave each one his work, and commanded the doorkeeper to be alert. Therefore be alert, since you don't know when the master of the house is coming – whether in the evening or at midnight or at the crowing of the rooster or early in the morning. Otherwise, he might come suddenly and find you sleeping. And what I say to you, I say to everyone: Be alert!"
- Mark 13:33-37 HCSB

The great day of the LORD is near;
It is near and hastens quickly.
- Zephaniah 1:14 NKJV

This know also, that in the last days perilous times shall come.
- 2 Timothy 3:1 KJV

"On that day, anyone on the housetop who has belongings in the house must not come down to take them away; and likewise anyone in the field must not turn back. Remember Lot's wife."
- Luke 17:31-32 NRSV

" 'In the last days, God says,
  I will pour out my Spirit on all people.
Your sons and daughters will prophesy,
  your young men will see visions,
  your old men will dream dreams.
Even on my servants, both men and women,
  I will pour out my Spirit in those days,
  and they will prophesy.' "
- Acts 2:17-18 NIV

"The day of the LORD draws near on all
      the nations.
As you have done, it will be done to you.
Your dealings will return on your own
      head."
- Obadiah 15 NASB

"When evening comes, you say, 'It will be fair weather, for the sky is red,' and in the morning, 'Today it will be stormy, for the sky is red and overcast.' You know how to interpret the appearance of the sky, but you cannot interpret the signs of the times."
- Matthew 16:2-3 TNIV

Establish your hearts, for the coming of the Lord is at hand.
                    - James 5:8 NKJV

"Nation will rise against nation, and kingdom against kingdom. There will be great earthquakes, famines and pestilences in various places, and fearful events and great signs from heaven. There will be signs in the sun, moon and stars. On the earth, nations will be in anguish and perplexity at the roaring and tossing of the sea. Men will faint from terror, apprehensive of what is coming on the world, for the heavenly bodies will be shaken. Be always on the watch, and pray that you may be able to escape all that is about to happen, and that you may be able to stand before the Son of Man."
                    - Luke 21:10-11,25-26,36 NIV

He who testifies to these things says, "Surely I am coming quickly." Amen. Even so, come, Lord Jesus!
                    - Revelation 22:20 NKJV

"For as the lightning comes from the east and flashes as far as the west, so will be the coming of the Son of Man."
                    - Matthew 24:27 NRSV

See also **Kingdom of Heaven, Prophesy**

Soldier of God

Fight the good fight of the faith. Take hold of the eternal life to which you were called when you made your good confession in the presence of many witnesses.
> - 1 Timothy 6:12 TNIV

The Lord God is my Strength, my personal bravery, and my invincible army.
> - Habakkuk 3:19 AMP

Indeed, we live as human beings, but we do not wage war according to human standards; for the weapons of our warfare are not merely human, but they have divine power to destroy strongholds. We destroy arguments and every proud obstacle raised up against the knowledge of God, and we take every thought captive to obey Christ. We are ready to punish every disobedience when your obedience is complete.
> - 2 Corinthians 10:3-6 NRSV

Train yourself in godliness, for, while physical training is of some value, godliness is valuable in every way, holding promise for both the present life and the life to come.
> - 1 Timothy 4:7-8 NRSV

" 'Today you are on the verge of battle with your enemies. Do not let your heart faint, do not be afraid, and do not tremble or be terrified because of them; for the LORD your God is He who goes with you, to fight for you against your enemies, to save you.' "
> - Deuteronomy 20:3-4 NKJV

"No weapon formed against you shall
  prosper,
And every tongue which rises against
  you in judgment
You shall condemn.
This is the heritage of the servants of
  the LORD,
And their righteousness is from Me,"
Says the LORD.
- Isaiah 54:17 NKJV

Put on the full armor of God so that you can take your
stand against the devil's schemes.
- Ephesians 6:11 NIV

" 'Do not be afraid or discouraged because of this vast
army. For the battle is not yours, but God's.' "
- 2 Chronicles 20:15 TNIV

He trains my hands for battle,
So that my arms can bend a bow of bronze.
- Psalm 18:34 NASB

As a good soldier of Christ Jesus you must endure
your share of suffering.
- 2 Timothy 2:3 CEV

I have fought the good fight, I have finished the race, I
have kept the faith. Now there is in store for me the
crown of righteousness, which the Lord, the righteous
Judge, will award to me on that day – and not only to
me, but also to all who have longed for his appearing.
- 2 Timothy 4:7-8 NIV

But you, O man of God, flee these things and pursue righteousness, godliness, faith, love, patience, gentleness.

- 1 Timothy 6:11 NKJV

Proclaim this among the nations:
"Prepare for war!
Wake up the mighty men,
Let all the men of war draw near,
Let them come up.
Beat your plowshares into swords
And your pruning hooks into spears;
Let the weak say, 'I am strong.' "

- Joel 3:9-10 NKJV

"You come against me with sword and spear and javelin, but I come against you in the name of the LORD Almighty, the God of the armies of Israel, whom you have defied."

- 1 Samuel 17:45 NIV

"All those gathered here will know that it is not by sword or spear that the LORD saves; for the battle is the LORD's, and he will give all of you into our hands."

- 1 Samuel 17:47 TNIV

"They will fight against you,
 But they shall not prevail against you.
For I am with you," says the LORD,
     "to deliver you."

- Jeremiah 1:19 NKJV

If God is for us, who can be against us?

- Romans 8:31 NAB

You armed me with strength for battle;
  you made my adversaries bow at my feet.
                        - Psalm 18:39 NIV

We do not wrestle against flesh and blood, but against
principalities, against powers, against the rulers of the
darkness of this age, against spiritual hosts of wickedness in the heavenly places. Therefore take up the
whole armor of God, that you may be able to withstand in the evil day.
                        - Ephesians 6:12-13 NKJV

Blessed be the LORD my Rock,
Who trains my hands for war,
And my fingers for battle.
                        - Psalm 144:1 NKJV

Fasten the belt of truth around your waist, and put on
the breastplate of righteousness. As shoes for your
feet put on whatever will make you ready to proclaim
the gospel of peace. With all of these, take the shield
of faith, with which you will be able to quench all the
flaming arrows of the evil one. Take the helmet of salvation, and the sword of the Spirit, which is the word
of God. Pray in the Spirit at all times in every prayer
and supplication.
                        - Ephesians 6:14-18 NRSV

See also **Courage, Protection, Strength, Victory**

Treasure

Do you not know that in a race all the runners run, but only one gets the prize? Run in such a way as to get the prize. Everyone who competes in the games goes into strict training. They do it to get a crown that will not last, but we do it to get a crown that will last forever. Therefore I do not run like someone running aimlessly; I do not fight like a boxer beating the air.

- 1 Corinthians 9:24-26 TNIV

Set your affection on things above, not on things on the earth.

- Colossians 3:2 KJV

"Do not store up for yourselves treasures on earth, where moth and rust destroy, and where thieves break in and steal. But store up for yourselves treasures in heaven, where neither moth nor rust destroys, and where thieves do not break in or steal; for where your treasure is, there your heart will be also."

- Matthew 6:19-21 NASB

In Him all the treasures of wisdom and knowledge are hidden.

- Colossians 2:3 HCSB

Command them to do good, to be rich in good deeds, and to be generous and willing to share. In this way they will lay up treasure for themselves as a firm foundation for the coming age, so that they may take hold of the life that is truly life.

- 1 Timothy 6:18-19 NIV

"Blessed are you when people insult you and persecute you, and falsely say all kinds of evil against you
because of Me. Rejoice and be glad, for your reward in
heaven is great."

- Matthew 5:11-12 NASB

We have this treasure in jars of clay to show that this
all-surpassing power is from God and not from us.

- 2 Corinthians 4:7 NIV

Looking at him, Jesus felt a love for him and said to
him, "One thing you lack: go and sell all you possess
and give to the poor, and you will have treasure in
heaven; and come, follow Me."

- Mark 10:21 NASB

See also **Eternal Life, Kingdom of Heaven**

Truth

"If you hold to my teaching, you are really my disciples. Then you will know the truth, and the truth
will set you free."

- John 8:31-32 NIV

We cannot do anything against the truth, but only for
the truth.

- 2 Corinthians 13:8 NCV

"You say rightly that I am a king. For this cause I was born, and for this cause I have come into the world, that I should bear witness to the truth. Everyone who is of the truth hears My voice."
                                        - John 18:37 NKJV

I was overjoyed to find some of your children walking in the truth, just as we have been commanded by the Father.
                                        - 2 John 4 NRSV

Send Your light and Your truth; let them
        lead me.
Let them bring me to Your holy mountain,
to Your dwelling place.
                                        - Psalm 43:3 HCSB

The church of the living God...is the pillar and foundation of the truth.
                                        - 1 Timothy 3:15 NLT

Jesus Christ – He is the One who came by water and blood; not by water only, but by water and by blood. And the Spirit is the One who testifies, because the Spirit is the truth.
                                        - 1 John 5:6 HCSB

It gave me great joy to have some brothers come and tell about your faithfulness to the truth and how you continue to walk in the truth. I have no greater joy than to hear that my children are walking in the truth.
                                        - 3 John 3-4 NIV

"When the Spirit of truth comes, He will guide you into all the truth. For He will not speak on His own, but He will speak whatever He hears. He will also declare to you what is to come. He will glorify Me, because He will take from what is Mine and declare it to you."
                                        - John 16:13-14 HCSB

For Your mercy is great above the
        heavens,
And Your truth reaches to the
        clouds.
                                        - Psalm 108:4 NKJV

Fasten the belt of truth around your waist, and put on the breastplate of righteousness.
                                        - Ephesians 6:14 NRSV

You were cleansed from your sins when you obeyed the truth.
                                        - 1 Peter 1:22 NLT

The truth lives in us and will be with us forever.
                                        - 2 John 2 NLT

"I am the way, the truth, and the life. No one comes to the Father except through Me."
                                        - John 14:6 HCSB

See also **Honesty, Integrity, Promise, Prophesy,
        Scripture**

Wonders of God

Whatever the LORD pleases He does,
In heaven and in earth,
In the seas and in all deep places.
He causes the vapors to ascend from the
       ends of the earth;
He makes lightning for the rain;
He brings the wind out of His treasuries.
                  - Psalm 135:6-7 NKJV

Stand still and consider the wondrous works of God.
              - Job 37:14 AMP

The heavens declare the glory of God,
and the sky proclaims the work of His hands.
              - Psalm 19:1 HCSB

How many are your works, O LORD!
   In wisdom you made them all.
              - Psalm 104:24 NIV

Great are the works of the LORD,
   studied by all who delight in them.
              - Psalm 111:2 NRSV

Say to God,
"How awesome are Your works!
Through the greatness of Your power
Your enemies shall submit themselves to You.
All the earth shall worship You
And sing praises to You."
              - Psalm 66:3-4 NKJV

Oh, sing to the LORD a new song!
For He has done marvelous things;
His right hand and His holy arm have
      gained Him the victory.
            - Psalm 98:1 NKJV

"He is your praise and He is your God, who has done
for you these great and awesome works your eyes
have seen."
            - Deuteronomy 10:21 HCSB

"Great and marvelous are Your works,
O Lord God, the Almighty;
Righteous and true are Your ways,
King of the nations!"
            - Revelation 15:3 NASB

I will praise You, for I am fearfully and
      wonderfully made;
Marvelous are Your works,
And that my soul knows very well.
            - Psalm 139:14 NKJV

The LORD has done great things for us,
    and we are filled with joy.
            - Psalm 126:3 NIV

He waters the mountains from His upper
      chambers;
The earth is satisfied with the fruit of His
      works.
            - Psalm 104:13 NASB

I thought it good to declare the signs and wonders that the Most High God has worked for me.
- Daniel 4:2 NKJV

O LORD, you are my God;
    I will exalt you and praise your name,
for in perfect faithfulness
    you have done marvelous things,
    things planned long ago.
- Isaiah 25:1 NIV

Known unto God are all his works from the beginning of the world.
- Acts 15:18 KJV

"God thunders marvelously with His
        voice;
He does great things which we cannot
        comprehend."
- Job 37:5 NKJV

He looks at the earth, and it trembles;
He touches the mountains,
and they pour out smoke.
- Psalm 104:32 HCSB

How great are His signs! And how mighty His wonders! His kingdom is an everlasting kingdom, and His dominion is from generation to generation.
- Daniel 4:3 AMP

This is the day which the LORD has made;
Let us rejoice and be glad in it.
- Psalm 118:24 NASB

"He performs wonders that cannot be fathomed,
    miracles that cannot be counted."
                              - Job 5:9 TNIV

They who dwell in the ends of the earth
            stand in awe of Your signs;
You make the dawn and the sunset
        shout for joy.
                              - Psalm 65:8 NASB

We give thanks to You, O God, we
            give thanks!
For Your wondrous works declare
        that Your name is near.
                              - Psalm 75:1 NKJV

On the glorious splendor of your majesty,
        and on your wondrous works, I will meditate.
The might of your awesome deeds shall be proclaimed,
        and I will declare your greatness.
                              - Psalm 145:5-6 NRSV

You have made the moon to mark the seasons;
        the sun knows its time for setting.
                              - Psalm 104:19 NRSV

"Of old You laid the foundation of
            the earth,
And the heavens are the work of
            Your hands."
                              - Psalm 102:25 NKJV

Declare his glory among the nations,
        his marvelous deeds among all peoples.
                              - 1 Chronicles 16:24 TNIV

When I consider your heavens,
   the work of your fingers,
the moon and the stars,
   which you have set in place,
what is man that you are mindful of him,
   the son of man that you care for him?
                              - Psalm 8:3-4 NIV

He counts the number of the stars;
He calls them all by name.
Great is our Lord, and mighty in power;
His understanding is infinite.
                              - Psalm 147:4-5 NKJV

See also **Creation, Power of God**

Afterword

Everything you receive comes with instructions, whether it is a new toothbrush, vacuum cleaner, vehicle, or a bag of vegetables. These instructions reveal the proper way to use or do something − and how to do it safely. Instructions enable us to understand and make the most out of what we have.

God did not withhold instructions from us about how to live. He provided them in the form of the Bible. The more you soak your mind in the Scriptures, the clearer your understanding will be about how God wants you to live. When you are living the righteous life that God has called you to live, He can then open the gates of Heaven and pour His blessings upon you relentlessly!

I hope *Verses by Virtue* has provided and continues to provide you spiritual support and joy for your faith in Jesus Christ.

I can do all things through Christ who strengthens me.
− Philippians 4:13 NKJV

Index

EternalLightPublishing.com

QUICK ORDER FORM

Online: Visit *www.EternalLightPublishing.com*

Postal: Eternal Light Publishing
P.O. Box 4378
Davenport, IA 52808, USA.   Send this completed form.

Ship to
Name: _____

Address: _____

City: _____ State: _____ Zip: _____

Telephone: _____

Email address: _____

☐ Check   ☐ Money Order   ☐ Visa   ☐ MC   ☐ Discover

Card #: _____

Exp. Date: _____ Signature: _____

Name as it appears on card: _____

	Quantity		Totals
Verses by Virtue (Hardcover, 448 pp.)	_____	x $24.95 USD	_____
Iowa sales tax: 6% ($1.50) per book when shipped to **Iowa** addresses			_____
*Shipping: $5.00 for first 2 books, $2.50 per additional book			_____
TOTAL Enclosed with Order:			_____

Thank you for your order!
May the Lord of peace Himself give you peace always in every way. (2 Thess. 3:16)

☐ Sign me up for Jeffrey Dunn's *Enlightening Word of the Week* with the email address I provided above. I understand this is FREE and I may opt-out at any time.

*For more shipping options order online at *www.EternalLightPublishing.com.*